STRATEGIC
COMMUNICATION
IN CANADA

STRATEGIC
COMMUNICATION
IN CANADA
PLANNING EFFECTIVE PR CAMPAIGNS

BERNARD GAUTHIER

CANADIAN
SCHOLARS

Toronto | Vancouver

Strategic Communication in Canada: Planning Effective PR Campaigns
Bernard Gauthier

First published in 2018 by
Canadian Scholars, an imprint of CSP Books Inc.
425 Adelaide Street West, Suite 200
Toronto, Ontario
M5V 3C1

www.canadianscholars.ca

Library and Archives Canada Cataloguing in Publication

Gauthier, Bernard J. M., 1963-, author
    Strategic communication in Canada : planning effective PR campaigns / Bernard Gauthier.

Includes index.
Issued in print and electronic formats.
ISBN 978-1-77338-076-6 (softcover).--ISBN 978-1-77338-078-0 (EPUB).--
ISBN 978-1-77338-077-3 (PDF)

        1. Public relations--Canada--Textbooks. 2. Communication in organizations--Canada--
Textbooks. 3. Strategic planning--Canada--Textbooks. 4. Textbooks. I. Title.

HD59.6.C3G38 2018   659.2   C2018-901794-5
                                                                             C2018-901795-3

Text and cover design by Elisabeth Springate
Typesetting by Brad Horning

Printed and bound in Canada

Canada

CONTENTS

INTRODUCTION
Setting the Stage for Strategic Communication Planning

CHAPTER OVERVIEW

This book begins with an overview of what is meant by the term *strategy* in the context of developing a detailed communication plan for an organization. This introductory chapter also includes a discussion of the military and sport analogies often called upon to explain and illustrate strategy. The drawbacks of these two analogies are discussed, and a new analogy—gardening—is proposed for strategy in the context of communication planning. Finally, this chapter lays out the structure for the remainder of the book.

LEARNING OBJECTIVES

1. Define strategy and discuss its role in the development of detailed plans for communication and public relations campaigns.
2. Differentiate strategy from the other approaches that can be taken when planning campaigns; explain the advantages of strategy over these other approaches.
3. Discuss the theoretical foundation for the approach to strategy development used in this book.
4. Appreciate the structure of this book and develop a clear sense of why this structure was selected.

DEFINING STRATEGY

It is fitting a book about strategy would begin with a definition of the term. What, precisely, is meant when the expression "strategic communication" is used in the title? How is strategic communication different from communication that is not strategic? The traditional approach is to start by looking at what dictionaries have published on the topic of strategy. The online *Oxford Canadian Dictionary* (2017), for example, defines strategy as:

1. an especially long-range policy designed for a particular purpose: *economic strategy.*
2. the process of planning something or carrying out a plan in a skilful way.
3. a plan or stratagem.
4. the art of planning and directing military activity in a battle or war.[1]

There is much in this definition that is useful to remember as you set out to learn how to develop strategic communication plans. Strategy is indeed best suited to long-range planning; your day-to-day plan is less dependent on an overall strategic approach and more focused on getting things done quickly. In the longer term, though, you need to know the things you have chosen to do will be strategic and lead you to your long-term goals and objectives.

Strategy is also skilful. It's not an easy process to develop a plan strategically, and it's even harder to implement that plan in a rapidly changing environment. Like all skills, however, strategy can be learned and the process does get easier with experience.

In terms of the third item in this definition, this book argues a strategy is not a plan; it is *part* of a plan. As we'll see, plans should also include a precise statement of goals and objectives as well as a detailed list of the tactics—or steps—you will complete to realize the strategy.

As for the fourth item in the definition, it is clear the concept of strategy has become closely tied to military exercises and battle planning. In addition to this, though, as businesses, charities, governments, sports teams, families, and individuals have shown, strategy is something any individual or organization can use for many, many kinds of activities. What they all have in common is the desire to meet specific challenges (not just battles) in the most carefully planned and directed way. Creating those plans and directions does, as the definition suggests, require a careful blend of science and art.

Arriving at an Alternative Definition

The definition of strategy proposed in this book was born not in a dictionary but in the offices of a rapidly growing public relations firm in Ottawa; it was born over more than 20 years as I met with clients and worked to develop public relations or communications plans that were truly strategic.

This definition begins by stressing strategy is one of *many* approaches an organization or individual can take to get things done. People and organizations don't *have* to be strategic; it could be argued many organizations and individuals are not actually strategic when they work. They turn instead to one of the three principal alternatives to strategy. By understanding those three alternatives, we develop a better sense of what strategy actually is.

The first alternative to strategy is *inertia*; some organizations just keep doing what they have always done. The fact that certain behaviour was done in the past becomes the reason to keep employing the same behaviour: "This company has always had a sales meeting in July and we will keep having a sales meeting in July." This kind of inertia is common because it feels safer and requires less thought and energy. It's easy.

The second alternative to strategy is *emulation*. Some organizations look around to their peers and competitors and copy what these organizations are doing. Without thinking too much about how their own situation and audience is unique, they take another's approach and emulate it. "If Apple uses music from contemporary 'indie' artists in its television commercials, so should we; after all, look what happened to their revenues over the last decade!"

The third alternative to strategy is *random selection*. Some organizations rely on luck as they plan. Someone (usually a senior executive or board member) gets an idea, the idea is implemented, and then the organization waits to see how the new idea turns out. Nobody asks critical questions about what might be lost as the new idea is implemented, how audiences might respond to the idea, or whether the money for the implementation of the idea might be better spent elsewhere. They roll the dice on a new idea generated at random and hope for the best.

This discussion of the alternatives to strategy leads us to define strategy as an approach to makings choices and decisions not merely based on inertia, emulation, or random selection. In contrast to these three alternatives, a strategic approach is very *outcome-oriented*. Strategic organizations know precisely *why* they are doing what they do. They have clear outcomes or goals in mind, and they insist on measuring their progress toward those goals. All decisions are taken in the context of the progress they are likely to bring about. Ideas that are borrowed, interesting, or novel must first pass the test of whether or not they can realistically help the organization achieve its stated goals and bring about its intended outcomes.

With this definition of strategy, old ideas that have been used for years must be tested to see if they address the organization's current goals. If the answer is no, the organization and its leaders go back to the drawing board. That makes strategy a *dynamic* process, with decisions and choices evolving as the organization, its stakeholders, and its external environment evolve.

A strategic approach is also an *informed* approach. Strategy always begins by gathering current and reliable information about the organization, the key stakeholders, and the current conditions in the external environment. Strategic organizations spend more time looking around, scanning, and assessing than they do making decisions. They know exactly what resources are available to them and how much of each is available, as well as the quality of those resources. Strategic organizations also know precisely what trends and forces outside the organization could affect the organization, making it harder or easier to succeed. They think hard about how best to overcome challenges and deploy the resources they have; this process of insisting on informed and customized decisions is also essential for a strategic approach.

Finally, a strategic approach is *consistent*. Strategic organizations insist on a coherent and overriding strategy that guides all the small, tactical decisions which follow. Without some overarching strategic directions, a plan becomes little more than a list of tactics that may—or may not—work together cohesively. In the absence of a consistent strategy, the temptation to simply do what you've always done, to copy others, or to try your luck can be overwhelming. Worse yet, the absence of a consistent strategy can lead organizations to keep changing their approach, hoping to find or stumble upon one that works.

All of this points to the qualities of the process that lead to effective strategies—the qualities this book will help readers develop. To be a strategic communicator, then, one must make careful choices and do so in purposeful and informed manner, so as to make optimal choices for the organization. It also suggests being a strategic communicator is to be outcome-oriented. Strategic communicators must be crystal-clear on the specific changes they intend the communication effort to bring about. If the campaign is intended to raise the awareness of a particular audience, strategic communicators know this and their understanding of the change and the particular audience is clear.

To be strategic is also to be thoroughly informed before communicating. Strategic communicators need to gather enough information on the audiences they hope to address with their PR efforts. They need to know about the audiences whose level of awareness or behaviour they want to change. Strategic communicators also need to know certain other audiences can reach and influence their primary audience in ways that help or hinder their efforts. To be strategic as a communicator is to know a great deal about the resources you can deploy. Strategic communicators carefully assess all the communication resources they depend on, and they must make decisions based on what they find. Strategic communicators are keenly aware of the complex series of forces and trends outside their offices that will greatly help or impede the PR efforts. Strategic communicators scan the environment and identify those changes and forces that will help or hinder the PR campaign. Most importantly, they must consistently make important decisions based on what they have learned about the world outside their office.

Finally, strategy is consistent. Strategic communicators must ensure the same strategy is applied consistently across all different communication vehicles. Consistency in communication strategy means a single strategy that guides every vehicle distributed, every experience created, every word and every image communicated.

ABOUT THE ANALOGIES USED TO DISCUSS STRATEGY

As the dictionary definition presented earlier in this chapter reminds us, the origins of the word *strategy* are rooted in Greek military history (*stratagem* is a Greek word meaning leadership of an army). This helps explain why so many books, articles, and lectures explain strategy using a military analogy.

In a business context, though, this turn to a military analogy has often meant equating competitors with "the enemy" and efforts to reach out to a market or segment or audience as "a campaign." Marketing buzz words with close ties to the military abound; think of "targets," "position," and "penetration," for example. So complete is the link between military and business strategy that the words of a 12th-century Chinese general—Sun Tzu—are now published and analyzed for the secrets they reveal about the art and science of winning customers in a competitive, contemporary market.[2]

There are certainly many advantages to this military analogy. To begin, the wisdom of ancient Chinese generals and their modern-day counterparts may indeed yield insights that can be quite useful to planning a business venture. As suggested above, the modern work of military strategists to precisely define the raw materials of strategy and map out rigorous processes for developing strategy have, in fact, helped give shape to a good portion of this book.

A second advantage of the military analogy is that it can help organizations rally their "troops" around a marketing mission. The "us-versus-them" mentality is a proven way to build cohesion and engagement within a team. Imagine the CEO of Home Hardware exhorting his employees to redouble their efforts in the face of a new campaign by Home Depot.

Finally, the military analogy brings a sense of credibility to business planning. By borrowing the language and methods of the military, the planning of a marketing effort or new business venture is given a sense of importance and rigour that might otherwise elude it. Those who lead these efforts and those who teach others how to do it all benefit by basking in the glow of military credibility and prestige built up over centuries.

Those who need to talk about or write about strategy but aren't comfortable with the military analogy often turn to a sport analogy. Sport, like war, is competitive. It's exciting. And most people have some knowledge and personal experience related to basketball, baseball, hockey, or football, whether as a player or as a fan. The analogy works by evoking powerful memories most people have of a big game and a winning strategy. And, much like the military analogy, the sport analogy brings with it the "us-versus-them" response that can help rally our team as we prepare to conquer the other team.

There are real limitations to the effectiveness of either analogy as a way to think about communication. Simply put, managing a modern organization—whether it's starting a business, running a not-for-profit, or administering a government program—is not war, and it's certainly not a game. The relationships, challenges, resources, and desired outcomes are all radically different. What works best on the battlefield or on the football field may not be the best solution in other types of organizations. General Sun Tzu, although we will never know for sure, might have failed miserably had he tried to launch a new government program to educate mothers of young immigrants or raise funds for a new cancer treatment centre. Scotty Bowman may be one of the finest hockey coaches in the history of the game, but it wasn't his job to help a client plan a national media conference.

Perhaps the biggest problem with the military and sport analogies is the relationship they create between the planning organization and the audiences with which it wants to interact. Those who use a military or sport analogy when they talk about strategy are much more likely to talk about "segments to be targeted and penetrated," "lines of defense that must be broken," and "adversaries to be conquered." This kind of language assumes the target audience is passive and their role will be to receive whatever it is the organization is about to send their way. The focus is on attacking and defeating an otherwise passive group of people in order to win.

Those with experience in public relations and marketing communication will have noticed, time and again, that nothing could be further from the truth. Audiences are never conquered; they are called upon, engaged in dialogue, educated, and motivated to understand how a certain proposition can improve their lives. Markets are not penetrated; they are cultivated over time. When the actions and messages of the organization are congruent with the audience, profitable relationships will emerge, to be nurtured by the organization once they realize those relationships are fundamental to their success. The big risk here is that the mere language of war and sport can lead organizations to make strategic errors as they plan their communication campaigns.

Finally, a subtler problem with the military and sport analogies stems from the unease many people feel with the intensely competitive culture within both these spheres. Many students feel a real discomfort when using planning tools and approaches designed by military strategists in an effort to destroy an enemy. Those who are not sports fans can feel the same kind of discomfort or detachment when strategy is explained using the language of sport. That level of discomfort could compel some people to abandon strategic thinking and revert back to "gut feeling," "habit," or purely random choices. The advantages of strategic thinking are significant; this makes finding an analogy and a language with which everyone will be comfortable a worthwhile effort.

Proposing a Better Analogy

This book proposes a much less violent and competitive activity as an ideal analogy for strategy: gardening. Successful gardeners are among the most strategic individuals in society today. The decisions they make, their sensitivity to their environment, and their clear sense of purpose make them an ideal example of solid, strategic thinking. That their pursuit is not destructive but reproductive, their intent to nurture rather than conquer, makes the analogy more appropriate for communication and public relations. It also makes the analogy more comfortable and more accessible to all.

Consider the many ways gardeners consistently display strategic thinking. First and foremost, gardeners—at least, those who are successful—are meticulous planners. You'll find them sketching plots, scouring seed catalogues, listing the supplies they'll need, and reading to learn from others—all of it months before the first shovelful of dirt gets thrown. The process and the outcomes for gardeners are rarely left to chance. The decisions they make are not random; they are strategic.

Gardeners almost always begin with a clear sense of purpose or outcome. They see a small piece of land and imagine it transformed into a bountiful source of fresh food, a fragrant oasis for the family, or a thriving ecosystem for particular species of birds or butterflies. Consider, for example, the Shelburne Museum in Shelburne, Vermont.[3] There, you will find three gardens, each built, as they would have been centuries ago, for a specific purpose: the first for food, the second for decorative and fragrant flowers for hats, and a third to grow medicinal plants. That well-defined sense of "why we are doing this and what it will look like when we are successful" is an essential ingredient in strategic thinking.

Gardeners are also strategic in that they take the time to learn about the plants and species with which they want to populate their gardens. They know what plants and species live well together and in what environments. Butterflies are attracted to milkweed. Corn, beans, and squash thrive when planted together—something Huron Aboriginals discovered centuries ago. Gardeners also take the time to learn about those plants and animals that pose a threat to their garden. They know which pests can destroy their plants and which weeds are most likely to invade. They also learn how best to prevent those plants and pests from getting started in the garden. The more they know about the plant and animals they will encounter, the better prepared they are to create an environment in which the right species will thrive.

Gardeners are also strategic in their constant efforts to maintain a very strong sense of the resources they have to work with and a clear understanding of how best to leverage those resources. They know the value of investing in quality seeds. They know from experience that the right tools can help them do more in less time and with less strain on their bodies. Gardeners also find innovative, strategic ways to overcome a lack of certain resources. Those who lack land turn to container gardening or find community gardens. Those who lack a long growing season find ways to extend the season by planting against brick walls that retain heat long into each evening. Simply put, gardeners know full well what is in their tool shed and work hard to leverage what they have and to overcome their deficiencies.

Finally, gardeners, perhaps more than any group, are also totally in tune with their external environment. They learn about their soil type and climactic zones. They study how the sun will shine (or won't shine) on their garden. They pay close attention to weather forecasts and climate change. They understand how the environment will guide them toward populating their garden with certain types of plants or species. They respect the limits imposed by Mother Nature but also learn from experience how to draw upon their resources to push those limits and how far they can go.

When it comes to gardeners, then, the four hallmarks of strategic thinking are all there.

1. Gardeners work with a clear sense of the changes or the outcomes they intend to bring about; they start with a clear sense of purpose and carefully defined goals.
2. They have a deep knowledge of the species (the plants and the animals) they want to attract, engage, and nurture; they read deeply and pay attention so they can learn even more.
3. Gardeners benefit from full knowledge of, and appreciation for, the many resources they have; they also know what resources they lack. In short, gardeners know what is in the garden shed.

4.   Gardeners pay continuous attention to the external environment; they know from experience about the limits and opportunities the environment presents.

This is strategic thinking at its best. And it offers a valuable model for strategic communication planning. It's a model with which many of us can identify. After all, who hasn't tried at least once to grow a few plants? Who hasn't walked through a public garden or admired a neighbour's garden?

Gardening presents a model for strategic thinking that looks on audiences (the plants or animals we want in the garden) not as enemies but as a species we must attract, engage, and nurture. Gardeners don't see success as conquest or victory over another but as a thriving, sustainable ecosystem—a win-win for both gardeners and the species they seek to attract. This makes gardening both appropriate and accessible as a model for the task of developing strategy and working strategically. The model works both to assist organizations trying to develop strategy and to assist individuals who are trying to learn about strategy and how to be more strategic in the decisions they make.

SOME THEORETICAL FOUNDATIONS FOR STRATEGIC COMMUNICATION

In this section, you will be introduced to a range of ideas about communication and about strategy, along with some of the key individuals who expressed and developed the ideas. We begin by discussing a U.S. Army general (there's the military analogy again) and then move to a list of communication scholars who have laid the theoretical foundations for this book by helping to shape our understanding of communication and public relations. Their ideas and the reflections on those ideas by other scholars have all deeply influenced this book.[4] This section of the chapter is focused on giving credit to the most influential of these scholars in this regard. While the chapter will not delve deep into the specific work of any of these authors, the hope is that readers will be intrigued enough to explore their works more fully.

General Norman Schwarzkopf and METT-T Analysis

The theoretical foundation for this book began early in my public relations career, when I was working in Toronto for a large life insurance company and was beginning to explore the role of strategy in successful campaigns. Around that time, I watched, along with millions around the world, as the U.S. Army's

General Norman Schwarzkopf, Jr., took to television each evening to announce and explain the start of the Gulf War and, specifically, what he and his troops were doing to move Iraqi forces out of Kuwait. Schwarzkopf was a talented communicator and the high-tech images he showed of bombs exploding on target were as riveting as they were troubling. I was moved by this, but was also taken with Schwarzkopf's brief explanation of the technique used by the U.S. Army to develop their military strategy, a technique called METT-T analysis.[5]

Schwarzkopf explained strategic decisions were made based on the commander's understanding of five different factors: the mission, the enemy, the troops, the terrain, and the time available for the operation (hence the acronym METT-T). He then went on to summarize what he and his allies knew about all these factors (which was a great deal, thanks to effective intelligence gathering) and how the strategy was developed on the basis of the conditions of each of the five factors. What the general made clear was that knowledge of the resources inside the U.S. Army (i.e., mission, troops, and time) and the conditions outside in the field (i.e., enemy and terrain) directly shaped the strategy he and his colleagues developed.

Of course, Schwarzkopf was talking about military leadership and planning, not public relations. Nonetheless, his careful explanation of the many factors to be considered while developing a strategy all had a significant impact on me and on the way I approached the process of developing communication strategy. The METT-T approach to strategic planning is explained fully in the U.S. Army's *Field Manual*.[6] Section 5–0 of the book in particular explains each of the factors that must be carefully assessed and considered as strategy is set. For reasons explained earlier, however, I chose a very different analogy and a very different set of terms to describe the approach. I was inspired by Schwarzkopf and the many authors of the *Field Manual* but chose, in the long run, to steer clear of military language and images to explain the approach developed for this book.

Edward T. Hall and the Palo Alto Group

The first scholar who deserves considerable credit here is Edward T. Hall. Hall was an American anthropologist who published most of his work in the 1960s. He focused much of his research and writing on the unique challenges of communicating across cultures.[7] He joined forces with two other researchers (Erving Goffman and Ray Birdwhistell) to form a research group known as the Palo Alto group.

What Hall, Birdwhistell, and Goffman did was greatly expand the range of elements and activities researchers looked at when they studied the interpersonal communication process. Hall paid close attention to how people use the space between themselves and others to communicate, and how different cultures perceive and use time very differently. Birdwhistell focused his attention on non-verbal communication and the messages we send using facial expressions, small body movements, and the placement of our hands, for example.[8] For his part, Erving Goffman explored (among many other things) how a person constructs an image using their acts, the settings they create, and the appearance they maintain. Think of how physicians carefully construct their professional image using these tools.[9]

The influence that Hall and his Palo Alto group colleagues had on this book is the understanding that communication is a complex and often subtle process that relies on much more than words. Time, space, subtle facial expressions, tiny movements, appearances, and settings all play a part in shaping the meaning that emerges out of communication; they are all part of the toolbox used by PR practitioners as they plan, prepare, and coach their clients. This challenges us to learn as much about the audience we hope to address as possible so we can anticipate how campaign messages will be interpreted using all of these channels. The range of audience-related factors communicators need to consider when planning a communication campaign will be presented in later chapters of this book.

Tony Schwartz and "Responsive Chords"

The second scholar whose work had a profound impact on this book is Tony Schwartz, a successful American advertising executive who wrote two highly influential books on communication and the media. One of those in particular greatly influenced the thinking in this book: 1973's *The Responsive Chord*. In it, Schwartz presents his resonance theory and explains how the meaning that people make when they encounter messages is shaped in large part by their own experiences and biases. "The resonance principle," Schwartz writes, "suggests that the starting point for understanding and creating communication lies in examining the communication environment you are living in at this moment, and the context within which any stimuli you create will be received" (p. 160).[10]

The chapters that follow will draw from Schwartz's ideas and provide advice and direction to help readers learn as much about the communication environment and as much about the intended audiences as possible, so that the campaign's messages will align with what's going on "out there" and resonate with what's going on inside the minds of the audience.

Uses and Gratifications Theory

The third type of communication studies research which has greatly influenced my thinking about public relations and strategy is attributed to a number of scholars but summed up in four words: uses and gratifications theory. The theory was born of a set of questions about why individuals choose to use one type of media (e.g., the web or social media) over another (e.g., newspapers or television) and what drives their decision to spend time consuming media in the first place, be it to find information, to be entertained, to protect themselves, or to connect with others, for example.

Successful public relations campaigns depend on organizations being able to consistently and reliably reach key audiences with certain information. The more communicators know about how an audience uses different media and channels to achieve certain uses and gratifications, the better prepared they will be to reach those individuals. Two scholars who helped shape this school of thought are Elihu Katz and Michael Gurevitch.[11] They wrote two highly influential papers on the topic in the 1970s and anticipated much of the contemporary discussion of new social media channels and questions about how and why people choose to use these channels.

Stuart Hall and Cultural Studies

Stuart Hall is the fourth scholar whose work has deeply influenced what is written in this book. Hall (who is in no way related to Edward T. Hall) wrote in Birmingham, England, in the 1970s and 1980s. He was part of a group of scholars who together introduced and refined a new way to study communication and society, which they called "cultural studies." As the name of the field implies, cultural studies scholars were most interested in how culture is created, repaired, and transformed through human activity and across history. Not surprisingly, they focused much of their attention on communication as a way to share, preserve, and repair culture.

One of Stuart Hall's most enduring and influential contributions to cultural studies was his research into the process by which the messages an audience listens to, watches, and reads are encoded by the sender or originator of the message, and then decoded by the receiver or audience of the message.[12] Hall proposed the receivers or audience members involved in communication play an active role in determining what the meaning is that they derive from the messages sent to them. Communication is much less of a hypodermic needle, sending precise messages to a recipient whether they like it or not. Instead, Hall suggested the process of decoding messages is complex, unpredictable, and a way that audiences actually use the power they have to make meaning out of messages. He focused particularly on the range of ways an audience can decode a text: the dominant or hegemonic position, the negotiated position that involves both the sender's intentions and the audience's interpretation, and the oppositional position that focuses more on what the receiver makes of a message than what the sender intended.[13] It is important for strategic communicators to learn as much about the audiences as possible, to anticipate how a particular audience is likely to decode a message, and to prepare for whatever type of decoding comes out of the encounter.

In Short ...

This book, then, is built on the premise that those communicators who understand the audience's preferences will be better able to reach them. Communicators who know why audience members turn to a particular medium or channel and what fundamental needs are driving that choice will be better positioned to craft messages that deliver information and connect with those audiences. Communicators who learn about the codes an audience uses and the approach they use to make sense of the messages around them will be better able to craft messages that work to inform those audiences, influence their behaviour, and foster their relationship with the communicator's organization. All of these insights and all of these decisions can shape a communication campaign and make it truly strategic.

This is not to suggest these scholars were communication or public relations professionals; with the notable exception of Tony Schwartz, they were not. They were scholars and academics who were motivated by questions about the impact of communication on the way we live as individuals and the way we come together as cultural groups and societies. Their questions were much broader and more fundamental than those asked by PR practitioners. Indeed, their questions and arguments were often critical of the mass media, advertising, and public relations. Nonetheless, the principles they developed and the insight they gained can be leveraged now to improve the ability of organizations to communicate effectively with important people inside and outside their organizations.[14]

HOW THE BOOK IS STRUCTURED AND WHY

This book is structured around the two major phases of developing communication strategy. In the first half of the book, readers will move through the main phases of conducting a situation analysis—a crucial first step to developing strategy. This book will bring a somewhat different set of questions and areas of enquiry designed to fit seamlessly with the model of strategic communication planning proposed in this book. They are questions and areas of enquiry that have been developed over several decades of strategic communication planning for hundreds of clients in all major sectors of the Canadian economy. They are proven.

Specifically, readers will be challenged to gather information about the four key elements of strategic communication:

- **Change**—Readers will be shown how to investigate the changes in awareness, attitudes, and behaviour the client is hoping to bring about with their communication effort.
- **Audiences**—You will be shown exactly how to gather additional information about the people and organizations the campaign needs to reach, engage, and persuade in order to achieve the stated campaign goals and bring about the changes the client seeks.
- **Resources**—Readers will be guided on how to gather objective data on the quantity and quality of the assets the client can deploy as they undertake the communication campaign.
- **Environment**—Finally, you will learn how to gather objective and reliable data on the external environment in which the campaign will be deployed. What's happening outside the organization that will make it easier or harder for the campaign to succeed?

Conveniently, the four words used to label each of the elements lead us to a memorable and appropriate acronym: CARE.[15] "Care" is an appropriate word to sum up this process and this approach to communication. After all, effective communication strategy will lead to your audiences caring more about what you propose for them and will allow your organization to listen effectively and send a clear signal to the audience that you care about them. Readers will emerge from this first section of the book with a clear sense of what information they need to gather and how to gather it.

The facts and figures you will be urged to gather serve as the raw materials of the communication strategy developed in the second section of the book. That second section will show how to move from raw materials to finished, polished strategy. Readers will be walked through the process of sifting through everything they have learned in the first section and identifying those pieces of knowledge of strategic importance. You will also learn how to use the planning model proposed in this book to help organize your knowledge and draw conclusions. Finally, you will be introduced to proven approaches for moving from knowledge to strategy, along with examples of past campaigns that illustrate these assertions.

In short, you will emerge from this second half of the book with a process and the conceptual tools with which to build the strategic directions that will orient and guide the plan, pointing to the best ways to deploy resources in order to maximize the chances of success.

This book will leave off where many people begin the strategic planning process: moving from broad strategic directions to precise recommendations for communication tactics (e.g., the vehicles and activities that will form the backbone of a campaign). These fine details of how best to conduct media relations, buy advertising, produce websites, and so on are already covered by other books. The intent of this book is to ensure you will be able to choose your tactics strategically and make the most of them by aligning all the elements of your plan around a common and informed strategy.

KEY TERMS AND CONCEPTS

As you review this chapter for any tests or assignments, you will want to pay particular attention to the following terms and concepts introduced in the preceding pages:

- strategy
- assessments
- change
- audiences
- resources
- environment
- tactics

QUESTIONS FOR CRITICAL REFLECTION

1. What other groups of people or occupations do you feel regularly behave in a strategic way? Who—other than military leaders, sports coaches, and gardeners—takes the time to clarify their intentions and goals, to learn about the individuals and organizations they will need to engage, to assess their internal resources, to scan the external environment, and to make choices that optimize the likelihood of success for their endeavour?

2. Not all plans are strategic. Many are based on simple repletion, copying what others are doing, or giving in to the allure of a new idea. Think of one activity or project you have been a part of (whether at work, at school, in your community, or in your family) that was not strategic. Describe which of the alternatives to strategy you and the others involved used instead. How might a strategic approach to the same activity have yielded very different results?

3. The CARE model proposes that there are four key elements of strategic thinking in the context of communication and public relations: change, audiences, resources, and environment. In your opinion, are all four equally important or does one of these four deserve greater attention from strategic planners? If so, which element is more important and why?

NOTES

1. Strategy. (2005). In K. Barber (Ed.), *Oxford Canadian Dictionary* (electronic edition). Don Mills, ON: Oxford University Press. Retrieved June 2, 2017, from www.oxfordreference.com.

2. For a brief but compelling example of the enduring influence of Sun Tzu's *The Art of War*, read the article in *Fast Company* by Mark McNeilly at: http://www.fastcompany.com/3021122/leadership-now/fighting-your-business-battles-6-lasting-lessons-from-sun-tzus-art-of-war.

3. More information on this unique museum and its impressive gardens can be found at https://shelburnemuseum.org/.

4. Harry G. Summers Jr. provides a nice introduction to the role of METT-T analysis in his February 6, 1991, article in the *Los Angeles Times* (http://articles.latimes.com/1991-02-06/news/mn-760_1_ground-war). Richard Hallion provides a more thorough discussion of how this strategy was developed in his 1992 book *Storm Over Iraq: Air Power and the Gulf War* (Washington, D.C.: Smithsonian Books).

5. Department of the Army. (2001). *U.S. Army field manual: Operations*. Washington, D.C.: Department of the Army. Retrieved August 25, 2016, from http://www.globalsecurity.org/military/library/policy/army/fm/3-0.

6. I was able to study every one of these scholars in detail and read much of their work as I completed a Bachelor's degree, a Master's degree, and a Ph.D. in the field of Communication Studies. I am grateful to the many professors with whom I studied and from whom I learned of these scholars and their work.

7. Edward T. Hall's 1959 book, *The Silent Language*, is a wonderful explanation of the powerful role culture plays in allowing or limiting successful communication (Garden City, NY: Doubleday).

8. See Birdwhistell's 1970 book *Kinesics and Context: Essays on Body Motion Communication* for a very thorough discussion (Philadelphia, P.A.: University of Pennsylvania Press).

9. See, for example, Goffman's 1963 book *Behavior in Public Places: Notes on the Social Organization of Gatherings* (New York, NY: Free Press).

10. Schwartz, T. (1973). *The responsive chord.* New York, NY: Doubleday.

11. Katz, E., Blumler, J. G., & Gurevitch, M. (1973). Uses and gratifications research. *Public Opinion Quarterly, 37* (Winter), 509–523; Katz, E., & Gurevitch, M. (1973). On the use of the mass media for important things. *American Sociological Review, 38*(April), 164–181.

12. Hall, S. (1980) Encoding/decoding. In S. Hall, D. Hobson, A. Lowe, & P. Willis (Eds.), *Culture, media and language* (pp. 127–139). London, U.K.: Hutchinson.

13. ibid., pp. 136–138.

14. I started my graduate studies after I had worked in PR for about a decade, and I was drawn to these scholars and their writing by my experiences in PR. None of these scholars was involved in public relations or strategic communication and, I suspect, none would argue the purpose of their research was to advance public relations practices in any way. Still, their contributions to our understanding of communication helped me realize the attention of an audience could never be taken for granted. Their research and writing allowed me to understand the meaning an audience would make of a message I prepared and distributed to them was not as simple to predict or control as once thought. I learned from these scholars the importance of understanding the audiences we address, the challenges of earning their attention, and the effort required to keep it. I learned I would have to use my knowledge of an audience to shape messages that had the best possible chance of being interpreted in a way that fit with my client's goals.

15. There is a considerable risk here in summing up this model for strategic communication planning by using the same four letters John Marston used to sum up the public relations process in his 1963 book *Nature of Public Relations*. Marston was writing more broadly about PR as a process that begins with research and moves to action planning and communication, before finally yielding to evaluation (hence his RACE formula). The CARE acronym proposed for this book is much more narrowly focused than the RACE formula. CARE describes only the process of developing a strategy to guide a PR campaign or program. The same four letters are used, of course, but each refers to quite different elements.

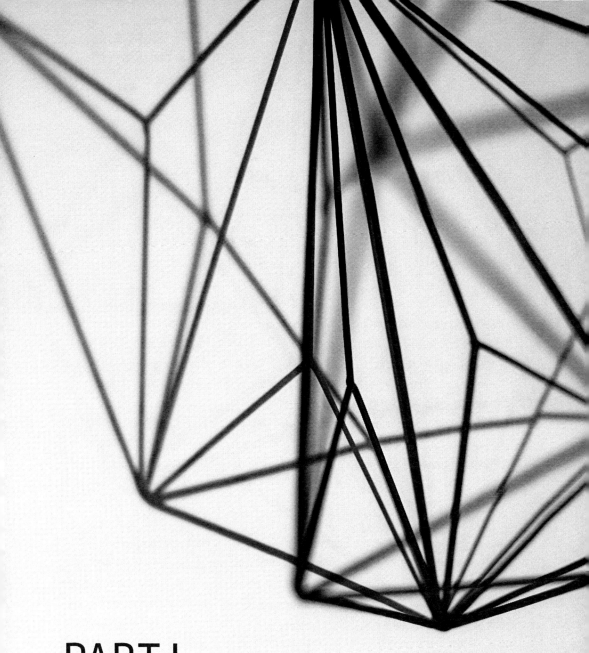

PART I
ANALYZING THE SITUATION

CHAPTER ONE
Identifying the Changes You Seek

The ground is covered with snow. The house creaks, and the furnace groans as the temperature dips yet lower. Even though you haven't eaten dinner yet, it is pitch dark outside.

You sit in the living room, fireplace crackling, and stare at a blank sheet of paper. "What do I want to get out of my gardening efforts in the coming year? What do I want my garden to yield? Will I aim for colour and shade this year—a vibrant oasis from the hot summer sun? Or will it be food? How about crunchy vegetables for my family? Or maybe it's time to do my part in nurturing the butterfly population?"

You try to imagine the ideal garden and what it would look like in early August. You pick up your pencil and start sketching the kind of changes you want to bring to the now-dormant soil hiding under a blanket of snow and ice.

CHAPTER OVERVIEW

This chapter starts at the very beginning of developing a strategic communications or public relations plan: determining precisely *why* you want to communicate and what *changes* you hope to bring about. Next, you will be introduced to challenges that often plague this first and critical step. You'll learn how to push beyond statements of awareness and attitude when defining the changes you seek. You'll be introduced to vision and mission statements and understand their potential to help define the changes you seek to bring about. You'll learn the value of understanding the desired changes as a series of steps you can accomplish in sequence, moving from simple awareness to motivation, instruction, action, and—ultimately—to habit and relationship. Finally, the chapter will touch briefly on the importance of considering both positive statements of change (e.g., residents will visit the public library more regularly) and more negative statements of the behaviours your audience needs to change or eliminate (e.g., citizens will stop smoking).

LEARNING OBJECTIVES

1. Develop a list of clear, actionable, and realistic changes that a PR or communication program can bring about.

2. Draw from the client organization's mission and vision statements to ensure the list of intended changes is tied to the organization's overall direction.

3. Define intended changes for a PR or communications program using small steps and ensure those steps are complete.

4. Ensure the intended changes you define are composed of both positive and negative statements: behaviours the audience must undertake and those they need to cease or modify.

IDENTIFYING THE CHANGES YOU SEEK: THE NEED FOR CLEAR OUTCOMES

Much like a seasoned gardener, it is often best to begin the strategic communication planning process by carefully defining why it is you want to communicate. Any communication campaign or public relations program, after all, is intended to generate some sort of change in the level of awareness, in the attitudes, and in the behaviour of a group of people; those changes are principally why organizations communicate. Organizations continually strive to influence how publics think about certain aspects of their lives and how they behave as a consequence. Some aim to change how members of a public buy food or take care of their bodies, while others aim to influence how people vote, where they travel, or how they drive their cars. The list goes on.

Different planners will call the changes "goals" or "outcomes" or even "results"; the point here is simply that Step One of any effort to plan a PR campaign strategically must begin with a concerted effort to define the precise reasons why precious resources will be spent communicating. Starting a journey without a clear destination is a sure-fire way to ensure you get nowhere.

As you set out to identify the changes you want to bring about, bear in mind the following cautions.

The Awareness Trap

The first and most important caution when it comes to defining the change you want to bring about is to avoid the awareness trap. "We want to create awareness," one client might explain. "We want to change attitudes," another might implore. Though these kinds of statements might be an important clue, they are not generally the actual final outcomes of the campaign. The "awareness trap" many communicators fall into makes an end of what is really a means to an end. Awareness is no more an end in itself than planting a seed is an end. We plant seeds because we want to grow a plant and perhaps harvest it later for food, décor, or medicine. In the same way, we create awareness or change attitudes to affect the behaviour of an audience. We communicate to generate action. We communicate because our organization's success depends on people buying, registering, donating, visiting, kicking habits, and building relationships with our organization over time. These are the true ends of any strategic communication campaign.

One of the surest ways to get out of the awareness trap is to pose the following question: What do we want the audience to do with their awareness? What actions do we want to make possible with a change in attitude? As you ponder this question, try to answer it with verbs. Those verbs, describing real changes in behaviour, are the stuff of which precise outcomes are made.

Those same verbs will later set the stage for the evaluation framework you will need.

Looking for Mission and Vision

Sadly, many organizations don't have as clear a sense of outcomes as a gardener planting a garden. Most organizations have only a vague sense that they need to communicate. They do it because, after all, don't all other similar organizations communicate? They communicate because they always have. Sensing that communication is something they *ought* to do is a far cry from knowing precisely *why* they communicate and what change they want to generate in the process.

Developing a clear and precise list of the changes they intend to bring about demands an organization's leaders get at the very heart of why they are investing in moving messages through space and time. In some way, they need to link communication to the very survival and ultimate success of the organization. The place to start this process, then, is with the broadest possible statement of the organization's *raison d'être*. Often dubbed the "mission statement," this is an elegant expression of why an organization does what it does. What greater purpose does it serve beyond its own survival? A publicly traded business exists to create value for its shareholders. A hospital's mission is to ensure the health of the population it serves. A school exists to foster the growth of its students into successful citizens. A state exists to allow its citizens to live with peace, order, and good government. A church's mission statement might be nothing less than to guide and save the souls of its parishioners.

The point here is every organization must have a clear sense of why it does what it does; that sense needs to go far beyond the obvious: "because it's what we do." The mission should be noble and inspiring enough to guide the organization and give momentum to its people. If it is, then in that mission statement you will likely find the seeds of the entire communication strategy. The communication strategy must—note the word "must" here, not "should"—be completely focused on driving the organization toward its mission. If the organization's mission is to create value for shareholders then the ultimate change brought about by the communication strategy must be to change the results generated by that company and to change perceptions of the company and its management, encouraging more people to change their behaviour and invest more in the company.

So, how do you get from a lofty mission statement to a set of precise changes for your communication campaign? You ask the fundamental question: If we are to achieve this mission, who must change their behaviour in what ways? It's not an easy question to answer, and it is one best answered by a group of people (perhaps a board or a committee), but the resulting statements of *who* (your audiences) and *what* (your verbs) will be well worth the effort.

Many organizations also wisely take the time to define what success will actually look like for them—a definition often summed up as the "vision statement." The vision statement guides the organization by helping everyone in the organization understand what future they are driving to and, to a certain extent, how they will get there. So, for example, the hospital whose mission is to ensure the health of the population it serves might want to be the #1 choice for prenatal care of expecting parents in the region. Getting to #1 will require changes in awareness, attitudes, and behaviour. It will require stronger relationships with more audience members. The beauty of this kind of vision statement is it's loaded with clues as to what the outcomes of a strategic communication program should be. If the hospital in this example is to realize its vision:

- expecting parents will recognize the hospital as being ethical and have confidence in their choice;
- parents and other health professionals will recognize the high quality of care offered there and be confident in turning to this hospital;
- parents will turn to this hospital for prenatal care services more than they turn to competitors; and
- health professionals working elsewhere will learn of this hospital's reputation for quality and for warm, friendly service and be attracted to come and work here.

With a little time and thinking, we can turn these kinds of lofty and broad statements into outcome statements that clearly set out "who" and "what" will change. The key to using the mission and vision statements as the foundation for the list of intended changes around which you will build the communication strategy is to find within them some indications of real behaviour by real audiences that will allow the organization to succeed. Creating changes in these behaviours are the reason your organization is communicating.

Help! We Have No Mission Statement

Not all organizations have taken the time to discuss and clearly articulate their mission and vision. Some organizations are brand new and not at a stage where they can yet focus on this long-term planning process. This is when you, as the strategic communications planner, will have to gather 'round you the leaders of the organization and have them contribute to the planning process. You and your colleagues or clients will have to consider a number of complex and important questions that are essentially the same as those discussed above.

- Ultimately, why does this organization exist?
- Other than ensuring its survival, what is the organization striving to do?
- How does this organization hope to touch the people around it (employees, shareholders, clients, the larger community, the world)?
- What will be the legacy this organization leaves behind?
- What does success look like for this organization? How will we know when we get there?
- When this organization reaches its ultimate success, what will be happening inside the organization and immediately around it?

The process of arriving at a mission and vision is nuanced and, at times, exhausting. Several excellent books and articles have been written on the topic and could serve as useful reference.[1] In addition, there are many consultants who specialize in facilitating the process through which an organization defines its mission and vision. A skilled facilitator who has helped organizations similar to yours through the process can help you and your colleagues move quickly and avoid the common traps that can grind the process to a halt. As such, they represent a solid investment for any organization serious about crafting a mission and vision to guide and energize the organization's strategy for years to come.

Step by Step

The mission and vision statements are clearly the place to start building the list of changes your communication strategy will bring about. Next, you can continue to grow your list by considering all of the steps involved in getting there. After all, a simple act like changing the donation behaviour of a donor involves a number of important steps for the audience. Donors must first learn about an organization and form a positive impression of the cause and the organization itself. Note again how awareness is an important means to an end but not the end in itself. The end here is a donor's cheque in the mail.

The steps involved are best understood as a continuum along which any public relations campaign must move as it seeks to alter the behaviour of an audience and the relationship that audience has with the PR client.

Awareness → Motivation → Instruction → Action → Habit/Relationship

To understand what this continuum is all about, imagine you're at home and hungry and not at all in the mood to cook. Will it be pizza? Chinese food? Indian cuisine? Or perhaps a simple burger? The range of options you consider at first will depend on your awareness. How aware are you of your options, based on your past experience, exposure to advertising, and conversation with friends and family? You might even decide to increase your level of awareness by reaching for your cellphone or laptop and conducting a little research.

Once you've arrived at a list of options, you choose among them. This is where the second stage in the continuum—motivation—comes in. You look for some reason to go with one choice over another: nutrition, taste, timing, impressing your friends, or price. The key is that you select your criteria and choose accordingly. Selecting criteria and choosing among options are behaviours; we're already far beyond the awareness trap.

The third stage in the continuum—instruction—involves learning what to do to get the food you've chosen. Is there a number to call? A URL or street address to find? An app to download? How can you pay? When should all this happen?

Now that you're aware, motivated, and fully briefed on your instructions, you take action. This is stage four on the continuum. You take action step by step: you call or click, you place your order, you give your credit card number, you wait for a while, and you enjoy the food once it arrives.

The last stage in the continuum is a subtler one and one we'll consider in more detail in later sections. Habits and/or relationships are formed when the actions we take meet or exceed our expectations. The pizza is great, and it arrived hot and five minutes earlier than you expected. The driver was friendly and seemed appreciative. You put the menu on top of the fridge and thought to yourself, "I have to order from this restaurant again." With each time you do order again and your expectations are met or exceeded again, the habit grows. Over time, the relationship between you and the pizza restaurant deepens, and your propensity to act in a certain way grows. You become a valuable customer to the restaurant.

This little story about ordering pizza demonstrates how a simple enough mission statement (to become the #1 pizza restaurant in the city) quickly expands into a series of changes that will orient the communications strategy.

- Potential customers will find our ad or website and consider us when they are hungry.
- Potential customers will learn of our great taste, low price, and rapid delivery.
- Potential customers will easily remember our phone number or URL (through a radio jingle perhaps) or easily find our restaurants (a big red roof would help).
- Potential customers will call or click and order our food.
- Customers will remember the experience, value the food, and come back to us next time; they will become regular customers.

The list of possible outcomes seems to suggest each step will happen in precisely that order, which is not necessarily true. Consumers are wonderfully unpredictable and might easily skip a step or switch the order of them. That's why it's important to remember all of these possible outcomes from a successful campaign; if they're the kind of changes you hope to bring about, it makes sense to have messages that speak to each one of them in every campaign you run.

The power of this approach to thinking about changes in behaviour as the goal of a PR campaign is each outcome is clearly stated as an action—a specific change in behaviour that a group or an individual (a public) may make on their way to the final destination. This kind of clarity—which publics will behave in what ways—is the essential building block for a successful strategic communication plan. We now know what to aim for. We know where we want to go and what it will look like when we get there.

Accentuate the Positive—but Don't Stop There

There is a tendency in defining outcomes to focus exclusively on positive statements of an action taken: "Customers will download our app." "Patients will choose our hospital." "Donors will send in their money." This is a fine starting point, but you need to think outside this box to fully capture all the possible outcomes for your campaign. Quite often, communication campaigns involve motivating people to *stop* certain behaviours (smoking and texting while driving come to mind). Your campaign might also be geared to *changing* existing behaviour—to take the same behaviour but alter it in a particular way:

- At a faster pace—Pay off your mortgage with bi-weekly payments.
- At a slower pace—Eat more slowly to help digestion and foster more communication with those around you.
- At a different time—Run the dishwasher in off-peak hours.
- More regularly—Buy ten bags of coffee beans and get the 11th free.
- Less regularly—Save water by watering your lawn only once every two weeks.

When arriving at a clear set of intended changes, be sure to consider all the options: adopting a new behaviour, ending an existing behaviour, or altering an existing behaviour. With your mind open to all these possibilities, you will be certain not to miss anything important.

Pick Your Battles

Before we move on to the second aspect of your situation analysis, it is important for you to stop and take a fresh look at the changes you have set out to bring about and think of them as a commitment. Each of the changes you accept for your strategic communication plan becomes an objective against which the success of your efforts will be measured. The changes you intend to bring about become a promise of performance you need to fulfill using the resources at your disposal. With this in mind, review the changes and ask yourself the following fundamental planning questions:

- Is it possible these changes are not *truly* linked to communication?
- Is the barrier really a public relations barrier, or is it possibly bigger than awareness, motivation, and instruction?

- Is something other than communication preventing this change from happening?

If you answered "yes" to all three questions, you should reconsider whether or not it makes sense to try and bring about the changes using only communication and public relations. As a communicator, it is often better to remain humble and focus on the levers we can truly move. What's bigger than communication should be left to others in the organization to handle, with communication playing an important supporting role, of course.

KEY TERMS AND CONCEPTS

As you review this chapter for any tests or assignments, you will want to pay particular attention to the following terms and concepts introduced in the preceding pages:

- changes
- awareness trap
- mission statement
- vision statement
- awareness
- motivation
- instruction
- action
- habit/relationship

QUESTIONS FOR CRITICAL REFLECTION

1. Why start the strategic planning process with a focus on the end of the eventual campaign? Wouldn't it make more sense to focus on the end of the campaign at the end of the planning?
2. Can you think of a PR campaign that got your attention, created awareness within you, but did *not* generate any change in your behaviour? What lessons can you draw from this campaign and its limited success?
3. Find the mission and vision statements of your school or your employer. Use these as the starting point to develop a list of the changes the organization

will likely strive to bring about through its communication and public relations activities.

4. Go back to the list of intended changes you developed for the question above and select one specific change in behaviour. Now build a continuum from awareness to motivation, instruction, action, and habit/relationship for it. What steps might be taken by one member of a public, and where will these steps ultimately lead?

NOTES

1. A good sample of articles can be found on the website of *Inc.* magazine, at https://www.inc.com/writing-a-mission-statement. A book that offers dozens of solid examples and some key steps to developing your own statements is *The Mission Statement Book* (1999) by Jeffrey Abrahams (Berkley, CA: Ten Speed Press).

CHAPTER TWO
Identifying the Key Audiences

After a long, harsh winter during which barely a bird or rodent showed its face, you decide to dedicate the garden this year to attracting colourful, moving life. In particular, you want to build a garden that will attract dozens or even hundreds of butterflies to your yard and bring you hours of colour and enjoyment.

With that in mind, you now have to answer some fundamentally important questions: (1) What kinds of butterflies even live around here and so could conceivably come across my garden? (2) What kinds of plants do these butterflies look for in terms of food, shelter, and nesting? (3) What types of conditions (soil, sun, water, nutrients) do these plants need to thrive? (4) What pests are likely to either destroy the plants I need to grow or deter the butterflies from setting up house here?

In short, you have identified a range of plant and animal species you need to engage in one way or another in order to succeed. The more you can learn about them, the more likely your efforts to attract some and dissuade others will be successful. You have a good deal of research to do.

CHAPTER OVERVIEW

You have already come a long way in your strategic planning. You have clearly defined the changes your communication campaign or program will endeavour to bring about. You are outcome-oriented. You have a destination to which you can aim your work. You know the link between communications and action and understand what must be done. Of course, clarity of outcomes is essential to any planning effort, whether it be planning a communication effort, marketing program, engineering project, human resources effort, or even organizational planning at the broadest level.

With this next step, however, you move into the domain of communicators. You now consider those individuals and organizations you must reach out to and engage—the publics for your campaign. In this section, we consider all the various publics with which we might communicate. We also discuss the different ways publics can contribute to the change you want to bring about. In particular, we focus on actors (those whose behaviours must change to ensure success), influencers (those who can reach and influence the attitudes and behaviour of our actor publics), and enablers (those in positions of authority who can allow our campaign to move forward ... or not).

You'll also learn how to classify and think about publics based on their place in a continuum that ranges from "awareness" to "relationship" (with stops at "motivation," "instruction," and "action" in between). Understanding whether a member of a particular public is only just becoming aware of your organization or whether they know you well and are forging a stronger relationship will help you customize messages to complete each step in the process.

Finally, this chapter will introduce you to a powerful way to structure your research into each public you decide to engage: BENCH analysis. BENCH is a simple acronym that sums up the five main areas to explore for each public you select: their biases, their expectations, their needs, their codes, and their habits. Each item is presented more fully in this chapter, and guidance is offered on how best to find information on each of the five elements.

LEARNING OBJECTIVES

1. Identify a complete list of key publics by considering the roles they will play in the success of the campaign.
2. Customize messages for each of the three types of publics (actors, influencers, and enablers).
3. Understand publics by considering their place on a continuum that begins with awareness and moves on to motivation, instruction, action, and habit/relationship.
4. Customize messages to fit more closely with publics at each stage of the continuum.
5. Conduct a thorough BENCH analysis for each public you identify for your campaign.
6. Think strategically about how your findings in each of these five areas can influence the direction your campaign takes and the messages you will communicate.

GETTING STARTED

Your task as a communicator will be to pick the right publics and learn as much about them as possible to ensure messages get through, publics engage, and relationships happen. You need to develop, in short, a deep understanding of your publics.

Once you have clearly defined the changes in the actions to be taken by individuals or groups as a result of your campaign, the choice of publics seems quite obvious; to a certain extent, it is. That's one of the advantages of beginning the planning process with clear intended outcomes expressed this way. Those whose behaviour we are trying to affect—the individuals and groups we want to move from awareness through to action and relationship—are logical publics for our campaign. As a group, these potentially active publics are what we can refer to as "actors." They take action. They make change happen when they buy, vote, volunteer, donate, recycle, or exercise regularly. Their behaviour makes the success of the campaign possible.

Who Are the Actors?

Building your list of potential publics begins with a review of the changes you have listed and the extraction of the actors identified in those changes. In our hospital example, our publics would include patients and potential patients, hospital staff, donors, and potential new employees. In the case of the pizza restaurant, our potential target publics would include current and potential customers. These actors constitute the first and often primary group of potential publics for the campaign.

Are There Influencers Out There?

The second group to consider in building a list of potential publics is composed of intermediaries or influencers. These individuals and groups stand between you and the actors you have identified for your campaign. They communicate with your actors and do so with influence (hence the name). There are two compelling reasons to consider influencers in your list of key publics. The first is access—influencers can often access your actors more effectively than you can. They may have better physical reach—meaning their messages simply get through the groups and individuals with whom you need to communicate. They may also have more prestige and credibility and hence influence over your key audience, allowing their messages to obtain a higher level of attention and more results. For example, consider a campaign that needs to reach teachers. Important influencers you might want to consider could include principals, professors at teaching colleges, or union leaders. All three have proven, highly credible, and influential means to reach teachers, from social media accounts and email to face-to-face meetings.

The other advantage of including influencers in your list of key publics is their ability to reach many of the people in your audiences at once. This multiplier effect can allow you to send your message to one member of a public and indirectly reach hundreds, thousands, or even millions. Indeed, media relations as a sub-field of public relations has grown because of this principle. When it is successful, media relations allows you to get your message to an editor or reporter who, in turn, shares your message (or some variant of it) with their entire audience of readers, listeners, or viewers. When that influencer is the producer of a nightly national newscast, the impact can be enormous. Your message is delivered in a credible way to millions. In a smaller but similar way, the editor of a newsletter published by a national professional association of teachers could also provide a multiplier effect and allow you to quickly reach hundreds of thousands of teachers.

If it sounds too good to be true, it's because it often is. There are no guarantees when it comes to using influencers to send your message. They may ignore your message. They may disagree. They may agree but choose not to send it on to your ultimate public. Worse still, they may amend, distort, or contradict your message and actually undermine your efforts—all of it quite legitimately. As you identify potential influencers who could help you reach actors, focus on:

- influencers you can indeed reach and convince to pass on your message;
- influencers likely to leave your message largely intact and not contradict it; and
- influencers who can effectively reach your ultimate public with precision and credibility.

When all three conditions look promising, you have good reason to include the influencers as a potential public for the campaign.

Enablers: Making or Breaking the Campaign

The third and final set of potential publics to consider—the enablers—includes individuals and groups who stand in some position of authority and who can decide whether or not your communications program or campaign can be implemented at all. Because of their power, they can enable your campaign to proceed, modify it in any way they want, or even block it.

There are many examples of enablers you will come across in your career.

- An association planning an ambitious communication campaign has to ensure the board is ready to approve the funding and a committee of the board approves the messages.

- A corporation planning a campaign has to ensure regulatory agencies will approve the messages.
- A non-governmental organization (NGO) planning to reach out to individuals who will be in a court of law needs to ensure judges are aware of the campaign and endorse the messages.
- A public hospital which had formerly been run by a religious order of nuns must secure the approval of the leaders of the order before changing the brand and promoting it.

Quite often, the authority of the enablers you need to consider is political or managerial. Think of CEOs, elected officials, and board members as important enabler publics. They have the demonstrated power to put a stop to your campaign or to boost it. You need to go further and also consider individuals and groups whose authority is more moral or bureaucratic. The voters who put the elected official in office have great power to enable or block, as do the community groups who can protest against the decisions of a CEO.

The key is to consider all the groups and individuals who, at some stage, can either approve of your efforts to change behaviour and allow them to proceed or in some way disagree and thwart your efforts. Often you won't require your enabler audiences to actually "do" anything but merely agree to not get in the way of your efforts. Nonetheless, the support of enablers should never be taken for granted. You have to ensure they are aware, motivated, and clearly called to support the campaign. Enablers generally don't like surprises. They like to know about your plans early and to be brought up to date often. In the long run, good and enduring relationships with enablers can ensure they allow your campaign to unfold and, in some cases, make additional resources available to you.

Consider, for example, the process you undertook to select the college or university you now attend. There's no question you were the principal actor in this case. Your parents likely handed that responsibility to you, even though they might well have been funding a good part of this adventure. As you sorted through dozens of possible schools and programs, you were surrounded by influencers, from friends and teachers to the news media and contributors to various websites you no doubt visited. There were also some key enablers in the process, however. Your parents likely had to be convinced you were taking the selection process seriously and doing your research, or they might well have changed the rules of the game considerably. And, of course, the universities and colleges in question (and their admissions staff in particular) were also key enablers; if you didn't present them with the right information and the right grades at the right time (and with the right cheques attached), your choice of college or university might well have been all for naught.

Focusing on the Principal Publics

So far, you have been focusing on the first step in determining the key publics for your communication campaign or program: developing a list of the actors, influencers, and enablers you *could* reach out to. The initial list of potential publics will likely be quite long and exceed the means of all but the wealthiest organizations. Don't let that stop you from adding important publics to it, however. The first step when developing a strategic communication plan is "going long." Gather as complete a list of the potential actors, influencers, and enablers as you can.

That long list will allow you to move to the second stage: distilling the potential publics to a more manageable number in a strategic way. The key to this stage is to identify the optimal publics to reach with your campaign or program. To do this, carefully review the list of actors, influencers, and enablers you have developed. Ask yourself the following six questions for each public on those lists.

1. Have we communicated effectively with this audience in the past?
2. Can we reliably reach this audience with our current array of communication vehicles and events?
3. Is the expense of reaching out and engaging this public likely to generate a strong return on investment? Will enough of them change their attitudes, behaviour, and relationship to warrant the expense?
4. Has our research allowed us to identify the reasons why this public would resist the campaign, and are we confident our creative strategy would overcome this resistance?
5. Has our research allowed us to identify why this public is likely to pay attention to our messages and likely to change their behaviour and their relationship as a result?
6. Are we likely to succeed in our efforts to create awareness, motivation, instruction, action, and relationship with this public? Are our messages up to the challenge?

If the answer to most of these questions is an enthusiastic "yes," then by all means include this public on your list of key publics for the campaign. If most of the answers are "no," then move on to other audiences. If you are split (i.e., three "yes" and three "no"), then consider doing more research into this audience before deciding. The section below will help you plan and design the research you will need.

USING RESEARCH TO UNDERSTAND YOUR PUBLICS

Once you have identified a number of publics to reach, you need to turn your attention to developing a deep knowledge of them. The better you know a public, the easier it will be to fine-tune your strategic approach to reaching, motivating, and engaging them. On the other hand, communicating without recent and reliable research is essentially gambling with your client's or your employer's money.

The first step in research to understand a public is to identify where each of your publics is along the path to taking action and building habits and relationships. Consider where they presently are on a continuum from awareness to motivation, action, and habit or relationship.

Awareness → Motivation → Instruction → Action → Habit/Relationship

The public's placement on this continuum will be your starting point and will help you identify exactly the gap that prevents each audience from moving to habit or relationship so your organization can succeed.

For each audience, ask yourself:

- Are they simply unaware?
- Are they aware but not at all motivated to act in the way we need them to act?
- Are they all set to go but lacking clear instructions?
- Have they acted once but still need time and reasons to develop a habit or lasting relationship?

Clarifying this starting point now will help you craft your messages more effectively later.

Situating your audiences on the continuum from awareness to relationship is a good first step. It clarifies the challenge you will face. In addition, though, you need to learn as much as possible about *how* the audience will find, interpret, and respond to your messages. This step of information-gathering is essential to your success since messages will be the primary means by which you try to move the audience to habit or relationship.

BENCH Analysis: What You Need to Know about an Audience

Your key audiences will bring five essential ingredients to the process: biases, expectations, needs, codes, and habits. These five words form a memorable acronym: BENCH. Using research to learn as much as possible about all five elements is termed a BENCH analysis of a public. By learning about all five elements for each public you hope to reach, you will be able to tailor the message and the channels to the audience and heighten the chances of success.

Biases

Communication is rarely an objective process that moves predictably from one sender to a wide range of receivers. Each member of a given public brings their own personal biases to the process, and these biases help shape what messages get through personal filters and how these are interpreted. Essentially, the biases we bring to the communication process are biases for and against (a) the sender, (b) the vehicle, and (c) the message. Biases against the sender can be the most challenging since they tend to cut the message off early and divert it to the overflowing bin of messages that were ignored. Imagine a politician you despise and disagree with is delivering a speech on television. Do you watch or change the channel? And if you do decide to watch, are you listening objectively to each point in their argument? Now consider that same politician is delivering a speech on the radio. You don't much like radio and would rather listen to the speech by watching an online video. Finally, consider the politician delivers a speech in which they acknowledge their mistakes and ask students to give them a second chance; the speech is funny, heartfelt, and beautifully delivered. Notice how fully a bias for or against the sender, the vehicle, and the message can dramatically affect the likelihood of success.

Finding out what biases your publics harbour for or against your organization can be challenging. Start by reviewing the feedback you gather from each public (you do gather feedback, of course!), but you should also consider going further to analyze media coverage, conduct surveys[1] of the publics, and, when particularly complex issues emerge, run focus groups[2] to get at the heart of the bias.

There are two important ways to understand a public's bias for or against a medium. First, evaluate your current efforts to reach that public and determine what vehicles seem to be most effective at getting through and generating action. Second, ask them! A standard audience survey will often reveal everything you need to know about the media and vehicles your publics find credible, attractive, and effective.

Finally, finding out about biases for or against the messages you create is not always easy, but it is always possible and always worth the effort. That effort should begin with the people on the front lines who actually communicate with potential voters, donors, customers, and so on. They hear and see the objections to your messages every day. They know the appeals that work best. Be sure to make these frontline people a core part of your situational analysis team. You can also learn about biases with surveys and focus groups. For maximum effectiveness, you'll want to hear from both those who are voting, donating, and buying *and* those who are not.

Your role as a strategic communicator is not to question but to understand these biases. You need to know as much as possible about the biases and to use this knowledge of the publics to craft messages with a high likelihood of being noticed, read thoroughly, and given a fair chance of motivating that public.

Expectations

Expectations are a much subtler element that members of a public bring to the process of communication; it is, in addition, an element that is becoming more and more important to the success of communication and public relations campaigns. Members of your key publics bring certain expectations about your organization and about the vehicles you use to carry your messages. This complex set of expectations helps the public deal effectively with the ever-growing flow of information around them. Expectations help them prepare, manage, and sift more effectively through the flow. Perhaps the finest example of the power of expectations is the classified ads section of any newspaper or online sales site (e.g., Kijiji or Craig's List). Those looking to buy a used car will know the used cars are grouped together and can be searched by make, model, and year. Because we expect this kind of organization, we can quickly find what we came for. It all seems logical because we expect to function in a certain way and it does. Without that logical order, we would be lost.

The expectations brought to the communications process by your audience will include the format of the message you send (e.g., table of contents at the start, appendices at the back). They will also include the actual content of the messages you send. Consumers expect ads will include a contact number, web address, and social media handles. They expect ads won't be offensive or repulsive. Editors expect your media release to be written in a journalistic style and contain essential information about the story. Voters will expect a politician's speech to feature promises, a critique of their opponents, and to build to some form of crescendo at the end.

The key to working with audience expectations is to carefully decide whether to conform to expectations or dash them completely. Either approach can, depending on individual circumstances, be quite effective. When the brand was first launched in 1985, General Motors' new Saturn division generated a good deal of excitement for its ads when they abandoned the traditional way to sell cars in favour of a subtler, personal approach. TV spots lampooned traditional car dealership commercials. The traditional haggle and "I'll have to run this by my manager" approach to sales was replaced with a fixed price and no-pressure approach. Expectations were dashed with—at the time—impressive results. Italian clothing retailer Benetton used a similar approach in the 1990s when it turned its magazine advertisements into powerful statements on contentious social issues. The clothing was often nowhere to be seen in the ads, and the messages broke all expectations. The result was strong brand awareness for Benetton and a truly distinct positioning in a competitive market. The ads, meanwhile, also offended some consumers and generated a good deal of negative publicity. The point here is that dashing expectations is often a risky approach to take but when getting attention is a priority, it may just be the optimal way to proceed.

How does one learn about the expectations members of a particular public hold? One asks. This is where a research panel[3] of your customers, donors, or voters can be an invaluable resource for planning effective communication and public relations campaigns. A good survey, series of focus groups, or even one-on-one research interviews[4] can help an organization learn more about what members of a public expect. Once you know, you can make a decision about whether or not to conform to those expectations or try dashing expectations.

Needs

Next, your knowledge of the audience should include a sense of the needs of the individuals. Consider needs in the broadest possible sense as you set out to do this. What are the basic desires driving the people in your key public to do what they do? It can be useful here to think in terms of loves and fears. Every human being has certain "loves" in their life—things of which they want more. Loves can include life, a sense of security, romance, sex, material objects, spiritual connections, and friendship. The list goes on. By the same token, individuals are also driven to want less of the things they fear in their lives: thirst and hunger, danger, exposure to the elements, poverty, loneliness, death, shame, being taken advantage of or lied to, and so on.

Communicators can leverage the knowledge they gather about the needs (loves and fears) that most drive the members of their key publics. Knowledge of needs can help an organization align its messages with those needs. When the messages you create are indeed aligned with the loves and fears of the audience, those messages will be far more successful in securing attention, engaging the audience, and motivating them to take action.

For example, consider a new father who is suddenly driven by a powerful need to protect and nurture his child. At the same time, the new father may also experience a new and different fear of dying—of no longer being there for his child. As you can imagine, these powerful needs will help shape both the choice of messages to which that father will pay attention and the way in which he will interpret those messages. Suddenly, a magazine ad for life insurance that shows a father resting on a hammock with a newborn infant sleeping peacefully on his chest will immediately get the attention of the father. The headline that reads "How will you provide for her if you are not there?" will strike a chord with that father, who is then very likely to read on. By the same token, the TV spot for a sports car, showing a young man with a bevy of beautiful women admiring the car may not get nearly the same level of attention and engagement. This spot is simply not as aligned with the needs of this individual as the TV spot for a sport utility vehicle showing a dad and his family unloading camping gear.

As powerful as this alignment between messages and the needs of the audience appears to be, it has to be used with a good deal of caution. The product or service you are proposing to the audience must in some *real* way be connected to the needs with which you are trying to align your messages. Appealing to a father's need to protect his children is a great way to sell life insurance, a car packed with safety features, or the need to plan an escape route in the event of a fire in the house. It is not, however, a sound way to sell jeans or a new schedule for garbage pick-up in the city. You may well get the attention of the members of your key public for a brief moment but your efforts to motivate these people to buy your jeans or take the garbage out on Wednesday nights is likely to fall flat. More importantly, you risk alienating the members of the public if they sense they are merely being manipulated. That alienation will be long-lasting and make it much more difficult to build the kind of habit or relationship with the public that is so often the ideal outcome of a successful communication program.

Discovering what needs are most driving the members of your key public is best done through qualitative research, such as focus groups and interviews. Qualitative research is better suited to getting a glimpse of the deeper needs that motivate individuals. The new father who buys a sport utility vehicle may not know the choice was driven by a need to protect his newborn. A skilful interviewer or focus group moderator can often tap into these more hidden motivations.

Codes

As the discussion of Stuart Hall in the Introduction made clear, communication is a very complex and profoundly human process. At its most basic level, communicating is a process of encoding, transmitting, and decoding messages. The ideas of the sender are coded using language along with oral sounds, images, and gestures (or paralanguage, to use the term coined by George L. Trager[5] and developed by Ray Birdwhistell). This encoding serves to package the idea so it can begin the journey through space and time from one head (the sender's) into another (the receiver's). Of course, the success of the process depends upon the sender and receiver using the same or similar codes. As a strategic communicator, your task is to learn as much as possible about the code your audience will use to decode the messages.

Basic language is a crucial part of the code we use, but codes often go much further. Consider how the language of teens can differ from that of their parents. In the past two decades, words like "post," "chat," and "tweet" have taken on a whole new meaning. New words like "blog" and "Instagram" have emerged and continue to emerge. Codes also differ according to the education level and profession of the publics with whom you communicate. To a public of lawyers, the expression "called to the bar" takes on a whole new meaning. Health professionals and administrators know the codes that allow them to make sense of an expression like "evidence-based best practices in primary care" in a way few others can.

There are many ways to learn the codes of your key publics. By far the most effective is to listen to what they say, read what they write, and watch what they do. Formal focus groups can be a place to start listening, but be sure to go further and build many opportunities in your communication program for the publics to provide feedback and input. Each of those opportunities can generate volumes of useful information and insight into your public's codes as you see the patterns they use when they communicate and reflect those when you reach out to them.

Habits

Finally, publics differ widely in terms of the ways they consume information each day and what they do with that information. The more you understand your key publics' media consumption habits, the better you can ensure you place the messages you create in the right channels and at the right times to connect with the members.

Finding this information is relatively easy, especially if your campaign might include a little paid advertising. Most media outlets spend considerable time and money making profiles of their readers, listeners, viewers, and visitors available to advertisers. They're usually only a site visit or telephone call away. Of course, unless the data at the heart of these reports has been audited by an independent organization, you'll want to read the reports with a grain of salt; they are, after all, designed to sell advertising, not to inform your campaign plan.

Beyond these reports for potential advertisers, you'll likely want to consider primary and secondary research into each of your key publics. Ask the questions that will reveal the media consumption habits these people share. What media do they turn to most regularly when looking for the kind of information you want to share? What media don't they use at all? What specific channels do they connect with most regularly and most deeply? What are the channels they have never connected with and likely never will? The strategy here, of course, is to go where the public is. Spend your time and money placing the right messages in the right place. That's only possible when you know a public's media consumption habits.

You will no doubt notice that a great deal of attention is being paid here to *learning* about the publics you hope to reach. The reason for this is simple: the members of those publics, in the final analysis, will determine the success or failure of every communication effort. They will choose whether or not to pay attention to the messages you send. They will choose whether to believe your messages and be moved or motivated by them. They will choose whether to act on the instructions you propose and whether they establish or maintain a mutually beneficial relationship with your organization.

For all of these reasons, it is essential your efforts to communicate with a key public be founded on a clear definition of the public, the barriers between its members and the action you propose, their biases, expectations, needs, codes, and habits. As each of these categories of information is gathered and considered, the likelihood of success for the communications program increases.

KEY TERMS AND CONCEPTS

As you review this chapter for any tests or assignments, you will want to pay particular attention to the following terms and concepts introduced in the preceding pages:

- actors
- influencers
- enablers
- awareness

- motivation
- instruction
- action
- habit/relationship
- BENCH analysis
- biases
- expectations
- needs
- codes
- habits
- survey
- focus group
- research interview
- research panel

QUESTIONS FOR CRITICAL REFLECTION

1. Think of a recent, high-profile PR campaign that reached people in your community. Now consider who the key audiences were for this campaign. Be sure to consider who the actors were, what influencers were reached and engaged, and whether there were any enabler audiences that also needed to be considered.

2. For the same campaign, map out where you feel each of the key audiences was at the start of the campaign. Were there any audiences that were not even aware of the organization and its reason for being? Were there audiences that needed solid reasons to change their behaviour (i.e., that needed to be motivated)? Were there audiences that simply needed clear instructions in order to act? Were their audiences already acting in the way the campaign intended? And, finally, were there audiences in a position to deepen their relationship with the organization on the basis of this campaign?

3. Select one of the audiences you identified in questions 1 and 2 and run a quick BENCH analysis for that audience. Learn as much as you can about the audience's biases, expectations, needs, codes, and habits at the start of the campaign. Given what you find, assess how appropriate you feel the campaign's messages and vehicles were for that audience. How might the campaign have been improved?

4. Your client is a government department that needs to communicate complex tax information to senior citizens. They are concerned the text they now have

will be too difficult for the average senior citizen in Canada to understand fully. How might you help them learn more about the codes this key audience uses and understands? Be sure to justify your answer.

NOTES

1.   A survey is one of the principal methods used by researchers to gather quantitative data. Survey questionnaires are presented on paper, using electronic channels (e.g., email, web pages, social media posts), via telephone, or face-to-face. Surveys typically contain straightforward questions that can be answered quickly using brief answers, multiple choices, or numerical scores (i.e., on a scale of 1 to 10 …).

2.   A focus group is an important method used by researchers to gather qualitative data. Focus groups typically bring participants together around a table to discuss points raised by a moderator. Increasingly, teleconferences and web-based conferences are being used to virtually gather participants from a wider geographic area and to make their participation easier. The power of focus groups stems from the careful transcripts of every word spoken by the participants. The analysis carried out focuses less on the precise number of people who answered one way or another and focuses more on the meaning of the answers delivered by participants and patterns in those different answers.

3.   A research panel is a powerful method of quantitative and/or qualitative research. The members of a research panel are selected from a given group (e.g., members, donors, employees) all of whom have an important quality in common. Rather than sending these people a single survey questionnaire or inviting them to participate in a single focus group, the panel—much like a committee—can be called upon multiple times to provide feedback and answers on questions and challenges that matter to them. Given the total commitment of time asked of panel members, some form of incentive is usually offered (e.g., money, discounts, special privileges, recognition, etc.). Panels have the advantage of allowing participants to learn about the organization or issue much more deeply than one-time research participants. Unlike a committee, a research panel should be randomly selected and its members should reflect the demographic profile of the group they are drawn from.

4.   Research interviews are a proven qualitative research method with several advantages over focus groups. Because they are individual conversations between a moderator and a participant, there is no chance the answers of one participant will be influenced by the answers of another participant. What's more, the introverted members of the group you want to study will likely be more comfortable in a one-on-one interview setting than in a focus group and so will be more likely to accept your invitation. This advantage is particularly important when the subject of discussion is personal and private (e.g., sexual behaviour, drugs, alcohol, abuse, etc.). The disadvantage

of one-on-one research interviews, of course, is the time required to use this method. Whereas a 90-minute focus group can gather data from 8 to 10 participants, 8 to 10 one-on-one interviews will take much longer to conduct (i.e., 20 to 30 minutes multiplied by the number of interviews you conduct). Much like focus groups, there is a growing tendency to conduct one-on-one research interviews over the phone or using a web-based channel such as Skype.

5. Trager, G. L. (1958). Paralanguage: A first approximation. *Studies in Linguistics, 13*, 1–12.

CHAPTER THREE
Assessing Your Communication Resources

As a seasoned gardener, you spend time carefully assessing what is in your garden shed. You know full well how the right tools can make your work lighter and more precise. You also have a keen sense of time and its value.

Gardening is all about time and the rhythm of the seasons. You know better than to rush a plant or an animal. Butterflies emerge from cocoons at a certain time each year and the wise gardener will put out food to feed the butterflies only once the metamorphosis has taken place. You also know rose bushes take years of nurturing and pruning before they consistently start yielding beautiful and fragrant flowers. If flowers are needed in a matter of weeks or months, a different, quicker plant will have to do.

Finally, you have a strong sense of your own capabilities. You know how much work you can accomplish in a day and where your expertise begins and ends. The workload in the spring is at its highest and extra hands have to be found. Pruning rose bushes is well within your area of expertise but dealing with a diseased tree may require outside expertise.

CHAPTER OVERVIEW

With this chapter, we begin the third stage in strategic communication planning. Our goals and objectives are set and the key publics to reach and engage have been identified. Now we can begin the process of analyzing the situation the organization finds itself in. This is a two-step process, and we begin by looking *inside* the organization and assessing the resources we can work with to mount a communication or PR campaign. The second stage of the situation analysis process—assessing conditions in the external environment—will be covered in our next chapter.

With this chapter, we will focus on how to review and assess the resources communicators need when they work. We will discuss each of these core resources and how to effectively assess them. We will learn about the principal indicators to look for—signs that point to a significant weakness or significant strengths in a particular resource area. This will set the stage for later developing strategic directions that will allow you to leverage your strengths and overcome the key weaknesses.

LEARNING OBJECTIVES

1. Assess an organization's key communication resources to identify both the strengths that can be leveraged and the weaknesses that will need to be overcome.
2. Assess both the quantity of a particular resource and the quality of it.
3. Differentiate all of the core resources communication and PR professionals draw from when doing their work, including both the hard resources (time, money, people, and vehicles) and soft resources (goodwill, strategic intelligence, internal cohesion, and stories to tell).

ASSESSING RESOURCES: FINDING STRENGTHS AND WEAKNESSES

In this chapter, we look deep *inside* the organization to assess the quality and quantity of its communication resources. Much like a gardener who walks through their shed in the spring to assess the gardening tools, seeds, and fertilizers they can use, we analyze our situation by assessing the hard tools of our trade and some of the softer resources we can perhaps put to work. Being communicators, we'll focus our attention on the most essential resources for our work. These will include both hard resources and soft resources. Hard resources can be measured and known with a great degree of certainty; you know precisely how much of a resource you can deploy and what the quality of that resource is. The softer resources are subtler, more intangible, but no less important to our success.

It's important to be clear about the importance of assessing resources; this truly is one of the most important steps in any strategic planning effort. That's because one of the most fundamental approaches to being strategic in any situation is to put your best resources to work. For example, if you need to get to the shopping mall quickly and you have a car, chances are driving that car to the mall is the most strategic approach you can take, as compared to walking or taking a city bus. You leverage your resource and you achieve your goal of getting to the mall quickly. On the other hand, if your car is running low on fuel and you need to get to the shopping mall quickly, the most strategic approach will be to put gas in the car and then drive to the mall. You overcome a weakness, avoid the delays of running out of fuel on your way, and you achieve your goal of getting to the mall quickly. Of course, all of this is only possible if (a) you know you have a car and (b) you know how much fuel there is in the car. Strategic choices are only possible if you have a recent and reliable assessment of the resources you have and those you do not.

Assessing Hard Resources: Time, Money, People, and Vehicles

Hard resources are great to work with because they are, more often than not, a known quantity. They can usually be measured with some objectivity and precision. The four primary hard resources for communicators to consider in their strategic planning are time, money, people, and vehicles. Knowing the amount and quality of each of these will help you prepare to develop an effective strategy that allows you to leverage the strengths and overcome the weaknesses you identify.

Assessing Time

One of the first and most important questions to ask when assessing the resources at your disposal is simply, "how much time do we have?" Much like a gardener has to know and respect the time it takes for certain plants and animals to establish themselves and thrive, the communicator needs to know and respect the time it takes for messages to make their way from the plan into reality and then into the consciousness of the key publics. From there, communicators have to recognize that members of a public often move slowly from awareness and motivation to action and, later, to habit or relationship. Donors have to be cultivated and brought along slowly. Loyalty from a customer is earned over time. The recycling habits of citizens are changed over months and years, not days and weeks.

The question "how much time do we have" is an important one to ask both for what it can make possible and for the limiting effects it can impose. If you find you have lots of time to work with, you can plan your campaign in terms of distinct phases, each concentrating on one step along the continuum. You can aim high, knowing you have the time to achieve great results. If, on the other hand, your boss or board or calendar indicate you have very little time to work with (e.g., the grand opening is in six weeks, what can you do to get our donors and the media out to the ceremony?), you will have to limit your campaign to certain vehicles, certain audiences, and certain messages. You may also have to limit the changes you hope to bring about with the campaign.

There is no hard and fast rule as to what constitutes "enough" time. With experience, you learn what can be done in any period of time. Successful media conferences can be organized in 24 hours. Then again, you can spend four to six weeks planning and preparing for a media conference. When assessing the time you have to develop and implement a campaign you will be doing for the very first time, it can be important to get the perspective of others who have done similar campaigns in the past. They will know from experience how much time is ideal for that kind of communication or PR effort. Generally speaking, however, communication efforts that have to unfold and deliver results in a matter of a year or more can be said to have ample time. Anything less than one month and you are beginning from a precarious position.

As you assess the time you have at your disposal (essentially, asking your organization's leaders, asking your peers, or consulting your calendar), be sure to consider what "quality" of time you have. Two months in the winter or spring are very different from two months in the summer, when the pace of work in many organizations grinds to a near halt with summer holidays. Likewise, if you have three weeks to work with and one of them is the week of Christmas and another the week of New Year's Day, you have much less time than you thought. Quality time is time that can be used for focused, uninterrupted work on a project. Be sure to get a clear sense of how much quality time you will be able to work.

Finally, try to keep an open mind as you assess the quantity and quality of time you have. Many deadlines are self-imposed and not real. When you feel strongly there isn't enough time to get the job done right, be sure to ask for more. If you can make the case that an additional three weeks will significantly improve the results, you just might be able to move people from the "we've always done it at this time" position.

TABLE 3.1: ASSESSING TIME

WARNING: YOUR TIME IS LACKING	GOOD NEWS: YOUR TIME IS A STRENGTH
Bringing about the change you want to happen will involve complex instructions and steps to be taken over time. Members of your target publics will need time to reflect, learn, and slowly embrace the behaviour you have in mind for them.	The kinds of changes you hope to generate are simple and straightforward. With enough information, the members of your target publics should be able to change with ease and speed.
Your goals are ambitious and involve moving target publics across much of the continuum from awareness to motivation, instruction, action, and relationship. Each step along the way will take time.	Your target public is already aware and largely motivated. Your challenge is to crystallize that motivation and move them to take action.
The members of your target publics have no existing relationship with your organization—you are strangers to them. You'll need time to build a foundation of awareness and goodwill before moving forward.	The members of your target publics know you well. They've interacted with you in the past, and you've done a great job of keeping track of each of them and their interaction. You are building on a solid foundation of knowledge and trust.

continued

The intended outcomes you hope to achieve represent a dramatic departure from the current behaviour of the target publics; there is a wide gap to jump. People change their habits slowly and often reluctantly.	The gap here is modest. People merely need to change how or when they act, not abandon longstanding traditions and embrace new ones.
Members of your target publics have a bias against the organization and the action it proposes. You'll need time to get their attention, set the record straight, and turn those biases around.	The bias here is all positive. People know the organization and they like it. They pay close attention to what you have to say. They are ready for action.

Assessing Money

This is likely what most communicators think of first when they consider resources. Much like time, money can be a known quantity and measured with great precision. Firm estimates from suppliers can provide a clear sense of what is possible with the given budget. And, much like time, money can either make a great deal possible or it can severely limit the options open to the communicator. Money, then, is a pivotal resource to assess and doing so is relatively straightforward. Ask the person in charge how much money they are prepared to spend.

Of course, what begins as a simple premise can quickly evolve into a complicated series of what-if scenarios. Answers like "it depends" or "let's just see how the first part of the campaign goes and then we'll determine how much to spend on the second half" can present a real challenge. PR professionals working in an agency setting will often find themselves working with clients who would rather not reveal their budget in the hopes of keeping a lid on the estimates prepared by the agency. The result, often, is a generic estimate that doesn't take into consideration the money available to the client. The key here is to persist in your research. Go as high in the organization as possible and get as strong a commitment as possible to the budget for the communication program or campaign. Communicators need clarity about money if they hope to work strategically.

Remember the further your planning horizon is, the less precise the budget estimate will be. Due to the annual budget cycle most organizations have in place, the majority will find it difficult enough to allocate money 12 months in the future; doing so 24 and 36 months in advance is often impossible.[1]

Although often not as straightforward as one might hope, measuring the financial resources available to you as a communicator is usually one of the simpler steps in assessing resources. Most organizations prepare a budget and are used to making and sticking with financial commitments. Is it enough money? The answer, of course, is "it depends." The budget for the campaign or program has to be measured against the outcomes of the campaign (i.e., how many goals and objectives are there? How many barriers stand in the way?). The budget also needs to be measured against the resulting key publics for the campaign (i.e., how many publics are there? How difficult are they to reach? How far along the continuum do they need to be moved?). A thousand dollars may be plenty of money to reach families in a small neighbourhood and inform them of a fireworks display in July. That same amount is not enough to launch a new business venture in a large urban market or reach a large audience dispersed across an entire continent. Assessing whether the budget for your planned communication campaign is sufficient or insufficient is a relative process and one that becomes easier with experience. Over time, communicators develop an innate sense of what scale of budget is appropriate for a given communications challenge.

Assessing the quality of money is a trickier process. Money is money, after all; it has a quantitative dimension but not really a qualitative one. Then again, money can be targeted for certain kinds of expenses; it is there to be spent on the communication and public relations activities you have planned. Money can also be placed in a "marketing" or "communication" budget. In that case, your plan will have to compete with other plans before money can be set aside for it. Money that can truly be considered a strength is money targeted for a communication or PR activity and money that can reliably be called upon when needed. Your ability to pay the printing bills will not depend on the success of next month's fundraising campaign.

As a starting point to assessing the quantity and quality of the money you can deploy, be sure check your budget for the flashing lights identified in Table 3.2.

TABLE 3.2: ASSESSING MONEY

WARNING: YOUR MONEY IS LACKING	GOOD NEWS: YOUR MONEY IS A STRENGTH
The changes you want to generate with your campaign and the target publics you must reach are numerous and diverse. Each change in behaviour and each public you must reach is an added strain on your budget. The less focused the outcomes and target publics, the more money is required.	This is a focused campaign. Only a few target publics need to be reached and the changes in behaviour you hope to generate are simple and modest.

continued

Your target publics are difficult to reach directly. You'll need to turn to paid advertisements in the mass media to get the message out—a more expensive proposition than direct contact.	Your own electronic media channels (e.g., social media, web, email) should be more than enough to reach the target publics. It's fast, inexpensive, and effective.
Your target publics have high expectations of the production quality of the messages and vehicles you send them. They expect high definition, interactivity, and lavishness. Be prepared to spend or risk losing their attention quickly.	Your target publics are more interested in what you have to say than in how slick your messages are. They trust the organization and generally value what you have to say. Your simple, direct messages have worked well in the past and should continue to do so.
Your target public's codes are largely unknown to you. You'll need to hire creative experts to craft and test your messages with the audience before going live.	You know this target public well. You have an experienced in-house team of writers, designers, and programmers who should be able to develop your messages effectively.
The organizations competing for the attention and engagement of your target publics are working with large budgets, and it shows. Getting attention in this competitive landscape will cost more.	Competition is modest with this target public and, in any event, the appeal your organization has with them means they will look for your messages and engage them almost regardless of the design or production value.
The budget set aside for your campaign is contingent on revenues that have not been earned yet. You hope the money will be there, but you don't know.	The budget set aside for your campaign is targeted, and the funds are already in place. You can move forward with confidence.

Assessing People

The people who will do the work of a communication campaign or program are also an important resource to consider when developing a strategic communication plan. These are the people who will actually implement the action plan: writers, designers, event organizers, and spokespeople. The list is as long and as varied as the list of tactics you will develop in your action plan. Most of them will work out of the department responsible for communication and PR in the organization, although spokespeople are often executives or board members. Quite often, part of the team will also be employed by outside firms and agencies. Indeed, finding good outside professionals is often a solid way to overcome a weakness in the organization's own people resources. Remember to also consider volunteers. These valuable people resources help many non-profit and charitable organizations by canvasing for funds, providing information to the public, and sitting on boards and committees. They are a valuable resource to be identified and leveraged fully.

In order to assess the people resources you have at your disposal, you need to identify the people who are available to implement the plan and measure a number of dimensions for each.

Quantity

The mere act of identifying and counting these people should immediately give you a sense of the scale of the communication program or campaign you can undertake and whether that scale is appropriate for the challenges you face. Other questions you should answer as you assess this resource include:

- Who are they and where do they work?
- What is the nature of their relationship to the organization? Volunteers? Paid staff? Board members?
- How many executives are ready and willing to play a part in your campaign?

Capacity

A little subtler, this measure relates to the actual time people can devote to the campaign. Your CEO, for example, may be a fine spokesperson, but may also travel extensively and only be available to help for an hour or two each week. Likewise, volunteers donate their time and often have work responsibilities of their own. Your assessment of capacity need not be a detailed estimate of how many hours per week the individual can allocate. Rather, identify an approximate fraction of their time you can expect. Volunteers and executives might rate a 0.1 (10% or about half a day per week), while the agency staff might be able to devote two days per week and rate a 0.4. Your full-time departmental staff might rate a 1.0 (i.e., five full days each week), unless they have other important projects and responsibilities, in which case the rating would have to be adjusted downward. By adding up the ratings, you can get a rough sense of the total capacity of your communication team.

Capabilities

Even harder to measure, this dimension relates to the knowledge, experience, and abilities of the people who can help implement the communication or PR plan. Although somewhat subjective and sometimes controversial, it is essential you consider the capabilities of your people. Are their skills and experiences up to the challenge at hand? Is this a kind of campaign (e.g., social media or special events) they have undertaken before or is it new for them? Are you dealing with seasoned professionals or enthusiastic, entry-level people? Are your spokespeople effective and graceful under pressure? Are your writers fast and fresh in their creative approach? The intent here is not to do a full performance evaluation but to identify whether your people resources are a strength to draw on or a weakness you will want to overcome before you implement (e.g., with training, with a strategic hire, with an outside agency to help with the campaign, or with some new volunteers recruited specifically for their particular skill set).

Assessing your people resources is not as easy as determining a budget or the amount of time with which you have to work. You will need to use your judgement and your discretion here; you are dealing with colleagues, not merely dollars or hours in a day. At the end of the day, if you've gathered the right information, you will have a clearer sense of whether or not the skills, experience, and capacity of your people resources are up to the challenge at hand. There are some important warning lights that may help you in your assessment, which are outlined in Table 3.3.

TABLE 3.3: ASSESSING PEOPLE RESOURCES

WARNING: YOUR PEOPLE RESOURCES ARE LACKING	GOOD NEWS: YOUR PEOPLE RESOURCES ARE A STRENGTH
There are simply too few people. Even when you consider staff, volunteers, and consultants, you only arrive at a list of two or three people. You need to consider whether a sustained campaign or program is possible without the money to hire more staff or retain an agency.	You have a large team of staff, volunteers, and consultants. They work well together and are eager to help with this campaign.
There is a clear mismatch between the experience of your people and the challenges you face. The people you have may be skilled and experienced, but it is with types of campaigns and programs different from what's needed here. You have great fundraisers but you're not sure they will be able to help you manage a PR crisis. Your marketing communication experts are at a loss for how to improve employee morale. Your newsletter editors don't seem to understand how to fully leverage social media channels.	Your team has exactly the skill sets you need to succeed. Every type of tactic or vehicle can be done and has been done by your team members. You can count on the team and leverage their many skills and great knowledge.

There is a lack of commitment. Beware a team of communicators composed entirely of volunteers or executives from other departments. Your campaign or program will not be a top priority for these people. You may well find their performance can't match your expectations. You need a core of people on your team who are very committed to the program or campaign.	Your team is 100% committed to the cause. They understand the long-term impact of their work on the organization's success. They genuinely want to see the organization succeed. Communication and public relations are their top priorities.
There are too many chiefs. Many of the small tasks that make a PR campaign or communication program successful are lacking in prestige, to say the least. Staffing a booth, stuffing envelopes, reading newsfeeds before sunrise—these and many more tasks may be required for your campaign to be a success. If your team is too heavily weighted with executives, high-level staff, and high-priced agency talent, you may find it difficult to get this work done and done at a price you can afford.	You have a talented team of people at all levels of expertise and experience. Your skilled and enthusiastic entry-level team members are backed by seasoned and smart senior-level team members.

Assessing Vehicles

The final hard resource you need to assess is the blend of existing and effective communication vehicles you can deploy to get your messages out to the audiences you've identified. These are, after all, the main tools at your disposal as communicators; these tools and your ability to use them are what most separate your work from the work of others in the organization. Assessing vehicles is both easy and difficult, owing to the fact any communication vehicle has a quantitative and qualitative dimension. In terms of quantity, it is relatively simple to measure the reach and capacity of any communication vehicle. This newsletter is 12 pages and sent to a mailing list of 4,000 readers each month. It either contains photos or it doesn't. It is either sent to a targeted mailing list or left on a counter and someone counts how many have been picked up at the end of the month. These are hard numbers that can be measured precisely.

Qualitatively speaking, communications vehicles need to be assessed for their readership and their credibility. Printing and distributing 4,000 newsletters doesn't mean 4,000 people eagerly await the latest edition each month, read it cover to cover, and accord it the highest possible degree of credibility. These softer assessments of a communication vehicle can only be gathered with some certainty by way of research (in this case, a readership survey[2]).

Of course, the quantitative assessment is often completed automatically with the latest generation of electronic methods. Websites and social media channels come with powerful analytics tools you can use to accurately and quickly measure how many have read, what they have read, and whether they shared it, liked it, or offered a comment. The numbers these tools generate are instant, reliable, and impressive. These same electronic channels, however, have no way to gather a more qualitative assessment. Yes, we are more likely to share and comment on posts we find credible and enjoyable, but the relationship between behaviour and sentiment online is much more complex and often difficult to measure instantly.

Whether you are using old technology or new channels, gathering readership data is a vital step in the resource assessment process that will help you determine if your current vehicles are strong resources you can put to work or weaknesses you'll need to overcome. Simply put, you need to ask your audience at least these three essential questions:

1. Of the last four issues or editions of a particular communication vehicle, how many did you read, listen to, attend, or otherwise engage?
2. Of the issues of editions you engaged, how thoroughly did you engage them (e.g., quick scan, read parts of it, read it all)?
3. In your opinion, how influential or credible is this publication (and its source)? Are the source and vehicle knowledgeable, reliable, ethical, and so on?

Table 3.4 sums up some additional indicators to watch for as you try to assess whether your communication vehicles are a strength you can leverage or a weakness you will need to overcome.

TABLE 3.4: ASSESSING VEHICLES

WARNING: YOUR VEHICLES ARE LACKING	GOOD NEWS: YOUR VEHICLES ARE A STRENGTH
No one seems quite sure how effective the vehicles you are using actually are. None have been properly and recently assessed to determine the number of readers or the trust and impact these vehicles have.	Your vehicles are all assessed yearly, and the results have been consistent and strong. Move forward with confidence!

There is little effort to target specific vehicles to specific audiences. Instead, one or two vehicles are intended for all audiences. The assumption is everybody reads the same things in much the same way, and all at about the same time. In this day and age, those assumptions are dangerous and lead to ineffective vehicles with no real following.	You have a full array of communication vehicles and many of them are customized for specific target publics. You can rely on proven electronic, print, video, and special events to get your messages out. Your readership survey confirms the members of your target publics actively read and share the content of every issue or edition.
The vehicles suffer from a dated and ineffective look and feel. The graphic design and the writing lack personality and style. The vehicles are functional containers, but they aren't fun to engage and play with. People spend a minute or two browsing and then turn to something else.	The vehicles all look great, and their design is modern and appropriate for the target audience. Your readership surveys tell you people find them engaging and, yes, fun.
The vehicles all seem old-fashioned in some way. There is too much paper and not enough interactive, electronic media. Young readers who consume most of their information on their smartphones are clearly not part of the picture here.	You use paper only when it's appropriate to the audience or the challenge. Other than that, your vehicles are electronic, mobile, and fully integrated. Your readers tell you the mix of vehicles is effective for reaching them regularly.

Assessing Soft Resources: Goodwill, Strategic Intelligence, Internal Cohesion, and Stories

Now we come to the softer resources on which communicators rely. They are often more challenging to assess and very subtle for the most part. These soft resources, however, are often the essential building blocks out of which the best campaigns are constructed. A campaign lacking in hard resources but blessed with soft resources can still be successful. Never underestimate the potential of proven goodwill, sound strategic intelligence, a tight team of willing people, and compelling stories to tell.

Assessing Goodwill

Goodwill is a resource that, while very soft, some accounting professionals have actually tried to quantify when determining the assets of a business.[3] Consider a brand-new lemonade stand, for example, with a table and glass pitchers and lots of lemons as its assets. The value of those assets would add up to a very modest amount. Now consider a second lemonade stand with the same number of tables, pitchers, and lemons but also with a sterling reputation in the market and dozens of long-standing relationships with clients who line up each day and refer other clients. Which lemonade stand would you be willing to spend more to purchase? That incremental amount in the market value of the business is listed as goodwill.[4]

As communicators, we take a somewhat broader view of goodwill, though one that stems from essentially the same principle. Goodwill is a measure of the extent to which members of your key public know your organization and like it. If the members of your public are aware of your organization and hold a positive bias toward the organization, you can expect:

a) the members of that public will be more likely to notice and pay attention to your messages;
b) the members will know more about your organization, allowing you to focus more on messages to motivate them to take action;
c) the members will be more likely to view your messages as credible and interpret them in a favourable fashion; and
d) the members will be more likely to share your messages and act on them.

All of these advantages will make it easier for your campaign to succeed and will save you money. Of course, the opposite is equally true. A key public whose members hold a negative bias toward your organization will make it considerably *more* difficult and expensive to achieve your PR goals and objectives. That's why goodwill is such a critical resource to be leveraged or overcome in your communication strategy.

Measuring goodwill is not as easy as counting tables, pitchers, and lemons, but it is possible. A customer satisfaction survey, public opinion polling, and focus groups can all work to give you a sense of whether your organization is well known and well liked or not. The trick with any of these research methods is to ask the right questions. Determining the trust the public places in your organization rates a 5.5 on a scale of 1 to 10 is not enough. You need to understand *why* the trust rating is as low as it is and explore what can be done to rebuild that trust. Similarly, if the public seems to feel your brand represents the best value for money, you need to find out more about the bias (e.g., whether it is it based on price, quality, or guarantees) in order to be able to make full use of the bias in crafting your messages. The optimal approach is to combine quantitative research (e.g., surveys of large numbers of people) with qualitative research (e.g., focus groups and in-depth interviews). The surveys help you identify the biases for and against the organization, while the focus groups and interviews help you explore the subtle reasons why the members of the public hold this bias.

One additional, though somewhat indirect, way to measure goodwill is a careful review of media coverage your organization has received. Looked at over time, has media coverage been positive, negative, or neutral? This is revealing for two reasons. First, the news media themselves are often an important public and their biases for or against your organization are usually evident in the words they write and the images they post, publish, or broadcast. Second and more importantly, the news media can have a significant influence on the goodwill people in the community have toward your organization. Years of continually negative media coverage can seriously erode goodwill, whereas positive stories about your organization, its leadership, and its contributions to the community can create goodwill.

A careful review of incoming communications from your audiences (i.e., what individual members of your target publics are saying, writing, and posting) can also help you assess the biases for or against your organization. Again, it's important to be comprehensive when analyzing these messages. Consider all the possible sources of incoming communications, including email, web, and social media channels you and the members of your key publics use. Don't forget to use more "old-fashioned" channels like meetings, comment cards, or phone calls. Keep track of the results in a database, and note the date and source of the communication, its tone, and the nature of the suggestion, praise, or complaint. Much as with media analysis, the important thing to look for is a trend or pattern over time and across multiple messages, rather than the meaning or tone of one individual message. Also remember incoming communications tend to be black and white, with only those who feel strongly for or against the organization bothering to write. These people are not necessarily reflective of the total population—another good reason to consider the big picture rather than the individual message.

Finally, a review of the relationships you have with clients, members, and donors will also shed light on the goodwill you have to work with. Every organization should keep some records of its most important relationships and note, if nothing else, when the relationship started and whether the nature and scale of the relationship has changed over time. How long has a donor been supporting your organization and has the annual amount of donations increased? Have your customers been with you for many years and has the range of product or services they buy from you expanded in that time? Have your partners deepened their relationship with your organization and for how long have they been partners?

Answers to these questions will give you a clear indication of the extent of the goodwill you can leverage in your strategic communication plan. Multiple relationships that have endured and evolved are a tremendous base upon which to build your campaign or program. These loyal customers, donors, partners, and other groups can be reached more effectively, and they can also be mobilized to speak on your behalf and bring added credibility and impact to your efforts. Table 3.5 identifies some other indicators you can look for as you assess the goodwill your organization can deploy.

TABLE 3.5: ASSESSING GOODWILL

WARNING: YOUR GOODWILL IS LACKING	GOOD NEWS: YOUR GOODWILL IS A STRENGTH
Consistently Negative Results—The results of the qualitative and quantitative research you undertake consistently points to a negative bias toward your organization. The biases are deeply held and not based on recent events.	**Positive Results Reign**—When members of key audiences participate in your surveys and focus groups, they are quick to tell you they feel very good about the organization and what it does. The bias is positive and has been for some time.
Media Bias—Your analysis of past media coverage shows a persistent and negative tone to the coverage. That tone negatively affects how your organization, its spokespeople, and its actions are portrayed. It also positively affects how your critics and competitors are portrayed.	**Glowing Coverage**—You get plenty of media coverage and, thanks to the people being interviewed and the results you have to share, the coverage is positive.
The Core Audience Complains—Your analysis of incoming communications from the members of your core audiences (via electronic, print, and face-to-face channels) shows a trend toward more negative messages than positive. The members of your target public are not satisfied.	**The Core Audience Praises**—The incoming messages from the members of your core audiences are almost all positive. People have been touched by what the organization does for them. They share powerful, positive stories. They make your people feel great!
Loyalty Lacking—Your analysis of the relationship between your organization and its core audiences shows mostly short-term, transient relationships. Long-term, growing relationships with customers, donors, volunteers, partners, and others are few and far between.	**Loyalty on Display**—The relationships you assessed are both long-standing and consistently positive. When people engage with the organization, they like what they find. They keep coming back. And they tell friends and family about you. Brand ambassadors are serving the organization well.

Assessing Strategic Intelligence

As has been made clear in the preceding pages, there is a great deal to know about an audience. What biases does the key public hold for or against our organization and the action we propose? What expectations does the public have and how can we use those to our advantage? What needs are driving the public's behaviour? What codes does the public use when it communicates? Finally, what are the public's media consumption habits? Having this kind of knowledge of your key publics is indispensable for the communicator. The more you know about the members of those publics, the more effective your communication can be—the messages, the vehicles, and the timing will all be stronger and more effective if they are based on deep knowledge of the people whose attention and engagement you want to secure. For all these reasons, knowledge of the audience is a powerful resource that must be considered when developing a strategic communication plan.

But your strategic intelligence doesn't end with the audience. As a communicator, you need a solid grasp of what is happening inside *and* outside the organization in order to make the very best choices. That's why assessing resources and scanning the environment both consume so many pages of this book. Some organizations invest in this kind of intelligence and can arm their communication team with current and reliable information. These organizations regularly monitor the news media; they regularly survey their external and internal audiences; they regularly dialogue with staff and management to ensure the pulse of the organization is loud and clear. They talk, formally and informally, with decision-makers and policy-makers in government to know what to expect and when. All of this information is a tremendous resource to strategic communicators and, as such, needs to be part of our resource assessment.

As a resource, then, strategic intelligence is the sum of knowledge an organization possesses of its audiences, its resources, and its external environment. Though the definition is simple, the process of measuring strategic intelligence is much more complex. The question "how much do we know?" is not one easily answered with a firm number. Rather, you end up with an answer like "nothing at all," "a little but not enough," or "quite a bit." That's why it is considered a soft resource. Measuring how much knowledge you have amounts to a judgement call. As a communicator, you need to gather the information you have on your audiences, the organization, and the external environment and ask yourself, "Do I know enough to determine key messages, select communication vehicles, and decide on timing with confidence?" If the answer is "yes," then get to work. Your strategic intelligence is a strength you can leverage to make sound decisions. If the answer is "maybe" or "not at all," you may well have identified an important weakness that needs to be overcome before moving forward.

Many of the best ways to gather more strategic intelligence on your audiences have already been discussed briefly, and include:

- conducting quantitative research (public opinion polling, surveys);
- conducting qualitative research (focus groups, interviews);
- analyzing news media coverage (remember, the news media can both reflect and help to shape public opinion);
- tapping into the insight of your frontline people;
- analyzing incoming communications from members of the key public; and
- analyzing your database of members of the public.

We have also covered ways to assess your communication vehicles and gather strategic intelligence on these, including readership surveys and focus groups with members of the audience. Gathering strategic intelligence on the external environment is quite a bit more complex and will be covered later in more detail. Your task at this point is to determine whether you know enough about your audiences, your external environment, and your resources to make informed, effective decisions. Table 3.6 will help you to assess your state of readiness to make strategic decisions.

TABLE 3.6: ASSESSING STRATEGIC INTELLIGENCE

WARNING: YOUR STRATEGIC INTELLIGENCE IS LACKING	GOOD NEWS: YOUR STRATEGIC INTELLIGENCE IS A STRENGTH
Same Old, Same Old—The overall approach your organization takes to communicate with core audiences hasn't changed in a decade. The world changes constantly, however, and organizations that steadfastly refuse to change often suffer from a lack of strategic intelligence. You just don't have the information that will signal to you and your organization's leaders how much the world is changing and in what directions.	**Definitely Dynamic**—Your organization is always changing and adapting to a changing world. The best part is those changes are based on a constantly refreshed source of strategic intelligence. You know what's going on inside and outside the organization, and you have the freedom to act on it.

Resorting to Gut Feel—Organizations that lack solid strategic intelligence often resort to gut feel when it comes to making big decisions. Ask leaders why they chose a certain direction and the answers will sound something like "it seemed like the right thing to do" or "I just sensed this was the way to go." These kinds of answers should alert you to a dangerous lack of strategic intelligence.	**Driven by Data**—Instead of gut feel, the big decisions are driven by quality data. Your organization values strategic intelligence and has proven adept at gathering it, exploring it, and using it to inform the key decisions of the day.
Copy Cat—Organizations that lack strategic intelligence are more likely to rely on the intelligence and decisions of other organizations. "If Nike's market research is telling it to target women consumers, then we should too" is the kind of thinking that results from a lack of strategic intelligence.	**Always Fresh**—The organization values originality. It rewards fresh thinking. Those who can gather, analyze, and use strategic intelligence to develop fresh ideas quickly rise to the top of the organization.
Old Intelligence—You can point to numerous key decisions based on strategic intelligence gathered two or three years earlier. Old surveys can be a dangerous thing. Some organizations will cling to the view of the world presented in an old survey because the survey results worked for a while, and they cost a lot of money to gather.	**Recent Data Please**—The survey findings keep coming in. They are planned well in advance, and the management processes are designed to ensure that new data can drive new decisions.

Assessing Internal Cohesion

Internal cohesion is among the most difficult of soft resources to assess. It is also, when lacking, one of the most debilitating weaknesses for any organization. Cohesion has two components, and it refers to the extent to which an organization is united in (a) its support for a particular goal or destination and (b) in its widespread commitment to doing what it takes to get there. A cohesive organization is one in which everyone agrees on which way to point the boat and everyone is happy to pick up a paddle and work hard to get to the destination. Having a cohesive organization brings many advantages to the strategic communicator and makes it easier to succeed. Money and time can be found more easily, as leaders and contributors are more willing to pitch in. People resources are more plentiful, with everyone in the organization wanting to do their part. People outside of the communication department are willing to align their efforts with the campaign.

Internal partners are ready and able to play their part. Best of all, everyone is communicating a consistent message so all efforts are cumulative.

On the other hand, a lack of cohesion can impede the success of a communication campaign in many ways. Decision-makers who are mixed or lukewarm in their support and understanding will invest less, demand more, and show less patience as results come in slowly. Communication staff will operate more in isolation, unable to secure the participation of other departments, volunteers, and partners. Synergies will be lost, every step will take longer, and the excitement that can sustain a campaign over time will be lacking. Worst of all, the same organization will often send contradictory messages.

It is admittedly difficult to assess an organization's cohesion when it comes to public relations and communication. Surveys will be of little use since respondents will most often resort to politically correct answers ("Of course I feel this goal is important!"). What's more, boldly proclaiming in your plan that board members and executives are failing to grasp the importance of strategic communication can be a career-limiting move of the highest order. Some diplomacy is called for when conducting the assessment and reporting the results. Having an outside consultant conduct the assessment and deliver the news can be a much safer and more effective way to go in these cases.

Assessing cohesion involves two steps. The first is to identify the individuals and units within the organization whose support and participation is central to the success of the communication effort. These will likely include senior decision-makers (e.g., the board and members of the executive) as well as those whose activities directly affect the activities of communication and public relations staff. These might include staff in the mailroom and staff in related departments such as fundraising, marketing, and IT. Finally, the list should include individuals who can play a role in communication but do so of their own accord—volunteers and local chapters of a professional organization, for example. These are especially important in the not-for-profit sector, where volunteers and provincial and local chapters are vital to the success of many national campaigns.

Once you've identified the internal players who can make or break the success of your communication effort, the next step is to assess their cohesion. This second step involves answering three basic questions:

1. Do they **understand** the importance of what we do and the strategy behind it?
2. Do they **support** (morally, financially) the effort to communicate?

3. Do they **participate** fully in the campaign, or are they prepared to do so when called upon?

The first two questions can be answered with conversations, with surveys and focus groups, or with anecdotal evidence. The senior communication person in the organization will likely have met with the important internal players, presented plans, reported results, and asked for support. That person will be able to assess the kind of questions, comments, and commitment they received. These are evidence of the level of understanding and support available.

The third question—whether internal players participate—is a little more objective. The actual behaviour of people will tell the story. Have executives been available for speaking engagements and media interviews? Have approvals of creative materials been quick and smooth or tortuous and slow? Have budgets been granted or withheld and cut back? Has the staff complement been increased to keep pace with growing demands or slashed when people were needed most? Have posters sent to provincial partners been mounted or kept in a box in a cramped closet?

To the extent that action is the best indicator of awareness and motivation (as argued earlier in the book), this third question is the most important to answer. You can guess at the level of understanding and support you enjoy in the organization. At the end of the day, the level of true participation will be the best measure. People can say they understand and support. But do they "walk the walk"? Did they attend, vote, donate, ask questions, and spread your message?

TABLE 3.7: ASSESSING INTERNAL COHESION

WARNING: YOUR INTERNAL COHESION IS LACKING	GOOD NEWS: YOUR INTERNAL COHESION IS A STRENGTH
Media calls to executives in your organization go unanswered.	Your executives know what to say and they say it well. They are trained, briefed, and always on top of media calls.
Approval of the campaign materials you create is slow and overly critical.	Approvals are quick and they usually bring useful feedback that improves the item being reviewed.
You are often unable to secure people for speaking engagements, photos shoots, and other communication activities.	Your list of potential spokespeople and models is long, and you sometimes worry those people aren't getting enough chances to get out and talk!

continued

Materials sent to partners are not passed along to the intended audience.	Your partners are very responsive. They provide not only a channel to key audiences, but real insight into those audiences and sound judgement you use to improve the messages.
Communication efforts by other units and chapters are not aligned, leading to overlap, contradiction, and competition for attention.	Your communication team is a team. Everyone knows their role and they all play it well. Work gets done well, on-time, and at low cost.
Funding for communication is unstable and subject to disproportionate cuts as compared to other areas of spending.	The organization "gets" communication and public relations. Budgets are realistic, they are stable, and—to the extent possible—they keep up with inflation.
Different units of the organization each hire different consultants and agencies, leading to even more competing voices, strategies, and messages.	There is a clear leadership structure in the organization. There is clearly a desk where the communication and PR buck stops. The messages are consistent, they're strategic, and they are unified.

Watch for the warning signs outlined in Table 3.7 as you assess the internal cohesion of the organization. When you find several of these, you likely have an important weakness to overcome as you set your strategic directions. On the other hand, if the opposite of these warning signs are in place, you likely enjoy an important strength that can be leveraged strategically as you make full use of the resources of the entire organization, its volunteers, and partners.

Assessing Your Stories

The final resource is perhaps the single most important for communicators: a good story to tell, or "content" as it is also called. It sounds self-evident, but consider how many individuals and organizations ramble on and on without generating any action because they don't have a compelling and moving story to tell. They call people to action all right but lack the tragedy, comedy, heroism, romance, and action to capture and hold our attention. Other than hawking their wares or ideas (which may or may not be relevant to the audience), they have little to talk about. Organizations and individuals with little to talk about should, perhaps, listen more and talk less.

Good stories for communicators must have the same essential ingredients as any good story:

- **A Protagonist**—Your organization, your people, and your intended audience should all be striving to achieve a noble goal. The audience always appreciates a "good guy" to cheer for.
- **Barriers**—Other people, organizations, or forces stand in the way of you, your people, and your intended audience succeeding. The presence of barriers—be they economic or environmental forces or an antagonist or "bad guy"—makes your story interesting.
- **Tension**—When success is not certain and failure is a possibility, the story holds our attention.
- **Solutions**—Someone somehow must have found an innovative solution that helps overcome the barriers. Tell the audience about the solution and its promise.
- **Climax**—The tension reaches its peak as the protagonist uses the solution to overcome the barriers.
- **Resolution**—The tension subsides, and the protagonist celebrates success.

Consider, for example, a local hospital trying to help patients overcome cancer. The goals—health and life—are clear, and the patients and hospital work together as protagonists. The barrier—a dreaded and complex disease—is also clear. The solution and climax may include a life-saving operation or a successful program to promote annual testing and early diagnosis. The resolution is equally clear: Lives are saved, and patients return back to their families and communities. In Toronto, the SickKids Hospital recently launched an impressive advertising campaign with very similar themes. The campaign is dubbed "SickKids VS the greatest challenges in child health," and it perfectly leverages the powerful stories a modern children's hospital has to tell.[5]

Granted, not every organization has stories of lives being saved. But if you're a small accounting firm able to help people navigate the rocky waters of taxation and help them free up time for their family, you just might find this seemingly simple story is incredibly compelling to someone who is overly busy and worried about the approaching tax filing deadline. A good story, in other words, has to fit with the biases, expectations, needs, and codes of the audience.

If any of the warning signs in Table 3.8 ring true for you and your organization, take heart: The great stories are there. They are always there. You just need to uncover them and share them with the world. The great stories will ultimately lie with one of two groups: (1) the people *within* the organization, or (2) the people *served by or touched by* your organization. In the first category, you might find you

TABLE 3.8: ASSESSING STORIES

WARNING: YOUR STORIES ARE LACKING	GOOD NEWS: YOUR STORIES ARE A STRENGTH
You and your writers simply have a hard time coming up with messages to communicate.	Your writers have a hard time limiting themselves to only a few messages. There is plenty to write about and it's all great.
Each campaign pretty much looks like the last. There is nothing new to say.	Your campaigns are always fresh. The creative strategy remains consistent but the messages are always new, innovative, and effective.
The news media don't return your calls and when you do manage to talk, they ask you for story ideas that are more interesting, more unique, or more in line with the interests of their readers, listeners, and watchers.	Your organization has a strong, positive presence in the news media. Reporters call you and ask about what's happening. They know the stories you have are exactly what the audience wants to read, hear, and watch.
Presentations and speeches you and your colleagues present generate little in the way of excitement.	Your team of spokespeople is sought-after. Audiences love the stories they share, and invitations continue to come in for repeat performances and referrals.
Communicating more with your intended audiences has little impact on their actual behaviour. You're getting in front of them, but you don't seem to be getting through.	Communication works. The stories you have gathered and presented work. The evidence is clear and compelling. You have strong stories to share.
Traffic on your website is limited and fleeting; those who do arrive move on in a hurry.	Traffic on the website is building, and people are spending increasingly long periods of time reading, connecting, and sharing.
Your social media editorial calendar is rather repetitive, with the same topic featured week after week.	Social media is growing quickly. Your editorial calendar is filled, it's diverse, and it's working. The number of followers and sharers of your material is at an all-time high.

have an executive with a real passion for the work of the organization—one that goes far beyond a paycheque. You might have a staff member who does something compelling (e.g., an Olympian, community leader, local historian). As you consider the stories within the organization, be sure to go back in time as well. The best story may be the one about the people who founded the organization and the reasons that motivated them in the first place. If those reasons still inspire the people in the organization today, then you have a powerful story to tell the world. Telling the story of the people inside the organization—yesterday and today—will help to define who you are by defining the people you attract and retain.

In the second category, you have people outside the organization whose lives have been touched in some positive way by the work of the organization. Perhaps your accountants saved clients time and money at tax time. Patients came to your hospital sick and left healthy. Students entered your program without market- able skills and left with skills and a job offer. These stories of success—call them testimonials—are the single most powerful way to help your audiences to (a) understand what you do, (b) have confidence in what you do, and (c) decide to turn to you when they need what it is you offer.

GOOD STORIES AND "GETTING IT"

I had a real "a-ha moment" in one of my PR classes on the importance of a good story told well. I had invited a local community group to serve as a client for a team of students throughout the semester. The group—Christophers—offered leadership courses at a very affordable price so people at all socio-economic levels could develop leadership skills and become more active participants in civil society. The students nodded politely, but I sensed they really didn't understand just what this group did or, more importantly, why. They didn't "get it."

As luck would have it, we were also joined that night by a gentleman rep- resenting another local not-for-profit serving as a client for a separate team of students. This second gentleman, Tim Kane, happened to also be my business partner at the agency he had founded when I was working in Ottawa (Delta Media, Inc.). He remains a close friend, and I credit Tim with teaching me a great deal about PR and how to run a successful agency. Tim raised his hand enthusiastically at the end of the leadership skills group's presentation. "I know this group," he ex- plained, as his voice broke a little. He stood up, took a deep breath, and reflected on a time many years earlier. "When I was just a boy, my dad took the Christopher Leadership Course. He had been a blue-collar railway worker in Windsor, Ontario, and he wanted to do more with his life. He wanted to make a difference.

"So he took this course, he gained all kinds of confidence and speaking skills, and he became a union leader, first at his local, then on the board of the Windsor & District Labour Council, and then on to national roles at his union and the Canadian Labour Congress. I still remember my mom and I walking down to Assumption University, where the course was offered and seeing how pleased he was after every class, and how proud I was of him."

continued

It was a simple but true success story and, thanks to it, the students all nodded their heads and suddenly "got" what a leadership course really is and how it
can help people rise to new challenges and new roles in society. When told well,
good stories can do that.

Your job as a communicator is to get to know all the good stories in an organization and the people behind them. It takes research, and it takes asking staff,
volunteers, customers, donors, and members to share their stories. The good
news, of course, is that new technology—from Facebook pages to smartphones—
is making it easier than ever for people to do just that. Indeed, we are increasingly
a society of media producers rather than merely media consumers. With a simple
invitation and perhaps a small gesture of recognition, most people will welcome
the opportunity to tell their story. When they do, they'll provide your communication campaign with an essential resource.

About Methods: How to Gather the Information You Need

There are a number of methods you can use to reliably gather the information
you will need to assess all of the hard and soft resources you can deploy for
your campaign. Most of these methods can be implemented at a low cost, but
you'll want to make sure you invest enough time in this critical, early stage of
the strategy development process. Typically, several weeks are set aside for the
situation analysis, which includes the assessment of resources. That won't always
be possible, but you will always benefit from spending more time gathering and
assessing information early on.

Table 3.9 proposes the most common methods used to gather information
on each of the resources discussed in this chapter.

TABLE 3.9: METHODS TO GATHER INFORMATION AND ASSESS RESOURCES

RESOURCES	METHODS TO GATHER INFORMATION ON RESOURCES
Time	Interview organization leaders and determine the schedule they have in mind Review past plans and determine the regular schedule of events your audiences will expect
Money	Interview organization leaders and determine the budget they have in mind Review organizational budgets from past years and determine the amounts with which you are expected to work If possible, negotiate with organization leaders to ensure an adequate budget is in place

People	Interview organizational leaders and determine their assessments of the capabilities and commitment of the people on your team
	Have members of your team perform self-assessments of their skills, capabilities, and commitment
	Reflect on the performance reviews you developed for the members of your team
Vehicles	Conduct a content analysis of the vehicles and assess their content, their style, and their frequency
	Conduct a readership survey and get a measure of the audience's attention to each vehicle, their assessment of the value of its content, and their assessment of the credibility and influence of the vehicle
	Have a third party (e.g., a PR agency) asses your vehicles and provide a list of the strengths and weaknesses they perceive
Strategic Intelligence	Interview organization leaders and determine their level of satisfaction with the intelligence they can gather on the organization and on the environment in which it operates; zero in on the current gaps in strategic intelligence they feel impedes decision-making
	Conduct a content analysis of the current sources of strategic intelligence to which the organization has access; identify gaps in information and the decisions that can be impeded by these gaps
Goodwill	Conduct a content analysis of communication received by the organization from its key target audiences; look for common concerns or complaints
	Conduct surveys of key audiences and include questions on the organization and the level of knowledge the audience feels they have, as well as the sentiment of the audience toward the organization and its operations
Internal Cohesion	Interview managers in the organization and determine their assessment of the extent to which their teams function effectively, with members agreeing on the intended direction and willingly contributing to the effort required to get there
	Conduct a survey of team members and determine the level of acceptance of the organization's goals and objectives, the willingness to contribute to the achievement of those goals and objectives, and confidence in the leadership of the organization
Stories to Tell	Interview organization leaders and determine their level of agreement on the key messages that need to be delivered—the stories that need to be told
	Conduct a survey of audience members and determine their knowledge of the organization's stories, their interest level in those stories, and their satisfaction with the way those stories are told
	Conduct a review of the organization's stories and assess the quality of the story and the manner in which it is told
	Conduct research into the organization and its people and find untold stories that will advance the organization and further connect it with its audiences

KEY TERMS AND CONCEPTS

As you review this chapter for any tests or assignments, you will want to pay particular attention to the following terms and concepts introduced in the preceding pages:

- hard resources
- soft resources
- time
- money
- people
- vehicles
- goodwill
- strategic intelligence
- internal cohesion
- stories
- leverage
- overcome
- quantity
- capacity
- capabilities
- readership
- credibility

QUESTIONS FOR CRITICAL REFLECTION

1. Of the four hard resources discussed in this chapter (time, money, people, and vehicles), which do you feel is the most important to have and to use? Be sure to provide the reasons behind your choice.
2. Of the four soft resources discussed in this chapter (strategic intelligence, internal cohesion, goodwill, and stories to tell), which do you feel is the most important to have and to use? Be sure to provide the reasons behind your choice.
3. Pick an organization you know well, review its public communication channels (e.g., websites, social media pages, publications, advertisements, etc.), and assess the organization's hard and soft resources based on what you find. For the same organization, map out other ways you could assess the resources if you had more time and an adequate research budget. What else would you want to know? How could you find out?

NOTES

1. Of course, this uncertainty over the amount of money available in the future can work to the communicator's advantage. I once presented a very ambitious strategic PR plan to a not-for-profit client. The final list of tactics was long and included many that were beyond the executive director's current budget. Her response was perfect: "I like this plan but you'll have to give me more time to generate the money we'll need to fund it." And that's exactly what she did. Her fundraising campaign was focused on making the campaign possible. Our strategic plan became one of her key fundraising tools. The one-year plan became a two-year plan that laid a foundation in Year One and built the more expensive tactics over top of the foundation in Year Two.

2. A readership survey is a particular type of survey conducted with the readers of a specific publication or online vehicle. Questionnaires can be distributed in print format via surface mail, included with the print edition of the vehicle, or sent via email and social media channels in the form of a link to the online survey. Readership surveys are typically implemented to assess a particular vehicle, the specific content within the vehicle, and the manner in which that content is presented. Ideally, the sample used for the survey will be randomly selected from the readers of the vehicle in question and not from the population at large. Readership surveys should indeed determine who reads a publication but should go further to explore why the audience chooses to read the publication and what improvements, if any, they would like to see.

3. Investopedia defines goodwill as "... an intangible asset that arises as a result of the acquisition of one company by another for a premium value. The value of a company's brand name, solid customer base, good customer relations, good employee relations, and any patents or proprietary technology represent goodwill" ("Goodwill," [n.d.], retrieved from http://www.investopedia.com/terms/g/goodwill.asp).

4. When I worked for a PR agency in Ottawa (Delta Media, Inc.), I instituted a system that named projects by using the acronym for the client organization's name (e.g., Industry Canada was IC) and the number of the projects we had completed for that client (e.g., IC100, IC101, etc.). This meant that on a daily basis we all had a clear idea of how much goodwill we had earned with any particular client; the higher the number in a project code, the more long-standing the relationship and the more important the client was to the agency.

5. For a look at how the SickKids Hospital Foundation has used powerful stories to make effective messages, visit http://www.sickkidsfoundation.com/#/.

CHAPTER FOUR
Scanning the External Environment

As a gardener, you spend more time than most moving slowly and deliberately through your garden. By mid-summer, as the weather heats up and the plants do the bulk of their growing, you walk carefully among them, sniff the air, and check the thermometer. Is it hot enough? Too humid? Just right? And what's with that little breeze coming in? What kind of weather is in store for the next week?

You squint at the sun and wonder if the total number of daylight hours is about right for this time of year. Is the shade from that small maple too much or not enough protection for those young flowers?

You reach down and grab a handful of soil. Too moist? Too dry? Too much clay? Time to mix in a little sand? Or maybe compost to add some nutrients?

You don't just look at the leaves of your plants; you turn them over and look closely for signs of trouble. Who's eating the edges of the leaves? Or is that rot setting in?

A walk through the garden is much more than a pleasant outing for a seasoned gardener. It is a chance to scan the environment and see if conditions are favourable or not. It is an important opportunity to know conditions now and anticipate conditions in the future. As a seasoned gardener, you know the importance of scanning the environment, and you know where to look and what to look for. More importantly, you know scanning the environment is something that must be done regularly, throughout the year. It's not simply a matter of scanning once before you plant the seeds and once when you go out to harvest.

CHAPTER OVERVIEW

This chapter introduces you to one of the key functions of a public relations professional: environmental scanning. PR professionals often function as the eyes and ears of an organization; they are the people who pay close attention to the complex and ever-changing world outside the organization and help ensure the strategy in place to maintain strong relations with key publics is still effective.

More specifically, this chapter will introduce you to a model of the external environment created by and for public relations professionals. The model simplifies and guides your environmental scanning process by dividing the world outside your organization's walls into eight distinct areas or fields. You will walk through each of these fields and learn about the important links between information you will find here and the communication strategy you are developing. You will also learn about how best to conduct research in each field.

LEARNING OBJECTIVES

1. Discuss why PR professionals are well suited to scan the external environment for their clients or employers.
2. List the eight fields of the external environment that are most important for PR practitioners to scan on a regular basis.
3. Discover each of the eight fields and explore their particular links to the practice of public relations. Why do they matter to PR practitioners? How can they help or hinder a PR campaign?
4. Learn how best to gather data on conditions in each of the fields in the external environment.

WHERE TO LOOK: EIGHT FIELDS OF THE EXTERNAL ENVIRONMENT

The strategic communicator must adopt a gardener's approach to scanning the environment. Reading a newspaper, listening to lectures, meeting industry and political leaders, and watching trends emerge—all of these activities become part of a continual process of scanning the outside world. The challenge, of course, is that the outside world is an incredibly complex place. Essentially, the task is for you to assess everything in the world that is not inside your organization! That could include weather conditions in the South China Sea, the pothole on the street outside your head office and the reluctance of the municipal government to repair it, and the rapidly changing price of corn on global markets. It could include those things but, more often than not, it won't. What's needed, then— and what this chapter proposes—is an approach you can use to structure your environmental scan. The model proposed here will help you focus on the areas that matter and will help ensure your environmental scan is complete.

   The model of the external environment proposes eight fields or places that most often yield information on trends and forces that will affect a PR campaign or program.[1] The fields are all constantly changing, and each touches on a sphere of modern life that will affect the members of your audiences and shape the ways they pay attention to and interpret your campaign messages:

1. Political
2. Economic
3. Social/cultural
4. Technological
5. Demographic
6. Competitive
7. News media
8. Natural

To go back to the three examples mentioned earlier in this section, your exploration of weather conditions in the South China Sea would fall under the "Natural" field; your concerns over the pothole on the street and how to get it fixed by the municipal government might well fall under the "Political" field; and the price of corn on global markets would fall into the "Economic" field. It is possible you will think of areas of life to consider for your strategic communication plan that do not fit neatly into one of these eight fields; if that happens, be sure to determine how changes and trends in that field could affect your PR campaign. If you find a way, simply create an "Other" category and forge ahead.

The point of the eight fields of modern life proposed here is these are the areas in which change is constant, and those changes will most often affect the success of your communication and public relations efforts. As the political, economic, and socio-cultural conditions change at a particular time and place, the lives of the people who live in that time and place will be affected. Changes to the technological, demographic, and competitive conditions will also shape the way the members of your publics live, feel, work, play, and make sense of the world. The very same can be said of the news media and natural spheres of life; they change constantly, and those changes affect the people who live, work, and play there.

The key to effectively scanning the environment is to know the areas on which you should focus your efforts. The world outside your organization is so vast and so complex that trying to scan it all without a clear set of limits is overwhelming. The aspects of the outside world that most merit the attention of strategic communication planners are those aspects most likely to directly affect the success of the particular campaign you are planning. The trends and forces in each of the eight fields listed above will have one of three possible effects on your efforts to accomplish the organization's goals:

1. they will make it easier for your campaign to succeed;
2. they will make it harder for your campaign to succeed; or

3. they will have little, if any, impact on the ability of your campaign to succeed.

For the purposes of strategic communication planning, any trends or forces which you feel would fall into the third category can likely be ignored. Focus your limited planning time and resources on trends and forces that will truly make a difference, whether for better or for worse. If you are running a fundraising campaign for a children's hospital and learn the price of wheat is projected to go down after a successful growing season in Europe, you can likely skip that development and instead focus on rising rates of obesity-related Type 2 diabetes among children. The price of wheat in Europe will likely have no effect whatsoever on your campaign, whereas the incidence of Type 2 diabetes among children could have a profound impact on parents, healthcare providers, and their young patients. Your attention, then, needs to be on trends and forces that will have a significant impact on two critical aspects of any campaign:

1. the size of the audience; and
2. the extent to which the audience is inclined or predisposed to pay attention and take the kind of action you want to bring about.

TABLE 4.1: ASSESSING TRENDS AND FORCES

IS THE TREND OR FORCE AN OPPORTUNITY?	YES	NO	UNSURE
Will it grow the size of your audience?	O	O	O
Will it increase the extent to which your audience is predisposed to pay attention to the messages of your campaign?	O	O	O
Will it increase the extent to which your audience is predisposed to act on the messages of your campaign?	O	O	O
IS THE TREND OR FORCE A THREAT?	YES	NO	UNSURE
Will it reduce the size of your audience?	O	O	O
Will it lower the extent to which your audience is predisposed to pay attention to the messages of your campaign?	O	O	O
Will it lower the extent to which your audience is predisposed to act on the messages of your campaign?	O	O	O

As Table 4.1 suggests, you need to reflect on the trend or force you are considering and assess the extent to which you feel the trend or force will affect the size of your audience. If you suspect the trend or force will grow your audience, you likely have an opportunity to capitalize upon; if you feel your audience may reduce in size, this may well be a threat you will need to mitigate. In much the same way, assess the impact you feel the trend or force you are considering may have on the predisposition of the audience, both to pay attention to your campaign messages and to act on those messages. Where you sense the audience will be more predisposed to pay attention and to act, the trend or force is likely an opportunity; where you sense they will be less likely to pay attention and to act, you likely have a threat to mitigate.

To illustrate, consider again the example of a hospital fundraising campaign; if the incidence of Type 2 diabetes among young people grows, then you can expect more parents, children, friends, and family members will be touched by the disease. Those people will suddenly be more predisposed to pay attention to a campaign focused on children's health and to messages about the hospital's efforts to care for children with Type 2 diabetes and prevent the disease. In other words, the increasing number of people touched by Type 2 diabetes may well grow the audience and make them more predisposed to pay attention and act on what they see, read, and hear. Paradoxically, the rising incidence of a troubling disease represents a strategic opportunity for communicators and fundraisers.

Those trends and forces that directly affect the principal audiences you hope to reach and engage are the trends and forces that will have the most profound effect on your campaign and its likelihood of success. Your strategy must be able to make the most of helpful trends and forces (i.e., those that will grow the number of members in your key publics and render them more inclined to pay attention and act on your messages) or to diminish the impact of the trends and forces that will make it harder to succeed (i.e., those that will render your publics less numerous and less likely to pay attention and change their behaviour). As you prepare to assess a field of the external environment, be sure to ask yourself whether and how a change in this particular aspect of the external environment can affect the likelihood of success for your strategic communication or PR campaign. How will the change affect the number of members of a public you hope to address? And how will the change affect the likelihood members of that public will pay attention to and respond positively to the messages in your campaign? If you struggle to arrive at any compelling answers to these questions, move on to the many other fields you can consider.

SPORT DRINKS AND TEEN HEALTH

Imagine you have been hired to develop a campaign to launch a new sport drink targeted to active teens. The demographics in this country are such that the number of teens in the country today is lower than it was 20 or 40 years ago.[2] This trend—a declining number of potential consumers—is going to make it harder to succeed. It is a threat you need to mitigate.

On the other hand, there is a political, social, and news media trend in this country to be more concerned about teen health. Some have even speculated Millennials might just be the first generation in centuries to have a lower life expectancy than their parents. This concern for the health of teenagers might make it easier for your campaign to succeed since a generation of teens, their parents, government health officials, and the news media will be more predisposed to pay attention to and act on messages about a product that could boost the health of teenage consumers. A trend or force that might make it easier for the campaign to succeed is, of course, an opportunity. Your strategy will need to include specific ways to capitalize on this opportunity.

ENVIRONMENTAL SCANNING: HOW TO LOOK AND WHAT TO LOOK FOR

Now let's consider concrete steps you can take to scan the eight fields of the external environment listed at the start of this chapter.

Scanning the Political Field

For organizations of all kinds, the priorities and actions of government legislators and policy-makers will have an important impact on their chances of success. Governments provide the funding that enables many organizations in health, education, and public safety to exist. Governments pass laws that limit what organizations can do and how they do it. Governments respond to the changing demands of society but also help shape the attitudes and actions of citizens. Consider, for example, how the percentage of the population who smoke continues to drop, driven as much by legislation that limits how and where cigarettes can be sold as by effective government public relations and advertising campaigns aimed at young people.

For all these reasons, strategic communicators will continually monitor the priorities and actions of governments at the national, provincial, or municipal levels. Whatever the level, the intent is the same: to identify current or imminent changes in priorities, policies, legislation, and funding programs that will affect the ability of the organization to reach its goals.

Scanning for Emerging Priorities and Policies

Speeches and statements by political leaders often indicate certain issues and ideals are rising on the agenda, while others are falling. Is this a government focused squarely on economic growth and job creation, or is social justice the top priority? Where do environmental protection and ethics in government fit in? The challenge is to correctly identify the priorities that most inspire the governments of the day, then determine where your organization fits or doesn't fit with those priorities. In Canada's parliamentary system, the Speech from the Throne is often an important indicator to read and consider carefully. Speeches during elections can also suggest what a government's priorities will be. Of course, priorities change often, so it is wise to scan for these continually on government websites, in media coverage, and in the speeches elected officials and department leaders will give on a regular basis.

Scanning for New Legislation

Beyond being inspired by certain priorities, governments also propose, debate, and pass legislation. This process can have profound impacts on organizations of every kind. The challenge here is to scan the environment and identify the legislation on the horizon that will most affect your organization's ability to realize its mission. This is possible, of course, because in most instances, legislative changes are the subject of debate and careful review by committees. Legislative assemblies will publish or post all of the bills that are currently being debated and will usually include means by which an organization could offer feedback on the proposed legislation. There are rarely any true surprises when it comes to legislation. Remember to consider all levels of government in your scan (i.e., federal, provincial/territorial, and municipal) as well as the most appropriate committees for the particular sphere or activity of your organization. Finally, be sure to pay particular attention to laws and regulations that will affect your ability to communicate effectively with key audiences.

Scanning for Changes to Funding Programs

Governments still help shape the world we live in by redistributing the wealth of taxpayers in ways that allow the realization of the government's goals and objectives. These funding programs are important for government departments, it goes without saying, since they often give birth to new offices and agencies and provide the funding for them. Government programs are also vital for many not-for-profit groups and businesses of all sizes. These programs can also have an indirect impact on all these organizations by strengthening or weakening competitors and partner organizations.

The challenge when scanning government funding programs is to identify those, if any, which can affect the size and predisposition of your organization's audiences. Most of your scanning can be carried out online, with funding programs often having detailed information on requirements and online applications posted to government websites. Once identified, be sure to get a sense of how secure that funding program is and what its growth or demise could mean for the organization. Finally, consider how new programs could affect your organization and your competitors and partners.

How to Scan the Political Field

The good news is that scanning the political field is now easier than ever. Major policy documents, budgets, and speeches by political leaders are widely available on government and party websites. The minutes from meetings of all-important committees are also often available online. The growing line-up of political and news media now provide in-depth coverage of the goings-on in national or provincial capitals like never before. Governments also increasingly announce their new programs, policies, and laws using social media channels. These readily available and largely free sources will quickly give you a good sense of where your organization and your cause stand.

What these free sources often give you, however, is the official version of reality—what leaders and parties and committees want you to know. To get an inside scoop, you may want to consider hired help. Public affairs or government relations consultants can offer a much more detailed and nuanced assessment of the current political environment. That assessment is often based on long-standing relationships with people inside government—a privileged position that offers a better view of the unofficial political situation. That assessment comes at a price, to be sure. Depending on how critical the political environment is to your organization, the price may be money well and strategically spent.

What Next: Working with the Information You Gathered

Once you've completed your scan of the political field, you need to step back, look at what you've gathered, and ask yourself, "Are the trends and forces in the political environment going to make my publics larger or smaller? Is all this going to make my publics more or less predisposed to pay attention and act? Will the changes affect my organization's resources in any way?" If the answer to all three questions is a confident "no," you should likely move on and focus your efforts on trends and forces that merit a strong "yes" to any of those questions.

For example, if your organization serves small business owners and new government programs are being introduced that will make it easier and more financially viable for people to start a small business, your audience is likely to grow. This is good and you should now look for ways to leverage this new program. If, on the other hand, your organization is dedicated to promoting music education among children and the government of the day is obsessed with getting math and science scores up to better compete with other countries, you will likely face an audience much less predisposed to pay attention and act; you will need to develop a strategy to mitigate this threat, which might include showing the government how music education actually improves math and science skills.

Scanning the Economic Field

Scanning the economic field is not intended to be an exercise in complex calculations and dizzying acronyms. Rather, the economic scan you carry out is designed to draw attention to a single, simple fact: Many of the actions you want members of your key audiences to take will require them to part with money (e.g., join an association, buy a certain product or service, donate to a worthy cause, etc.). The more money members of your audiences have to dispose of, the more likely they will be to take that action. In the same way, the less expensive your action, the more likely they will be to undertake it. Your economic scan, then, is simply designed to give your organization a sense of whether future economic conditions will make it harder or easier for you to succeed.

An economic scan designed to support a strategic communication plan should consider statistical measures like consumer confidence, unemployment rates, and rates of economic growth or decline. These measures help you determine how predisposed members of your key publics will be to part with their money. It should also consider the prices of any materials or resources (including labour) that go into the delivery of your organization's products or services. This last point holds whether your organization is in the manufacturing business or any public or not-for-profit sector. After all, a strategic communication plan for a hospital will be stronger if it considers the implications of physician and nurse salaries increasing. By the same token, a national charity's plan will benefit from knowing the costs of delivering the services it delivers are about to rise significantly.

As you scan the economic environment, resist the trap of getting bogged down in pages of statistics. Remember you are a communicator and not an economist. Stay at the high level, and focus your mental energy on understanding the impact of economic trends and forces on your audience and your organization. As always, make sure you focus on economic trends and forces that will directly affect the members of your key publics or your organization. If the price of corn in Europe is irrelevant, move on.

How to Scan the Economic Field

Where can you find this high-level economic information? Start with the news media, which faithfully reproduces the latest economic indicators, along with pages and hours of expert analysis. Whether from business television specialty channels, business sections of the major dailies, business magazines, or credible business bloggers, you will find more than enough economic information to complete this aspect of your environmental scan. If you feel you need more detail, consider government sources (e.g., the Bank of Canada and Industry Canada), not-for-profit organizations (e.g., the Conference Board of Canada), and major financial institutions (e.g., banks, insurance companies, and trust companies), all of which publish detailed economic analyses for the benefit of their customers and the news media. The reports they publish are usually offered free of charge and are readily available online. Finally, as is the case with political scans, if your needs are quite detailed and specific (e.g., your organization depends on exports of specific commodities to specific international markets), you may be wise to retain the services of professional economists who can dig deep to find and analyze the specific information you need.

What Next: Working with the Information You Gathered

The key question to ask as you review the economic data you have gathered is simply this: Will the members of my core audiences have enough money to take the actions on which the success of our campaign depends? Will changes and trends in the economic field make it more or less likely members of these audiences will pay attention to our campaign and act on the messages we communicate?

The relationship between economic conditions on the one hand and attention and likelihood to act on the other is not necessarily a simple, one-way relationship. Some products and services will be easier to sell when economic conditions are bad (e.g., low-cost alternatives or options with financing included). Government programs that help the disadvantaged will also be easier to promote when economic conditions drive up the number of people who need those programs. On the other hand, your campaign to promote luxury cars or announce tax cuts for the wealthy may find a more supportive audience when economic conditions are strong.

As with all elements in the external environment, then, ask yourself if the economic changes you have identified will render the audience you hope to reach more numerous and more likely to pay attention and act on the message.

Scanning the Social and Cultural Fields

The definitions of what is social and what is cultural vary and tend to be rather all-encompassing.[3] As communicators, there are a few aspects of these very large and broad categories to which we need to pay particular attention. The simple matter is, on some larger, "social" scale, people in a particular society are constantly changing. Our collective sense of what is fashionable, what is acceptable, what is important, what is worthy of praise and criticism will change over time. It is important for communicators to scan the social environment because what is "in" or "right" in one year can virtually disappear in the next 6 or 12 months. People in Canada spent the early 1980s buying "green" products and worrying about the depletion of the ozone layer. Those same people spent the 1990s and first few years of the 2000s buying giant SUVs and worrying more about towing capacity and heated leather seats. Now, many people are back to worrying about climate change and looking for energy-efficient alternatives. Social change is continual, and those changes will have a profound impact on your campaigns.

Carefully scanning the cultural environment will allow you to see how the cultural industries (notably social media, television, the web, film, magazines, theatre, and literature) reflect and deepen social trends and sometimes spark new social trends entirely. Consider a film like *An Inconvenient Truth*[4] and the way it both reflected society's growing concern over climate change and helped to deepen that concern for many consumers (thus affecting the economic and political fields at the same time). Consider how the news media's intense coverage of social media channels like Twitter and Facebook is helping to drive ever more users to social media sites. As communicators, we scan the social and cultural environment so we can deepen our understanding of what is happening today and what is likely to happen in the near future.

How to Scan the Social/Cultural Field

Scanning the social and cultural fields of the external environment is best done on a continual basis; you also need to be focused in your approach. Think first about the trends and forces you need to scan and then select your sources. You'll find yourself otherwise quickly overwhelmed with a vast amount of information only marginally relevant to your campaign. As you set out to scan, pay particular attention to the forces and trends that might affect how people think about the following:

- your organization's work;
- the people who work for your organization;
- the people or interests your organization serves or represents;
- the products or services your organization offers; and
- the values and principles that guide the organization.

Though the subject area is vast and complex, scanning for information on these kinds of social and cultural trends and forces is relatively easy; it's relatively easy because many people like to keep up to date on these trends and enjoy learning about them. That's why the news and entertainment media are chockfull of stories about the latest in style, fashion, technology, food, the arts, and more. The web, social media, and bookstores are loaded with the works of professional predictors like John Naisbitt and Faith Popcorn who work to predict what will be the latest trend. Sources on future trends abound.

As a communication professional, you need to carefully select those you feel are the most qualified and insightful. You also need to focus on those who regularly cover the trends and forces that can affect your cause or organization. Once you've found the top sources of information about the future, you need to subscribe and/or visit them regularly to see what they have to say.

In the same way, the trade media for film, television, music, advertising, video games, and publishing can provide you with detailed information on what projects are now in production and when we can expect them to hit the shelves, airwaves, and the big screen. Sources like *Variety* and the Internet Movie Database (IMDB) provide detailed coverage of major projects in production and in theatres. In Canada, government agencies like the Canadian Radio-television and Telecommunications Commission (CRTC) and Telefilm Canada do a great deal to support the industry, and both their websites provide solid research into the film and television industry in this country.

What Next: Working with the Information You Gathered

As a single category, the social and cultural field is incredibly vast and complex. To make full use of the data you gather as you scan this field, be sure to identify those forces and trends that could make it more or less likely your audience will

(a) pay attention and (b) act in ways that will bring about your success. Focus your efforts on the aspects of the social/cultural environment that will really make a difference. If you're working for a software development firm, chances are fashion trends are not going to have a profound impact on your success as a firm; trends in how consumers use technology, however, likely will. Similarly, if you're developing a campaign to promote the legal profession, societal concerns about obesity likely won't be of much concern; the way lawyers are portrayed in the popular media will be. You'll want to know if John Grisham, whose lawyer characters are usually either the bad guys or somehow morally challenged, is planning to publish a new novel or if Hollywood is looking to turn another of his novels into a blockbuster.

As these two examples suggest, there is more judgement involved in working with data from the social/cultural field. The relationships between social and cultural trends and forces and the awareness, motivation, actions, and relationships of your key audiences are far less predictable. Nobody knows for certain if a book, movie, song, or television program will be popular and whether it will actually influence your audience. Nobody knows for certain if a hot new trend will grow or disappear after a few weeks. Nonetheless, it is important to scan this field and proactively plan how you will respond to the opportunities and threats you find there.

Scanning the Technological Field

To scan the technological field of the external environment is to look into the future in an effort to identify major trends or forces that could fundamentally alter your organization, the business you are in, and your relationship to your audiences. Like any trend or force in the external environment, technology can make the number of people in your key public expand or contract. It can also make those people more or less predisposed to take the action you need them to take in order to succeed. The trick is to know what to look for and how to look. There are four key areas every strategic communication planner should consider.

1. Technology and "the Way You Do the Things You Do"

A good scan of the technological environment should always include some consideration of the way technology will affect the manner in which your organization will develop and deliver its products and services—the ways the organization achieves its mission. New diagnostic equipment and telehealth are changing the way hospitals deliver medical care. Social media is changing the way governments dialogue with their citizens and deliver information and services. Robotics, computer-aided design, and manufacturing and new materials are all changing the way everything from a toothbrush to an automobile is designed and made.

All of these changes have implications for communicators. Technological innovations will change the way your organization organizes its work and does business. Many PR professionals can still remember a world without faxes, relying instead on surface mail and courier to get drawings and documents to others; some practitioners remember a world without email and PDF! As the way your organization does what it does changes, your messages will need to keep up, ensuring audiences are aware, motivated, and well-instructed on how to "do business" with you. Where once you instructed people to visit one of your three locations to pick up your forms, now you instruct them to "like" your Facebook page and download all the forms they need from your website. Technology is reshaping the way we shop, compare, order, complain, and maintain contact with organizations. The set of instructions has grown to keep up with that pace.

2. Technology and "What" Your Organization Does

Technology not only changes *how* you do the things you do, but also *what*— the array of products and services you offer. Hospitals offer MRIs, banks offer sophisticated projections of your investment accounts, electronics companies offer impossibly small and powerful smart phones, and grocers now offer a dizzying array of gluten-free products and a bizarre apple that smells like grape juice! As the "what" of your organization is reshaped by technology, your messages to motivate and instruct audiences must also keep pace. Audiences will need to understand and embrace new products and services and learn the ways to use them. The iTunes phenomenon was built on years of consistent and strategic communications to dramatically change both how people listen to music and how they buy it.

3. Technology and the Audiences You Connect With

Apart from profoundly changing your organization and the way you communicate, new technology may also change the nature of the audiences you address. Technology can dramatically open up the range of audiences you can reach and engage. With a simple web site, a small mustard shop can now profitably sell to customers all over the globe. Alumni associations now keep track of alumni all over the world and use social media, the web, and email to keep in touch more cost-effectively than ever. Changes to communications technology are making it possible and reasonable to connect with very small and very dispersed audiences. There is no longer, it seems, any audience niche so small it doesn't make sense to reach out to them.

This point was made definitively in Chris Anderson's 2006 book *The Long Tail: Why the Future of Business Is Selling Less of More*.[5] Anderson is an author and was the editor-in-chief of *Wired* magazine. His biography nicely drives home the need to scan both the social/cultural field and the technological field. *Wired* has long been and continues to be an influential magazine. Anderson was editor-in-chief of the magazine until 2012 and today serves as curator of the TED Conference; his foundation owns the organization behind the now-famous TED Talks.[6]

4. Technology and the Way You Connect

Perhaps most importantly for communicators, new communications technology is dramatically reshaping the expectations of audiences in terms of dialogue and interaction. The defining feature of social media is that audiences are no longer required, nor do they expect, to be passive recipients of your messages. Increasingly, audiences are active participants in the process. They post videos and photos, they share content they like, they blog, they visit consumer forums, and let loose with their praise and criticism. Audiences still read the news but then post their own responses to the headlines, share the article with others, or respond to other readers' responses.

All of this presents both a threat and an opportunity for communicators. The threat is that our professional tendency toward monologue ("Your attention please for this important message …") is increasingly causing audiences to tune out. Their expectations have not only been raised but, frankly, shifted entirely. Members of your key audiences want, expect, and value your attention as much as you value theirs. If you can't or won't provide a constructive forum within which they can express themselves, chances are someone else will—only it may not be that constructive.

The opportunity created by the new generation of communications technology is that interaction and dialogue are precisely the building blocks of lasting relationships. Finally, communication professionals have the tools at their disposal to quickly and easily keep track of their most important customers, donors, voters, or members. PR professionals can now create dynamic communication vehicles that customize the messages they send to the biases, expectations, needs, codes, and habits of each member of their key publics. Organizations of all kinds can now create engaging new ways for audience members to talk with them, so the organizations can learn from, better understand, and better reach these individuals in the future. The trick, of course, is to change the prevailing mindset so organizations can see and capitalize on these opportunities. By adopting this new mindset and continually scanning the technology available to you as a communicator, you can capitalize on new opportunities and keep pace with the rising expectations of your audiences.

A SMALL CHANGE WITH A BIG IMPACT ...

For an example of the impact new technology can have on a wide range of people in society, consider the addition of long handles and small wheels to most suitcases.[7] Since their introduction in 1970, those little wheels and handles have transformed how many airports around the world look and how passengers flow through them. Thanks to this small technological advancement, there are now far fewer luggage carts for passengers to load with their suitcases. These large carts used to clog up space in many airports; everyone used one so getting through a door was often slow and perilous. In addition, with the arrival of suitcases with small wheels on them, most airports now hire far fewer porters than in the past. Consider how such a relatively small change in the technology of suitcases could have such a profound impact on the design of international airports and on an entire occupation. If your client was either an airport or the national association or union representing porters, you would have done well to spot this technological trend early and prepare. This is one small example of why scanning the technological environment is essential for the practice of strategic communications.

How to Scan the Technological Field

Scanning the technological field of the external environment requires time, an open mind, and an appreciation for how quickly science and technology can advance. It also requires a good understanding of those areas of science and technology that most directly affect your campaign and your client or employer. As a communicator, you may not have enough background in science and technology to gather and make sense of all this information. This information and insight, however, can often be found in the pages, airwaves, social media pages, and websites of major trade publications, research journals, and news media outlets that cover your sector or areas of interest. Make sure you take the time to read or scan these outlets and familiarize yourself with the most important writers focusing on technological changes that will affect your client or employer. Let these seasoned reporters, bloggers, and analysts become an extension of your communication team and turn to them for a sense of what new technologies are emerging and how they might affect your audiences.

What Next: Working with the Information You Gathered

Done properly, your scan of the technological field can allow you to peer into the future of what your organization does, how it does it, with whom it connects and how. The more you know about these trends, the better you can prepare to capitalize on those that will make it easier for you to succeed and mitigate the impact of trends that could make success more difficult to achieve.

As with all the environmental fields you will scan, you need to stay focused on those trends and forces that will affect the size of your audience, your ability to reach them, and the extent to which they will be predisposed to take the actions your organization needs them to take in order to succeed. If a particular technological trend or force will do none of these things, you can safely leave it off your radar screen. If a particular trend or force seems poised to affect your audience and the way you connect with them, then you will definitely want to pay close attention. Try to get a sense of when the new technology will be introduced, to whom, and under what conditions. Find out who the most influential writers and thinkers are on the topic and start following closely what they say and write. Ask the members of your key audiences questions about the new technology to get a clearer sense of how likely they are to dive in once it arrives.

Scanning the Demographic Field

The science of determining whether your audience is growing, shrinking, or moving is vital to a successful strategic communication plan. Changes to the demographic profile[8] of a population can change both the size of your potential audience and the extent to which those people are predisposed to pay attention and act. Think of it: If your challenge is to convince 1,000 individuals to donate part of their estate to your alumni fund and the total number of your aging alumni is expected to shrink from 100,000 to 50,000 over the next decade, your task just became twice as hard. At the same time, those aging alumni are entering a period of their lives when their thoughts are more likely to turn to charitable giving and, in particular, gifting portions of their estate to the organizations that made a difference in their lives. The same demographic trend then, can create a threat (a shrinking audience) and an opportunity (an audience more predisposed to your messages).

Scanning for demographic changes is all about determining the extent to which your markets or publics are changing in terms of age, address, occupation, education, and other basic demographic criteria. Once you know the trends, you need to think through (or perhaps research) the implications of those changes. Ponder what the demographic change will do to the size of your key public and to the ways they will make sense of your messages.

How to Scan the Demographic Field

The good news is governments have long understood the importance of monitoring demographic trends in their area of responsibility (i.e., city, province, or country). Starting with Statistics Canada and moving on to provincial and municipal departments with similar mandates, governments hire very skilled and educated people to gather and analyze data that lets them know what to expect as the population changes. In most cases, the work of these professionals is then published to websites and readily available. These websites should be bookmarked and visited frequently by someone on the PR or strategic communication team. That is likely the first place to find recently gathered data on changes that could profoundly affect the organization.

The not-so-good news is much of the data published by different levels of government often comes in the form of rather large tables filled with thousands of numbers; there is data in these tables but not necessarily information. If the person responsible for monitoring this field has the expertise needed to make sense of the data, then there is no problem. The members of a PR or strategic communication department often won't have the background necessary to sift through complex sets of data and find the nuggets of insight there. Depending on the state of resources in your organization, you may be able to hire such a person to your team. Oftentimes, you'll need to bring that expertise on board for a temporary rather than permanent assignment. Many consultants in fields like demographics, labour market analysis, and sociology will analyze demographic tables and answer your questions, billing you on an hourly basis for the services.

An even less expensive option is to turn to the experts in demographic trends and forces who publish their thoughts and insights. They are often academics, industry leaders, and experts who work for the government departments and agencies that gather much of the data. Even the country's leading polling firms will share many of the insights developed by their analysts with the news media and with visitors to the firm's website. It's often a good idea to start your scan of the demographic field by reading stories about influential trends and forces in the news media and in specialized media related to your organization. From there, you can dig for more detail by connecting with the business, government department, university, or college that actually gathered the data. You can often contact the researcher or researchers who led the study to ask them specific questions. The more closely you have read the reports on the study, the more precise your question will be and the more likely you will be to have that question answered.

What Next: Working with the Information You Gathered

As with all of the fields you analyze in your environmental scan, your work with demographic data should be focused on determining whether your audience is growing or shrinking in size and whether the audience is more or less predisposed to pay attention to and act on the messages you send them. Demographic data will be of greatest use in helping you determine the changing size of the audience; you'll learn most about changes to the size of the population and the distribution of segments within that population.

Demographic data, however, can also point to important changes in the likelihood that the members of a population segment will pay attention to messages and act in a certain way as a result. Indeed, much of the analysis of demographic data you will find moves from the basic numbers in a population table to discuss the implications of the change. Yes, for example, the youngest members of the baby boomer generation are now at or approaching the age of retirement. But what does their entry into their 50s and 60s mean about the kinds of messages they will pay attention to? How might this affect their behaviour? What types of organizations might they now be ready to enter into a relationship with that they would have ignored during the earlier years of their lives? These are the kinds of questions that most concern strategic communicators. Demographic data may well reveal the changing age and size of a particular segment of the population; it will not, however, tell us how the members of this segment are thinking and behaving. The answers often emerge from careful analysis of the data and from additional research with members of a particular segment.

SHIFTING TO A MORE DIVERSE AUDIENCE

Consider the impact on a professional association of a decided shift in their membership profile to a more ethnically diverse membership and a greater proportion of female members; this shift has indeed been felt in a wide number of professions I worked with as a consultant, from healthcare professions to construction, engineering, and law. The new audience these professional associations want to reach is changing in many important ways, as summed up by the brief BENCH analysis below.

Biases

Your old membership brochure with its faded pictures of smiling Caucasian males and its appeals to "tradition and solidarity" is no longer doing enough to motivate your new potential members to join. You'll need to better represent your membership's gender and ethnic diversity and discover the reasons that most compel them to join a professional association. Those reasons to join have changed as surely as the demographic profile of the membership has.

Expectations

Our expectations about how organizations approach us and persuade us are largely based on our past experience, so many people educated in other parts of the world will arrive in this country with different expectations about things we may take for granted, like association social media sites, online membership surveys, and membership renewal at the click of a button. How and when do new potential members expect to be approached?

Needs

Your members who are raising children will likely have very different needs in terms of how they want to access services like continuing education and annual conferences. The time pressures of being a working parent should compel the association to rethink what it offers and compel you to rethink how you promote those services.

Codes

Literacy skills in English may not be as high for your new members educated in other countries. The colloquial language you use and the references to popular culture you include in many stories and posts may also not be as readily understood by a more ethnically diverse audience. Take the time to learn how best to communicate with your changing membership.

Habits

People born and raised in different countries around the world may well have developed very different habits when it comes to researching and accessing media channels. They may be more sophisticated and savvy than Canadian audiences, they may be far less so, or they may be just as savvy but more likely to turn to the channels they have known and used in the past. In much the same way, women in Canada have quite different media consumption habits as compared to men. The key is to recognize that different audiences will have different habits and make sure you do the research to learn as much as possible about the current habits of your new audience so you can be certain your messages find them quickly and effectively.

As this simple example demonstrates, the more you know about the demographic changes affecting your audience and the more you reflect on and research what those changes will do to the size and predisposition of the audience, the better your communication strategy can be.

Scanning the Competitive Field

This section starts with a simple truth: Every organization faces competition when it communicates. No matter what the nature of your organization's mission, you compete with others for the attention and engagement of audiences. Your success in that competition will in large part determine whether or not you succeed in realizing your mission. Businesses compete for investors and customers. Charities compete for donors and volunteers. Governments compete for the support of citizens, advocacy groups, and businesses. None of these vital forms of action—investing, donating, or voting—is possible unless those organizations can first secure the attention of the audience and engage them in a communication process. Now for a second truth: The more you know about the competing voices in the external environment, the better you can capitalize on the opportunities they create and mitigate the very real threats they represent.

The first step is to identify your competitors. You need to spot the other organizations in a similar line of business as yours and who are reaching out to the same audiences. In other words, they are after the same people, for roughly the same reasons. They will compete with you for attention and for action. For example:

- A chain of restaurants will want to consider other restaurants that target the same market segment, but also look further to see what other eating and entertainment options are being offered to that market segment (e.g., prepared meals in the grocery store, dance clubs, movie theatres, etc.).
- A government in power wants to look closely at what the opposition is doing and saying, along with advocacy groups.
- A national professional association will want to look for other groups a member could join to further their career and deepen their knowledge; that could include local, regional, or international associations, as well as more specialized associations and organizations more specifically focused on learning or research in a particular field.

You need to look for those competitors most like your organization and for competitors who are different yet are meeting similar needs and moving your principal audiences to similar types of behaviour. Those are the competitors that matter. Once you have identified the competitors that matter, you need to learn four key things about each.

1. The Publics Your Competitors Reach

First and foremost, we communicators are in the business of reaching, engaging, motivating, and instructing the members of our key publics. We obsess over these people and work mightily to nurture relationships with them. It behooves us to know exactly who is out to nurture relationships with the same people. Your scan of the competitive environment should therefore include some sense of what audiences your competitors will reach. Be as specific as possible here. Are they out to reach the same age groups? The same income brackets? The same geographic regions?

Knowing which audiences your competitors will focus on reaching will help you aim more strategically. If your competitor is out to woo upper-income beer connoisseurs, you may choose to shift your attention to younger, more blue-collar drinkers. If their fundraising next year will focus on the Pacific Northwest, you may choose to aim for the Prairies or the Maritimes. Making these kinds of strategic choices starts with scanning the competitive environment for competitive intelligence.

2. The Timing and Channels Your Competitors Use

Make sure your competitive analysis also allows you to learn *when* your competitors plan to be most active and in which channels. This will allow you to plan around their efforts, rather than run headlong into them. You'll have the opportunity to speak to your audience first and frame the messages your competitors are about to send ("Some people will tell you price is the most important consideration when buying a car. We think wise decisions are based on quality, reliability, and the value you derive over time."). You'll be able to enjoy the last laugh by reacting and countering the claims of your competitors ("Why settle for just 10% off when we offer 15%?"). You'll also be able to plan your efforts so they reach out to the audience when your competitors are quiet, making for less interference with your message.

TURNING THREATS INTO OPPORTUNITIES

Of course, sometimes the channels and timing chosen by your competitors' campaigns create real opportunities more than threats. My firm was hired to stage a special event introducing a new online service being offered and allow people to sign up. Our competitive analysis revealed a major new IKEA outlet would be opening in the city at the same time as we were asked to hold our event. We had a sense of how lavish the communication budgets were for other IKEA openings in other cities, and we knew we could not match it. We developed a strategy that allowed us to turn the competitive threat into a wonderful opportunity. We staged our event in the same mall parking lot as the exciting new IKEA. That way, most everyone who came to the grand opening (lured there by blanket newspaper and radio advertising and news coverage) also walked over to our sales event to see what we were offering. By capitalizing on the opportunity, we were able to triple the client's expectations. The point is knowing your competitors' plans for communications will allow you to react in a strategic way to their timing and their channels.

3. The Competitive Claims They Make

Your organization will not be the only one sending messages on the topic of your organization, your products and services, and your cause. Your competitors may also be busy telling the members of your key publics all about how their products and services compare to yours. And, like it or not, what they have to say will have an impact on the overall impressions formed by these people. The key to preparing your audience and responding to the competitive claims is to know as much in advance just what those claims will be. Will your competitors call into question the integrity of your organization's leaders? Will they cast doubt on the relative quality of your product or the speed of your service? Will they suggest their organization is more efficient in channelling donations to where the money is needed? Knowing now will put you in a position to respond to the threats quickly and make the most of the opportunities your competitors present.

4. Their Own Promotional Claims

Your competitors, of course, will not talk to your audiences about your organization alone. They will, if they are wise, spend at least as much time telling all who would listen about themselves. They'll trumpet their accomplishments, sell their products and services, and celebrate their people, values, and history. "Tomatoes are loaded with antioxidants." "The most powerful hybrid engine available." "The hospital with the most pediatric cancer specialists in the country." "The country with the best quality of life in the world." Whatever their boast, the more you know and the sooner you know it, the better you will be able to plan a strategic response. You'll be able to map out a unique market position—a beachhead where your competitor is not dug in and where the route to your audience is less crowded. You'll be able to forge a Unique Service Proposition or USP—a statement of the value you can offer your audience that is truly unique and memorable. Rosser Reeves, a legend in American advertising, coined the phrase and mastered the practice,[9] giving the world such enduring USPs as "M&Ms melt in your mouth, not in your hands," "Wonder Bread builds strong bodies eight ways," and "Certs—the only breath mint with Retsyn." The key to Reeves's success was in understanding that overloaded audiences (and he wrote this before email, the web, social media, and digital cable) could only effectively remember one strong claim about a product. Success would come to those who made their claim unique and memorable. That process, of course, must begin by knowing what claim your competitor will make. Only then can you be sure your claim will be unique.

How to Scan the Competitive Field

There are many ways to gather competitive intelligence. No one of these will suffice, and a blend of some or all approaches is the best way to ensure you gather the most and the highest quality intelligence.

Learn from Your Competitors

You will often find many of your competitors will provide you with competitive intelligence. Often times, a simple phone call or chance encounter is the best way to find out what they're up to and when. There are limits, of course. Samsung's marketing team will not likely tell anyone from Apple what their plans for launching new phones are. On the other hand, one hospital in the city might be quite willing to work with another to coordinate their efforts and enhance their impact by not tripping over each other. One government department might be happy to share plans with another for the same reason. It's a win-win proposition when duplication and overlap are kept to a minimum. When you approach communication as a gardener might, the benefit is obvious. When you approach it as a military general, it might be harder to see.

Beyond talking to them, you can also learn a great deal about your competitors by thoroughly reading their publications, social media feeds, and websites. Annual reports of major businesses, for example, will often include a look ahead to complement the detailed look back over the past year. The Facebook pages of charitable organizations will often announce their latest fundraising campaigns months in advance. Government officials and political leaders will often proudly announce their plans in speeches which are then dutifully posted to their websites and shared with the news media. In all these ways and more, the organizations that compete with you for attention will share their plans and enable you to gather valuable strategic intelligence. You only reap the rewards, of course, if you pay attention and see this information for the resource it truly is.

A third way to learn from your competitors is to look backward as a way to see forward. Organizations, for reasons discussed earlier in this book, often fall into the trap of doing what they do simply because "we've always done it." There is never any guarantee but chances are, if a competitor has always run a big fundraising direct mail campaign in November, they'll do the same this year. The same holds for their annual June golf tournament. Whether strategic or not, organizations develop rhythms and habits. The more you know about these, the better you can tell *when* they are likely to be most active in reaching out and engaging the key audiences you share with them, and *how* they are likely to proceed. Once you know, you can develop a strategy that makes the most of this knowledge.

Scan the Industry and Trade Media
The second way to scan the competitive environment is to scan the industry and trade media. Big plans for marketing, advertising, and public relations campaigns make good news. That's why trade publications like *Advertising Age* in the U.S. and *Marketing* magazine in Canada are filled with considerable detail on the best-laid advertising plans of your competitors. Similar publications in PR, fundraising, and investor relations can also hold clues on what your competitors have planned and achieved. The key is to read these publications strategically. Treasure the information you'll find in those pages and on those websites; understand how the stories fit into your situation analysis. Look for strategic intelligence on when the big ad campaigns will break, when the major events will take place, and when the blockbuster movies will be released. The better you can build your campaign around these dates, the more effective you will be.

Here again, the risk is you will quickly be overwhelmed by too much information. Stay focused on who your key competitors really are and ignore the rest unless it really strikes you the campaigns in question will reach your key audiences and compel them to take action in ways similar or diametrically opposed to what you have in mind.

Talk with Suppliers
Talking to your suppliers can also be a helpful way to scan the competitive environment. Your favourite printers, web developers, and photographers are busy

meeting your needs but those of your competitors as well. They may know what your competitors are up to, why, and when. Make a point of networking regularly with all your suppliers with a view to understanding what they're busy doing. They're as proud of their successes as you are and will most often be delighted to chat with you about their latest projects. Do not, however, ask for confidential information; your success is not worth the damaged reputation and client relationship your supplier will have to endure. Often, you won't even need to meet with suppliers to gather strategic intelligence; many will boast about their clients on their websites or in their social media feeds.

The key is to stay focused on your major competitors and to see networking opportunities with suppliers as an opportunity to gather strategic intelligence on those organizations.

What Next: Working with the Information You Gathered

As suggested above, the most important thing to achieve as you work with the competitive intelligence you gather is differentiation. You need your campaign's messages, timing, and vehicles to be distinct from the competition. Carefully review the *timing* of your competitors' efforts and find ways to launch your campaigns at different times and avoid overloading your audiences. Even a small difference of a few weeks can allow your campaign to reach more people and hold their attention more closely. You will also want to review the *creative strategy* your competitors are using: the claims they make, the calls to action they communicate, and the way they tell their stories. While still holding true to your overall communication strategy, try to find unique ways to tell your stories, call your audience to action, and describe your product and service. A truly distinctive campaign will stand out, be noticed, and be remembered more fully by the audience. Finally, try to get a clear sense of the blend of *channels and vehicles* your competitors will use. While still paying attention to your research into the media consumption habits of your audiences, try to use a unique blend that will allow your campaign to stand apart. If your competitor is focused on television, focus your resources on social media and the web. If competitors are using special events, focus on media relations. That way, it's much more likely your messages will appear in an environment as free of your competitors' messages as possible.

The more you can learn about your competitors' creative strategy, campaign timing, and the channels and vehicles they will select, the better you can ensure your messages, timing, channels, and vehicles are different and the impact on the audience is not diluted by what your competitors have planned. It happens, of course, the competitive intelligence you gather is incomplete and there is some overlap between your campaigns and that of a competitor. If this happens, your success will be driven by the overall communication strategy you have developed; if it is better informed, more consistently applied, and more professionally executed, chances are your campaign will come out ahead.

Scanning the News Media Field

News media outlets remain the most important "influencers" in many organizations' external environment. Even in this age of the web and social media, millions of Canadians turn to news gathering organizations (e.g., major television and radio newscasts, newspapers, magazines, and their respective websites and social media feeds) every day for a sense of what is going on in the world. And, since many Canadians still buy into the idea reporters approach stories and issues more thoroughly and objectively than, say, a blogger or anonymous author of an unknown website, they give more weight to what they read, watch, and hear on the news. For reasons of reach and influence, then, what is happening in the news media environment is something most organizations need to give close attention.

How to Scan the News Media Field

There are several aspects of any news story you will want to capture and analyze as you scan this field. Scanning the news media field should include a close look at how your organization is portrayed in the news media (if at all). That coverage is just the beginning, however, and there are other equally important forces and trends for you to consider.

Sources

Reporters need sources, and the sources they find and turn to regularly are given a tremendous, credible voice. When it comes to coverage of your issues and causes, that voice will either belong to your organization or to one of your competitors. Remember here that "competitors" can include organizations whose positions are opposed to yours (i.e., adversaries), but they can also include organizations that hold the same positions as yours (e.g., in support of additional funding for cancer research) but that compete with your organization as they reach out for attention and funding. For these reasons, a scan of the news media environment should include an assessment of which organizations are being cited as sources and how the coverage of competing organizations compares to the coverage your organization receives. This comparison will serve as a useful index of the credibility and visibility of your organization with the news media.

Agenda

Owing to the constant hunger for something new and different, the list of "hot" stories in the news media changes constantly and quickly, even though the list of news values is remarkably constant. Since coverage of specific issues or ideas is driven by what is hot and what isn't, a thorough scan of the news media environment should include an assessment of how the news media agenda is changing over time. Specifically, you need to track your organization's ideas and issues as they rise and fall on the agenda. Be sure to think broadly as you undertake this scan. The issue of funding for cancer research may be important to you, but news coverage of cancer research, celebrities with cancer, funding for health research, and the cost of cancer to the healthcare system could all create important opportunities for your organization to tie its messages to the news of the day. Simply put, when your issue or idea (or one closely related to it) is on the news media agenda, you have an opportunity to exploit. When your issue or idea falls off the agenda, you have a threat on your hands as your media relations effort will be more likely to fall on deaf ears. For example, imagine you represent oat farmers. Think back to 2013, when health claims about the beneficial impact of oat bran on cholesterol levels were all the rage in the media. Now search your daily newspaper's website for the past week and see if oat bran merits even a brief mention. Agendas change quickly and the impact on your organization can be massive.

Tone

The news media take great pride in the objectivity they bring to their work. In spite of their best and noblest efforts, however, it is clear some subjectivity enters into nearly all media coverage (reporters are human, after all). Tracking that bias and how it influences the tone of media coverage on a collective, long-term basis is an important part of assessing the news media environment. Assessing news bias and tone should include coverage of your organization, as well as the causes and issues your organization espouses. As you review coverage of these, keep track of whether the coverage is:

- *Neutral*: No opinion is reported, just straight facts.
- *Positive*: Either the reporter or a person quoted expresses a positive opinion toward your organization or your cause.
- *Negative*: Either the reporter or a person quoted expresses a negative opinion toward your organization or your cause.
- *Balanced*: Both positive and negative opinions are expressed by the reporter or a person quoted in the story.

Finally, if you regularly face stiff competition from a particular organization, you may also want to track how this other organization is portrayed in the news media. A sudden shift in the bias for or against a competitor could create an important opportunity or threat for your organization.

How to Scan the News Media Field

Of all the fields of the external environment to scan, the news media is in many ways the easiest. After all, most media outlets survive by making themselves and their content accessible. All major outlets now have websites that display most or all of the content they generate. Many include archives of past coverage for free or for a small fee. Many public libraries and commercial vendors also offer services that gather past media coverage into sophisticated databases and allow you to search them for very specific coverage of narrowly defined topics. Looking back at past coverage is now easier and less expensive than ever in the history of the news media.

Of course, tracking the news media can also be done in real time, allowing you to monitor coverage and adjust strategy on a day-by-day basis. If you have the budget, hiring a media monitoring service to sift through millions of words and images and find those most relevant to you is a worthwhile investment. If not, try using Google News Alerts as a no-cost way to keep your finger on the pulse of many of the most influential media outlets in the country and the world. If you use this option, be sure to be very limited with the number of keywords you include; too many keywords can quickly lead to so much information coming in that none of it gets read.

As easy and inexpensive as real-time media monitoring can be, there is real value in looking back on what you have assembled (doing so on a quarterly basis, for example) to see the emerging trends and the lessons that reveal themselves. Over time, you can see which of your employer's or your client's messages are getting through; which of the spokespeople are most effective; and which of the media releases, media conferences, and speeches are actually generating positive coverage. You can then develop recommendations to help the organization improve its visibility in the news media in ways day-to-day media monitoring does not allow.

What Next: Working with the Information You Gathered

At the risk of sounding repetitive, there is a risk that your scan of the media coverage will generate electronic folders chockfull of megabytes of stories. You will have more than you can handle and will likely pretend those folders don't exist.

Make the task manageable by focusing on the topics that matter most to your organization and the media outlets that truly reach your key audiences. If your interest is promoting the use of modern ceramics in automobile parts manufacturing, make sure your stacks and folders aren't cluttered with news of ceramic tiles in kitchen renovations. Similarly, the British Broadcasting Corporation (BBC) is an important outlet, but if your campaign is designed to reach and engage young single mothers in Atlantic Canada, your detailed scan of the BBC archives will likely yield little of value to you and your campaign. The key, as in all aspects of scanning the external environment, is to focus on what will truly make it harder or easier for your campaign to succeed.

The next step is to find a concise way to represent all the information you have gathered so you can share it with others. Many of the top media monitoring firms will do this as part of their paid services. They will prepare tables and charts that allow a reader to quickly grasp an emerging trend or pattern in thousands of new stories. If you choose to analyze media coverage yourself, be certain to learn how to use a spreadsheet program to calculate and produce tables and charts. A simple pie chart showing the tone of media coverage of your organization over the past quarter, for example, can replace pages of text and draw much more attention than mere words. If the bright green slice of the pie (i.e., positive tone of coverage) is much wider than the bright red slice (i.e., negative tone of coverage), then all is well.

Scanning the Natural Field

The natural field is in many ways the most fundamentally important field of the external environment. After all, the survival of human beings on the planet depends on clean air, clean water, and climate and soil conditions that allow food to grow. Beyond this very fundamental level of impact on humanity, though, the natural environment can also influence the extent to which audiences will pay attention to your messages, the way they will interpret those messages, and the likelihood of them acting on the messages.

Consider, for example, the impact a warm, sunny summer has on sales of beer, swimsuits, and sunscreen. Consider how a cold winter can affect how often people go outside and what they do when they're there (e.g., shovel snow, ski, fall and hurt their backs). Consider how the arrival of a new strain of the influenza virus during that winter can make hundreds of thousands of people ill and cost many lives. Consider how the arrival of an invasive species of fish like the Asian carp in the Mississippi River can affect what we eat, what sports we engage in, and whether we swim or boat in that river (or in the connected Great Lakes). Whether it is weather, climate, land, or animal species, the trends and forces in the natural environment have a profound impact on what we do, how we do it, where we do it, and when we do it.

How to Scan the Natural Field

The challenge for communicators is to know what aspects of the very complex and ever-changing natural environment to focus on. You cannot scan the entire natural field, and you should likely not even try. Instead, learn what elements deserve attention and be sure to focus on those. The knowledge of which elements of the natural field are worthy of close tracking is something experienced people within the organization will likely know. They will have seen the impact heat waves, ice storms, and flu outbreaks have (or do not have) on the organization. They will have developed the strategic intelligence to know what variables matter and which don't. Make sure you spend time talking to experienced people within the organization to identify the aspects that matter most.

In addition, do some brainstorming with the members of your team and organizational leaders to explore the possible impacts different aspects of the natural field and external environment could have on the success of your campaign. Be sure to consider elements such as climate, plant life, animal life, soil, water, microorganisms, and disease-causing bacteria and viruses. Here again, you need to look for trends that will grow the size of your audience (e.g., a cold winter in Canada drives more snowbirds travelling to Florida) and/or make them more predisposed to pay attention to your campaign and act on its messages (e.g., a sudden spike in the number of people stricken by a preventable disease gets the public's attention and makes them think about immunization). Those will be your opportunities. The threats will be the trends or forces in the natural environment that shrink your publics and/or render their members less predisposed to pay attention and act (e.g., a forest fire that causes the evacuation of an entire city will easily do both).

Gathering information on the natural environment is often simpler than the other fields described in this chapter. Weather forecasts, crop reports, public health announcements, and updates on endangered species are regularly compiled and shared by government agencies, academic researchers, and news media outlets. Much of the new content is quickly scanned by search engines, which makes it possible to receive updates in your inbox.

The only risk is you will be overwhelmed as you scan this field. There is a great deal of information available on the natural environment, it is often very complex, and, depending on the source, can be highly political and biased. For this kind of information, more than any other, be sure to carefully select your sources, staying away from advocacy groups and preferring authors that are neutral, rigorous, and focused on science rather than politics. For this same reason, you may also want to consider hiring a consultant to scan this field and provide a report. This is best done after you have determined which aspects of the natural field are most likely to influence the success of your campaign; that way, you can find someone who specializes in that field (e.g., weather and climate vs. viruses and disease) to run the scan.

What Next: Working with the Information You Gathered

Your scan of the natural field will almost always yield the most diverse information from the most diverse sources of any field you scan. That's why your efforts to limit the range of topics you search for early in the process is so important. If you have done so successfully, you will have a manageable number of articles on a focused range of topics to consider. Ideally, all those articles and posts will come from credible scientific sources.

So long as this is true, you will notice there is a fair bit of repetition in the articles and posts you have gathered; many will deal with similar topics, present similar evidence, and reach similar conclusions. This repetition is a good sign some sort of scientific consensus is emerging on a particular topic. You can have more confidence in the findings when you discover this consensus. You can also use the emergence of consensus to limit the number of articles and posts you read; if you have already read six or seven articles all articulating the emerging consensus, you can quickly scan the next dozen you find. Save your time and effort for any articles or posts that challenge the emerging consensus.

Once you have identified the emerging consensus on a trend or force in the natural environment you feel could affect the success of your campaign, you then need to review the findings and ask yourself the now-familiar questions:

1. Will this trend or force affect the size the audience we are trying to reach?
2. Will this trend or force affect the predisposition of the key audience to the messages we are sending? In other words, will it affect the likelihood members of the audience will pay attention to the messages and act on them?
3. Will this trend or force affect the resources this organization can deploy to run this campaign?

Together, these questions will help you remain focused on the trends or forces that matter most. The answers you arrive at will later help you develop strategic directions to help you capitalize on opportunities and mitigate any threats.

KEY TERMS AND CONCEPTS

As you review this chapter for any tests or assignments, you will want to pay particular attention to the following terms and concepts introduced in the preceding pages:

- **external environment**
- **political field**
- **economic field**
- **social/cultural field**
- **technological field**
- **demographic field**
- **competitive field**
- **news media field**
- **natural environmental field**

QUESTIONS FOR CRITICAL REFLECTION

1. Why is it so important for organizations to have effective ways to monitor what is happening in the world outside the organization? What negative outcomes could come about for an organization that doesn't bother to scan the external environment?

2. Of the eight fields proposed for research into the external environment, which do you feel is most likely to yield important information and insight for PR practitioners looking to plan strategically? Which field is least likely to have a strategic impact? Be sure to support your answers.

3. Your client is a provincial association representing faculty at universities and colleges. They have asked for your help in planning a campaign to encourage taxpayers and government officials to increase funding for postsecondary education in the province. Consider each of the eight fields and identify at least one strong trend or force in each field that could create either an important opportunity or a threat you would want to consider as you develop your strategy. Identify which one of these trends or forces is the single most important to consider and explain why you feel this is the case.

4. Your boss calls you in to discuss the weather and the impact it has had on the sales of your company. The past winter was one of the coldest in the past decade, and sales during the coldest month were down more than ten percent. Your boss is understandably concerned and wants you to find a way to predict the weather next winter so she can revise sales estimates and perhaps adjust the marketing strategy if need be. How would you approach this challenge of predicting the weather many months in advance? How else might you gather strategic intelligence to help your boss with the key decisions she faces?

NOTES

1. These eight fields are based in part on the PEST acronym, which draws attention to the factors in the political, economic, social, and technological fields of the external environment. This combination of four factors is often attributed to Francis Aguilar. See Aguilar, F. J. (1967). *Scanning the business environment*. New York, NY: Macmillan.
2. Statistics Canada. (2016). CANSIM, Table 051-0001. Retrieved October 24, 2016, from http://www.statcan.gc.ca/tables-tableaux/sum-som/l01/cst01/demo10a-eng.htm.
3. Consider, for example, the definition of the word "social" on Merriam-Webster's website (https://www.merriam-webster.com/dictionary/social).
4. Guggenheim, D. (Dir.). (2006). *An inconvenient truth: A global warning*. Hollywood, CA: Paramount.
5. Anderson, C. (2006). *The long tail: Why the future of business is selling less of more*. New York, NY: Hyperion Books.
6. TED. (2017). Chris Anderson: TED Speaker. Retrieved July 10, 2017, from https://www.ted.com/speakers/chris_anderson_ted.
7. The history and impact of this small invention was wonderfully summarized in the following *New York Times* article: Sharkey, J. (2010). Reinventing the suitcase by adding the wheel. *New York Times*. Retrieved July 11, 2017, from http://www.nytimes.com/2010/10/05/business/05road.html.
8. The demographic profile of a group of people looks at the most fundamental aspects of that population: the number of people; birth rates and mortality rates; the distribution of those people around the city, province, or country; the age distribution and gender distribution of the population; and the marital status of the population. Some definitions of the term "demographic profile" will go beyond these fundamental measures to consider the racial profile of the population, as well as levels of education, employment, and income.
9. Reeves also wrote a book that included references to USPs and how to build them. See Reeves, R. (1961). *Reality in advertising*. New York, NY: Alfred A. Knopf.

CONCLUSION TO PART I

You have now been introduced to four elements of strategic communication planning: the intended changes, the audiences or key publics, the resources, and the external environment. Gathering information on all four elements is the first stage in any strategic planning process. It may now seem like an overwhelming task. You may well feel that if you were to take the time to gather all of this information, you would surely be swamped and completely unable to do your job. There is no doubt the risk of being overwhelmed here is great. That's why readers are cautioned in Part I of the book to focus on what really matters. If, after a bit of reflection, you can't imagine how a particular audience, resource, trend, or force could affect your ability to implement a successful communication campaign, move on. You have enough to focus on with those elements that definitely will have an impact. The key is to take some time to carefully reflect on any particular trend or force in any field before you dismiss it.

The next question, of course, is what to do with all this information. The next section of this book will guide you through the following stages in the strategic planning process. In particular, you will learn how to sift through the information you have gathered and focus on what is most important. Next, you will learn how to use this information to actually build an effective communication strategy—the very reason why you gathered the information in the first place. Finally, you will learn how to present a strategy to your client or employer.

PART II
DEVELOPING A COMMUNICATION STRATEGY

CHAPTER FIVE
From Information to Insight

The vision for your garden is clear and ambitious. You have visited your garden shed, tested the soil, asked neighbours about the pests to expect, and done your research on how best to ensure success. You've even read the gardener's almanac and have a good idea of the kind of growing season you can expect. You've mapped out the garden in copious detail, complete with a row-by-row planting plan. You called the seed catalogue people, asked dozens of questions. Your head is full of information, but, alas, there is nothing in the garden at this point except soil and promise. You take a deep breath and realize this is the moment of truth; it's time to move from gathering information to actually using that information to make strategic decisions.

CHAPTER OVERVIEW

The first section of this book challenged you to think like a gardener in the late winter and gather as much information as you can. Your research helps you clarify what it is you will do with the plants and animals that will thrive in your garden. You learned more about the species of plants and animals, their preferences, the conditions under which they will gather and thrive. You also looked deep inside the tool shed and carefully evaluated every tool, every seed, and every fertilizer at your disposal. Finally, you scanned the environment, walking slowly and purposefully around the garden, paying attention to the soil, the light, the water, and the air.

If the process outlined in the first half of the book was successful, you now have a series of rather long lists. You perhaps also have a looming sense there is a lot you don't yet know and need to find out. Those lists you gathered are not a strategic communication plan. The information you have on the change you seek, the audiences you must reach and engage, the resources you can deploy, and the environment in which your campaign will run are what I like to consider the *elements* of strategic communication. They are the raw materials, the building blocks of the strategic communication plan you will now develop.

This section of the book will now guide you in mining the intelligence you have gathered. You'll learn how to quickly convert your findings into strategic directions and then mould those directions into a complete strategic communication plan. That process of "getting to strategy" starts by taking the lists and distilling them into something more precise and potent. This first chapter in the second section of the book, then, is all about how to get from long lists of intended changes to short lists. More importantly, this chapter helps you do so strategically, so the intended changes that remain are the most important, most focused, and most realistic changes you can aim for. The work you need to do now will move ahead in the same order as the situation analysis work you did earlier: you will start with strategically shortening your list of intended changes and then move on to narrow the list of audiences; focus on the most strategic strengths and weaknesses in your resources, and identify the most important threats and opportunities in the external environment.

What you have gathered may not look like much to you right now: random words and observations jotted down on papers or typed into documents. They are essential and ready to reveal their full value.

LEARNING OBJECTIVES

1. Distill a list of intended changes to a more realistic and strategic list of intended changes on which to focus the efforts of the campaign.
2. Distill a list of audiences into a tighter, more strategic list of groups and individuals to reach and engage with the campaign.
3. Focus in on the most strategic resources you can deploy and begin identifying ways to leverage strengths and overcome weaknesses.
4. Focus on the most strategic observations from the scan of the external environment and begin identifying ways to capitalize on opportunities and mitigate threats.

———

DISTILLING A LONG LIST OF CHANGES

There is such a thing as too much of a good thing. Your list of intended changes can easily outreach the resources with which you have to work. To go back to our garden analogy, you may decide you would like to have a garden that provides food, a habitat for the butterflies you love, natural medicine, a quiet place for meditation, and all the flowers you'll need to decorate the house over the spring and summer. The trouble is, you have about an hour each week to devote to your garden and a small balcony in which to do it all. As Johnny Mercer wrote, "Something's gotta give."

It's important at this point to consider ways to shorten the list of intended changes a little. This is a strategic process—it's not one we leave up to chance, habit, or imitation. You need solid reasons why you chose to focus on Outcome A and not on Outcome B. The strategic techniques below will help you consider your options as you work to a shorter, more strategic list of intended changes.

1. Begin with the Beginning

This first technique is obvious but often overlooked. The eventual change in behaviour or relationship you need people and organizations to take in order to be successful doesn't happen all at once. It is built out of small steps. If your audience has to learn about a cause *before* it can consider donating to that cause, then begin with a campaign to educate the audience. In later phases, you can move to ask for donations. If customers need to try your new detergent for the first time *before* they can become regular customers, focus on generating product trials first and move to generate repeat sales and referrals later.

This is why it's so important to break down the broad change in behaviour you are trying to generate into component steps. The more limited your resources, the more you will need to focus on a few of those steps at any one time. The place to begin this, of course, is the beginning. Focus your list of intended changes on ensuring the conditions are in place for later success. Build a foundation of awareness and goodwill, and grow from there.

Consider the following list of simple questions to prompt thinking and discussion. These can be projected onto a smart board, printed onto flipchart paper, or handed out individually to members of your planning team.

The intended change is that this audience,_____.

will _____.

For this to happen, the audience must first_____

_____.

For this to happen, the audience must first_____

_____.

For this to happen, the audience must first_____

_____.

If the change in behaviour you are trying to bring about involves a particularly large number of steps, feel free to move on to two or even three pages; take the time to identify all of the steps involved in the process. It's important that the final list of steps is complete and each step is in the right order.

So, for example, we might end up with a list such as:

The intended change is that this audience, engineering school graduates, will choose to become members of the professional association for engineers in their province.

For this to happen, the audience must first learn about the association and the specific services it offers members, and understand how those services are tailored to the needs of recent graduates.

For this to happen, the audience must first find and visit the association website or attend one of our information sessions on campus.

For this to happen, the audience must first (a) learn there is a professional association that represents them and (b) value what a professional association can offer them.

For this to happen, the audience must first develop a positive attitude to professionalism and understand its relevance to their career.

Note how each step in this process suggests a clear set of messages; you now have a much better sense of *what* to say and *when* to say it. You also know where to begin: in this case, with developing a positive attitude to professionalism; the last item on your list is the first challenge your campaign needs to take on.

2. Mind the Gap

A slightly different way to narrow your long list of outcomes is to clarify where your audience or key public is on the action continuum:

Awareness → Motivation → Instruction → Action → Habit/Relationship

Essentially, the approach here is to always focus on the next step in the process, to identify the precise gap members of the audience must move across as they travel from awareness to habit and relationship. If your audience is already well aware and motivated, focus your efforts on providing instructions. If, on the other hand, the audience is aware but not at all motivated, your instructions will fall on deaf ears, so focus on motivational messages. Move the audience across the gap they face.

The more you know about where your audience or key public is on the action continuum, the better you will be able to focus your resources on moving them through the continuum without wasting resources on steps they've already taken. You'll also be able to create and disseminate messages that meet the needs of the audience. Intuitively, as we move across the continuum, we know to look for information related to the next step.

As you move the audience, however, you need to mind the gap. Trying to move a public too quickly across too many steps of the continuum can overwhelm an audience and encourage them to tune out. An audience that has never even heard of your charitable group is not at all likely to make a donation or volunteer. Asking the members of that audience or public to do too much will discourage them and result in many tuning out your messages; asking them to do too little will waste much of the effort you put into reaching them and getting them to consider a change. Instead, you need to figure out a realistic gap for the audience to cross over the period of time of the campaign.

Moving across multiple steps can also require tremendous resources. Be realistic about what you can accomplish and be sure to consult your assessment of resources as you set the goals and objectives for the campaign. Focus on one or two gaps at a time so you can devote more resources to each rather than spreading yourself too thin.

3. Go for the Core

Nearly every organization has a mission and a vision to guide it. These statements serve as a core for the organization, providing both energy and direction over the long term. The more closely aligned you are with the core mission and vision, the more support you will receive from others in and around the organization and the more their efforts will naturally and holistically support yours.

If you're faced with too many intended changes to bring about, focus on those most obviously and fully aligned with the mission and vision of the organization. After all, a gardener who needs to feed his family would do well to see fruits and vegetables as the core purpose of the garden, with flowers for hats relegated to the periphery. In the same way, a university communication team that focuses on attracting new students first and promoting the new E-Z Pay parking meters later is being strategic by aligning itself to the very reason universities are in business—teaching students. Running parking lots for profit is very much on the periphery.

To narrow your list of intended changes in a strategic way, then, always select those most closely aligned with the core of the organization and leave the changes on the periphery for later.

4. Build Early Momentum

Nothing succeeds like success. After sorting through your long list of intended changes using the first three techniques, if you find you still have too many, you may want to focus your attention on those changes that can be brought about more easily and more quickly; these early wins will allow you to build momentum. Your audiences and your colleagues will notice the early success. Customers, donors, members, voters, and colleagues will all rally around the success. Everybody loves a winner. We are drawn to busy restaurants, to popular clothing labels, to buzz-worthy charities.

The opposite is also true. Media reports of a car whose sales did not meet expectations will hardly encourage customers to go for a test drive. Those same sales reports will do little to encourage senior management to continue with this particular strategy. Lack of early momentum can undermine what could have been a very sound strategy in the long run.

Summing Up

In short, as you look at the possible intended changes your communication efforts hope to bring about, shorten the list by highlighting changes that should be brought about first, changes that will move audiences across the gaps they currently face, changes that are truly aligned with the core mission and vision of the organization, and changes that will generate early momentum as they are brought about.

Is there a magical number of intended changes at which to arrive? No. The optimal number will depend on the resources you have at hand and the other challenges your organization faces. If a change is foundational for later success and aligned with the organization's mission and vision, it needs to be addressed in your plan, no matter how long your list is. If you have a choice, however, always err on the side of doing only a few things and doing them well.

DISTILLING A LONG LIST OF AUDIENCES

Working from too lengthy a list of audiences can also be a big problem for strategic communicators. Each additional audience we include will draw on our limited resources. It takes time, money, skilled people, and effective communication vehicles to reach and engage an audience. If you try to reach too many audiences with too few resources, you will achieve little. You may, in fact, turn an audience away from your organization. Nobody is impressed with communication that is generic, of low quality, riddled with errors, or sent via the wrong channels. You only get one chance to shape first impressions, so be sure to focus your efforts on the right audiences.

TOO MANY AUDIENCES

I once volunteered my time to give a lecture on strategic communications planning to the regional police force in Ottawa. I explained the importance of being clear on a strategic list of changes and audiences. I warned the participants that setting out to generate too many changes among too many audiences would quickly overwhelm their limited communication resources and leave them with a campaign that generates little in the way of results. I then left them for half a day to develop their own list of changes and audiences. I returned to the lecture hall the next morning to find two walls full of flip chart paper, each sheet bearing the name of one or more "key audiences." There were, to be conservative, close to 50 different audiences the participants were determined to reach, engage, and motivate to change.

It should have come as no surprise to me to find so many audiences listed on the walls. After all, these are administrators and police officers whose entire focus is on the public good. Distilling the number of audiences must have felt like abandoning a group of people in need; shortening a list of audiences cuts right against their nature. They couldn't bear to abandon "seniors" or "youth" or "educators." It was clear we had a dilemma.

I presented these well-meaning participants with some ways to think about their audiences and the same strategic approaches to narrowing their focus presented in this chapter. They were very quickly able to create a much tighter list of the audiences that mattered most.

It can be politically charged and difficult to do, but here are proven, strategic approaches to paring audience lists down to a more manageable number.

1. Ensure a Clear Intended Change for Each Audience

Remember the goal of any communication is to generate change of some sort; there should be a clear outcome against which your work will be assessed. If you have an audience on your list but can't quite imagine what outcome it is you want to generate or what change in their behaviour will mark your success, you can likely remove that audience. The exception would be those audiences you intend to use as influencers or enablers; even they, however, will be directly tied to a particular outcome or intended change. The key is to focus your resources and your efforts on those who will either make specific changes in their behaviour or relationship with your organization or who will help you bring about those changes. There are typically fewer of these audiences, which means more resources for each of those truly key audiences.

If you followed the first step in this chapter and narrowed the list of changes you intend to generate, you may find you can now easily narrow your range of audiences by eliminating those who were specifically linked to changes you've omitted. If you no longer have "convincing grandparents to take their grandchildren to the zoo" as an intended change, you may be able to now strike grandparents from your list of audiences.

You may be able to put some sort of intended change beside many of the listed audiences. Look for those associated with truly active verbs—the ones who will move beyond changes in awareness and motivation to really *do* something. The audiences to keep will be those to whom you assign real action like "donate to the foundation," "vote to increase our funding," "buy our entire line of products or services," or "stop smoking." There is great power in active verbs like donate, vote, buy, and stop. They are a signal to you the audience in question is one worthy of your time and attention.

This first approach to narrowing the focus of a campaign is often sufficient to distill the list to less than half of its original length. You likely still have work to do, however.

2. Know What Audiences to Reach First

This second approach is linked to the advice to "begin with the beginning," which was shared earlier. When it comes to limiting the number of changes you set out to generate, you want to focus on those changes that must be accomplished first. If you want to reach school children in school, you'll have to communicate with and engage school board officials, teachers, and parents first. The children might better be considered as part of a second phase of your campaign. If you want public servants to take action, you'll want to consider motivating their political leaders first, to ensure moral and financial support will be there when the public servants need it. If you want to communicate to the news media about a planned expansion, you'll want to make sure your board members, employees, and regulatory agencies are well advised and on side first. There are often compelling reasons to communicate with one audience before another, and this alone can help you pare back your list. Do the first things first.

3. Look for the Multiplier Effect

Some audiences have an innate ability to take your messages and communicate them to others. They are multiplier agents and, if handled correctly, they can have an enormous impact on the reach and influence of your campaign. Consider a group of people known to researchers as "opinion leaders"[1] or "influencers." Opinion leaders have strong opinions on one or more topics and a tendency to share them. What's more, opinion leaders tend to operate from a position of prestige, status, or expertise with the topic in question; their opinion is more likely to sway others whose opinion is not yet formed.

KNOWLEDGE AND OPINION LEADERS

One example of an influencer or opinion leader is my older brother, who is a long-time car buff. He has owned many different cars, taken them apart, and also managed to put most of them back together. He has strong opinions on automakers and the cars they build. What's more, he's a respected and experienced automotive engineer who has worked in Canada, the U.S., and Europe. Needless to say, he's an opinion leader when it comes to cars. He reads a great deal about automobiles, talks a lot about what he's learned, brings proven expertise to the subject, and is able to secure both attention and influence when he does.

Finding opinion leaders is never easy but it is possible. Look for people in your community or market who are very educated on the topic at hand or who teach on the subject in local universities and community colleges. Look also for people who have shown a tendency to voice an opinion, for example, people who have written letters to the editor of the local newspaper on a topic. Look for people in leadership positions in organizations related to your subject. They're managers and executives, board members and committee chairs. The good news is all of these individuals can be found using a good search engine, often with contact information for them.

In many instances, your list of opinion leaders will be quite small and manageable. You should be able, for instance, to reach opinion leaders with a special email list or via their social media accounts. You can often invite them to a special event. Whichever way you do it, if the messages and channels are strategic, you might begin a chain reaction that will carry your message to other key audiences in a credible and convincing way.

The news media are often the most important multiplier agent you can reach. A popular columnist or reporter with a respected outlet can easily reach several hundred thousand or even millions of people in a day. The challenge is not to find these people—their names and faces appear on the page or screen, and many online directories exist to help you find their contact information. The challenge here is to sway these people and convince them your position is (a) interesting to their readers, listeners, or viewers; (b) correct; and (c) worth writing or talking about. It's a big challenge, although, as we'll see in subsequent chapters, not an insurmountable one.

4. Assess the Risks of Not Communicating

We are, as Aristotle pointed out, a political animal.[2] There are rules—formal and informal—that we break at our own peril. Breaking rules (or expectations) can leave people insulted or incensed. For these reasons, it is important to think carefully before removing an audience from your list of key audiences. Though it may be the right thing to do strategically (i.e., the answers to the three questions at the start of this chapter suggest you should), the political price of dropping them may be too high.

You'll find this is particularly true with the enabler audiences we identified in the first half of the book. Unlike actors and influencers, we often expect very little action from enablers. Enablers tend to have less of a multiplier effect than influencers. Enablers are more likely to know about your organization and so aren't often considered important audiences for the early stages of your campaign (which are more likely to focus on awareness messages). What enablers can do, however, is put various sticks in your spokes, as it were. Enablers can allow your campaign to proceed and succeed, or they can bring the whole process to an abrupt halt. If you were planning on expanding your garden so it reaches into your neighbour's yard, you would likely want to start by talking to your neighbour, maybe offering her a nice bottle of wine and a share of the harvest. Enablers, after all, are those audiences we don't want to surprise. We want to show respect by keeping them informed and doing so early. Enablers need to be reminded their support matters. Think long and hard before removing enablers from your list. The added investment will pay off in a smooth campaign in which all your doers and influencers are able to interact with you and take action, free of any interference or directives from above to cease and desist.

All this is to say politics will sometimes surpass strategy as a rationale. Your head will tell you that you can make better use of limited resources by omitting an audience. Your gut will tell you the political price to pay may be too high and too long-lasting. At that point, keep the audience on the list but be clear on why you are doing so, what the outcomes are for this audience (i.e., support our efforts, don't impede them), and invest your resources accordingly.

DISTILLING A LONG LIST OF RESOURCE ASSESSMENTS AND ENVIRONMENTAL CONSIDERATIONS

Congratulations! Your lists of audiences and intended changes are now much shorter and more realistic given your resources. Better yet, you have narrowed your focus strategically. Now comes the time to look more closely at the other two lists you gathered in Part I of this book—your assessment of resources and your environmental scan. You can tackle both of these at once with the power of SWOT analysis. SWOT[3] is an acronym and one of the most effective thinking tools for the strategic thinker: strengths, weaknesses, opportunities, and threats. SWOT analysis is a fast and strategic way to make sense of what you've gathered. And it all begins by sorting all the strategic intelligence you've gathered into six piles.

Sorting the Findings from Your Resource Assessment: Strengths, Weaknesses, and Question Marks

Let's start with the strategic intelligence you've gathered on resources. Divide those findings into three: strengths, weaknesses, and "question marks." Where a resource you need is of high quality *and* you have lots of it, you have a strength. Strengths will help you reach your key audiences and generate the kinds of change you need to be successful. You'll want to make sure you make the most of the strengths you identified when it comes time to develop strategy.

If, on the other hand, a resource you need is lacking in terms of quality and lacking in terms of quantity, file it under weaknesses. You'll also have to carefully consider weaknesses when you get to developing strategy, trying to find ways to overcome the weakness and generate results in spite of them.

What do you do with a resource that is not so easily categorized? Perhaps you have a resource (say people on staff) in abundance, but the quality is not what you need (e.g., none are experienced in social media campaigns). Or maybe the quality is there (a really well done and recent survey of donors), but the quantity is lacking (you have no other reliable strategic intelligence on any of your other audiences). You may even have resources that are of "sort of" good quality and "kind of" good quantity. These should be rated as question marks. Later, you can take note of the question marks and pay particular attention to the ones that could be fixed most easily (and so turn them into strengths). Generally speaking, though, question marks don't play a great role in most strategies. They aren't strong enough to leverage, and they aren't so weak they absolutely must be overcome. In short, you would do well to focus your strategy on the real strengths and real weaknesses you have identified. Be mindful of the question marks in your resources, but don't dwell on them.

DISTILLING LONG LISTS OF STRENGTHS AND WEAKNESSES

Consider, for example, a campaign my colleagues and I undertook with a local hospital called SCO Health Services (today the hospital is known as Bruyère Continuing Care). Our situation analysis revealed some very clear strengths for the organization. They had an abundance of internal cohesion; people at every level of the organization were rallied around the same mission and the same values. To this day, this is the most cohesive organization with which I have ever had the pleasure of working. They also, and not unrelatedly, had an abundance of talented people who could act as ambassadors for the organization—credible and effective staff, volunteers and patients who could genuinely get the message out. These two strengths became the foundation for our strategic direction for the campaign, which was to give voice to that unique sense of shared mission and to those powerful spokespeople.

This client also had significant weaknesses, not least of which was a lack of goodwill in the broader public. Too few people knew of them and the great work they did. This lack of broad public awareness was combined with a lack of communication vehicles and activities with which to reach this wider audience—another significant weakness. Our campaign worked hard to overcome both weaknesses by building a series of external communication vehicles and activities specifically designed to broaden the base of people within the community (potential donors) who were aware of the hospital, its work in the community, and its many unique qualities.

The point here is our situation analysis revealed all kinds of complex strengths and weaknesses, with many question marks. In the end, though, we were able to focus on two key strengths (that we leveraged fully) and two key weaknesses (that we worked hard to overcome). We distilled a long list, focused our efforts, and generated measurable results.

Sorting the Findings from Your Environmental Scan: Opportunities, Threats, and Question Marks

Now that your resources are neatly sorted, it's time to do the same with the observations you made about the external environment. Here too you will find good news, bad news, and question marks. You will find trends and forces that will make it easier for you to generate change by (a) growing the audience in terms of number of people you can reach and motivate, (b) making the audience more predisposed to pay attention, and (c) making them more predisposed to undertake the behaviour you need to generate. These are the opportunities on which you can capitalize. Of course, you will also find trends and forces in the external environment with the opposite effect—making your audience smaller and more difficult to reach, or rendering them less predisposed to pay attention and make the necessary change. These are threats, and they will need to be effectively mitigated if your organization is to be successful. And, once again, you'll no doubt find many trends and forces whose impact on the attention, predisposition, and size of the audience is entirely unclear. It might be that, at this point, it's not at all apparent whether this particular trend or force will have any impact on your audience's numbers or leanings. These are your question marks.

KEEPING AN OPEN MIND REGARDING OPPORTUNITIES AND THREATS

Consider, for example, my firm's work with Human Resources Professionals Association of Ontario. Our scan of the external environment revealed immense interest among governments, employers, and the news media in a number of HR issues, from managing younger workers and replacing the soon-to-retire baby boomer generation to integrating foreign-trained professionals in the Canadian workplace. The widespread interest in the very issues this association's members deal with each day was a key opportunity that would help our client secure attention and succeed. We also, on the other hand, spotted a crowded marketplace of professional associations, each trying to shout above the others for attention, prestige, and the interest of postsecondary students (to replace those soon-to-retire baby boomers). This competition for attention was clearly a threat that would make it harder to generate the required change in career choices of postsecondary students.

Opportunities and threats are rarely quite as simple as strengths and weaknesses. The same trend or force can be either a threat or an opportunity based on how you look at it (i.e., is the glass half full or half empty?) and how you respond. The opportunity created by government interest in the need to integrate foreign-trained workers can also be a threat if the government decides your organization is part of the problem, rather than part of the solution. Likewise, the threat of so many competing associations vying for the attention of college and university students can also be turned to opportunity if some of the associations decide to collaborate and integrate their efforts into a single, blockbuster campaign. So remember as you sort the results of your environmental assessment to keep an open mind and consider the possibility that the same observation can belong to two columns—opportunities *and* threats.

This process of distilling long lists and focusing on what matters most is much more than reducing workload; it's an essential step in developing strategy. The choices you are making are themselves strategic. You are choosing to focus on some items and not others. You are making decisions about where best to deploy your resources for maximum impact. You are also sharpening your thinking and setting the stage for the move to strategic directions.

THE MOVE TO STRATEGIC DIRECTIONS: FOUR IMPORTANT VERBS

Once all of your items are organized into strengths, weaknesses, opportunities, threats, and question marks, you are ready to craft a series of strategic directions to point the way for your communication campaign or program. The simplest way to approach this is to remember four verbs: your strategic directions will identify how you intend to **leverage** strengths, **overcome** weaknesses, **capitalize** on opportunities, and **mitigate** threats.

TABLE 5.1: THE FOUR TYPES OF STRATEGIC DIRECTIONS

Resources	Leveraging Strengths	Overcoming Weaknesses
Environment	Capitalizing on Opportunities	Mitigating Threats

In the simplest terms, when you have a great tool in abundance, it makes strategic sense to put that tool to work. On the other hand, if a resource is of poor quality or lacking in abundance, the strategic thing to do is to try to improve the quality and quantity of that resource before you deploy it. As for trends and forces in the outside world, you want to make strategic use of those that are helpful (i.e., capitalize on an opportunity), and you want to minimize the impact of those that can hurt (i.e., mitigate a threat). We explore all four of these approaches in the coming chapters.

And so we come to the heart of strategic communications planning—developing strategy. It has been a long haul to get here, but the work you've done so far is what makes strategy possible. Without it, the decisions you make would necessarily be based on luck, imitation, or habit. Now, thanks to the information you've gathered, analyzed, distilled, and sorted, you are in a position to make the very most of the precious resources you have, while finding ways to succeed in spite of the resources you lack. You are ready to reap the benefits of the opportunities happening in the outside world and soften the blow of the threats.

KEY TERMS AND CONCEPTS

As you review this chapter for any tests or assignments, you will want to pay particular attention to the following terms and concepts introduced in the preceding pages:

- **component steps**
- **mind the gap**
- **core mission and vision**
- **multiplier effect**
- **opinion leaders**
- **SWOT analysis**
- **question marks**
- **leverage**
- **overcome**
- **capitalize**
- **mitigate**

QUESTIONS FOR CRITICAL REFLECTION

1. Review the four methods for distilling lists of intended changes. Discuss which of the four you think is likely to be the most valuable for most client organizations. If you could only use *one* of these methods, which one would you choose? Why?

2. Now consider the four methods for distilling lists of audiences. Which of these methods do you feel is more strategic and will yield the best results? Why?

3. Thinking of the process high school students use to select the college or university where they will study, who would you say are the key influencers? What could a college or university marketing department do to reach and engage these influencers? Did any of these influencers have an impact on your choice of college or university?

4. Classifying a resource as a strength or a weakness can sometimes be a very subjective process. The same can be said of classifying a trend or force in the external environment as an opportunity or a threat. Your feelings and emotions can affect your judgement one way or another. What are some steps you could take to reduce the risk of subjectivity in your assessment of the resources you can deploy and the trends and forces in the external environment?

NOTES

1. The term "opinion leadership" is often attributed to Paul Lazarsfeld, who co-wrote two very influential books about communication research. Both *The People's Choice: How the Voter Makes Up his Mind in a Presidential Campaign* (Lazarsfeld, Berelson, & Gaudet, 1944) and *Personal Influence: The Part Played by People in the Flow of Mass Communications* (Katz & Lazarsfeld, 1955) suggested some individuals in society are more likely to consume the news and more likely to share what they learn with other, less active people around them. Those people were dubbed "opinion leaders" and the label has stuck ever since.

2. In *Politics*, book 1, section 1235a.

3. Though widely used by academics and business leaders in much of the world, there does not appear to be a widely recognized author of the original paper or book on SWOT analysis. For a brief discussion of this continuing search for the originator of the term, see http://www.marketingteacher.com/history-of-swot-analysis/.

CHAPTER SIX
Strengths, Weaknesses, and Strategy

It's early spring and, in an optimistic mood, you put on your rubber boots and make your way across the melting snow to the garden shed and pry it open for the first time in nearly four months. The first thing you notice is the instruction manual you purposefully left open on your workbench—the one that tells you how to start your brand-new, automated sprinkler system for the first time after a cold winter. You smile and think of the varieties of vegetables you'll be able to grow now that you can rely on a steady source of water for them. This is one new resource of which you can't wait to make full use.

As a bonus, of course, the automated sprinkler will save you a good half-hour of watering every day—time is such a valuable resource you can put to good use by finally building the pagoda at the back entrance of the yard.

"Gardening," you think to yourself as you admire the new sprinkler, "is all about making the most of your resources."

A moment later, though, you scan your rack of gardening tools and notice, with some dismay, how rusted and worn most of them are. You wonder if a thorough cleaning and oiling will be enough this year or if it's time to finally replace some of these well-worn tools.

"Gardeners," you think to yourself as you scan the rack of aging tools, "are only as good as their tools."

CHAPTER OVERVIEW

With this chapter, you will begin the process of transforming the facts and figures you gathered in the first half of this book into actual strategy. You will learn how to methodically review each of the resource types that communicators most often work with and determine how best to put your strengths to work and bolster or replace your weaknesses. You will be introduced to strategic directions that will allow you to leverage the hard resources of high quality and abundant supply (i.e., time, money, people, and vehicles). You will also learn strategic directions that will allow you to leverage strengths among your soft resources (i.e., strategic intelligence, goodwill, internal cohesion, and stories). Just as important, you will learn proven strategic approaches to overcoming weaknesses in these same resource areas. These approaches and your selection of the best ones for any given challenge constitute the very essence of strategic thinking and, more specifically, strategic communication planning.

LEARNING OBJECTIVES

1. Review each of the principal resource categories used by communicators, understand the impact each can have on the success of a campaign, and discover the fundamental differences between strengths and weaknesses in each resource area.

2. Realistically and thoroughly assess each resource area to determine if that resource constitutes a strength, a weakness, or an uncertainty for the strategic planning process.

3. Effectively leverage strengths and overcome weaknesses in hard resources, including time, money, people, and vehicles.

4. Effectively leverage strengths and overcome weaknesses in soft resources, including strategic intelligence, goodwill, internal cohesion, and stories.

5. Summarize your efforts in the form of clear strategic directions.

SETTING STRATEGIC DIRECTIONS

Strategic directions are the essential building blocks of a strategy. They are decisions, based on evidence, that guide the way your resources are allocated and your campaign unfolds. Most strategies are composed of as few as two or three strategic directions; others are made up of as many as 10 or 12 directions. There is no magic number, as each organization and each challenge is unique. As was suggested in the previous chapter, there are essentially four types of strategic directions, summed up in Table 6.1.

TABLE 6.1: THE FOUR TYPES OF STRATEGIC DIRECTIONS

Resources	Leveraging Strengths	Overcoming Weaknesses
Environment	Capitalizing on Opportunities	Mitigating Threats

You assessed the organization's communication resources and now you must find ways to leverage the strengths among your hard and soft resources. You must also find effective ways to overcome the weaknesses among your hard and soft resources. You worked hard to scan the external environment and now comes the time to determine how best to capitalize on the opportunities you identified and, of course, mitigate the threats you pointed to.

Leveraging Strengths: Making the Most of a Good Thing

This chapter begins with a discussion of strengths (rather than weaknesses) for two good reasons. First, it's the order in which the four elements of the familiar SWOT acronym are presented (strengths, weaknesses, opportunities, and threats). Second, and more importantly, the chapter begins with strengths because strengths are the most important of the four strategic elements to consider. Experienced communicators quickly learn the most successful campaigns are built on the greatest strengths of the organization. Good strategy almost always begins by identifying the key strengths an organization has and finding ways to leverage those resources.

You'll remember the first half of the book presented eight different types of resources, each of which can be assessed for quantity and quality to determine if the resource is a strength, a weakness, or a question mark. Let's take each of these resources in turn and consider what abundance and quality looks like and what you can do to leverage it. We will also discuss what a lack of abundance and lack of quality look like and consider ways to overcome these weaknesses. You will find examples of past campaigns I have been involved in as well as some notable campaigns led by other practitioners to illustrate the key points in this chapter.

Time as a Strength

Ah, the luxury of abundant time. It seldom happens, of course. More often than not, you need to generate results fast (lacking quantity of time), and you have a dozen or so other priorities competing for attention (lacking quality of time). But once in a long while, it happens. You will know time is a strength you can leverage when the expectations set for a particular campaign are realistic; the board or your VP is thinking in terms of months or even years, not days or weeks. You will also know time is a strong resource when the priority given to a particular campaign is high enough that you can focus on it; it is not one of a dozen "top priorities" competing for attention. This project is the #1 priority and everyone around you knows it.

When these conditions are met, you will have time in abundant quality and quantity. So what can you do to fully leverage time? First, look to the heavens and give thanks. This is a rare privilege, so appreciate it. When you're done giving thanks, consider the following strategic directions.

Work Step-by-Step
One of the best ways to leverage time as a resource is to work in steps rather than feeling you need to somehow accomplish all your goals all at once. Remember the action continuum?

Awareness → Motivation → Instruction → Action → Habit/Relationship

You now have time to move your audience across this great divide one or two steps at a time. You can focus the first part of your campaign on tilling the soil—getting the audience ready by focusing on messages of awareness and motivation. In some instances, this comes across as a teaser campaign. You strike a chord with the audience, remind them of a need or desire, and promise an amazing solution. You just don't tell them what the solution is … yet. Later, you move into a second phase and start issuing your call to action, moving your audience to take that definitive first step. Finally, in a third phase, you go back to those who have taken action and move them to make it a habit and to establish a relationship, rather than limiting it to a single transaction. These phases can take months or even years each. You've got the time, so move in phases built on each small step. It's more realistic and generates results that last.

Moving in steps or phases also allows you to take time to reassess at certain intervals as you go along. As Phase One draws to an end, evaluate your progress. Look for indicators of success. Look for signs of failure. Adjust your course accordingly before moving to Phase Two. These kinds of iterative campaigns extended and adjusted over time are the most successful in the long run.

Get to Know the Audience
How else can you leverage an abundance of high quality time? Use that time to research the audience. You can never know too much about an audience, its biases, expectations, needs, codes, and habits (remember BENCH analysis). The reason strategic communicators usually move forward without knowing everything they should about an audience is lack of time. If you're told on November 1 you need results by Christmas, you really can't take five weeks for focus group testing, can you? If, however, you do have abundant time, you can leverage this resource by

converting it into another valuable resource: strategic intelligence. Take the time to commission a poll, run some focus groups, or simply get out and talk to your frontline people. Take a block of the time you have in your critical path and label it "gathering strategic intelligence." You'll emerge with sharper messages that resonate more with the audience and the right blend of communication vehicles to generate greater results.

A further way to leverage an abundance of time is to test your messages before you distribute them. If you're producing a TV spot, have the storyboards tested with audience focus groups. Your new website is almost ready? Spend some time on usability testing and really get it right. Different versions of a new fundraising letter could be sent to a random sample of your mailing list and the results used to select the best version. Testing and fine-tuning messages takes time but you've got it, so make the most of it by leveraging it to produce stronger messages. That's what strategy is all about.

Sustain the Campaign

The last and perhaps most important way to leverage an abundance of time is best summed up in three words: Keep it going! Sustain the communication campaign for as long as you can (recognizing this also often takes money, of course). Moving an audience across the action continuum takes time. Trying to move the audience too quickly usually encourages the audience to tune out; nobody likes to be pushed around, after all. If you have a year or two to generate results, craft your campaign and keep it going that long. Don't change the campaign's messages halfway through because you are bored with the creative. Unless the results clearly indicate you're headed in the wrong direction, sustain the campaign and give the audience time to come across the messages a number of times, digest them all, reflect on them, and slowly change.

THE HOSPITAL THAT TOOK ITS TIME

A PR campaign my colleagues and I did for a local hospital (back then, it was known as SCO Health Services) was designed to set the stage for what was then the largest fundraising campaign in its history. The main strategic resource we had to leverage came from the fact the hospital and its board of directors were wise enough to allocate the time to run public opinion research and then run a year-long PR and advertising campaign to raise the profile of the hospital. Our research showed clearly the organization was not nearly well-known enough to ensure success in fundraising; they had the lowest name recognition of any hospital in the region. We designed our campaign strategy to begin by focusing on building awareness and motivation before then, and only then, passing the baton to a fundraising firm who ran an 18-month fundraising campaign, shifting the campaign's strategy to generate action and build relationships.

By the time we handed off to the fundraising firm, we had significantly raised the profile of the hospital, thanks to extensive news media coverage, a dramatically enhanced website, special events, and paid advertising. Needless to say, this set a solid foundation for the fundraising campaign, which exceeded its goals and did so ahead of schedule.

Not every campaign will allow you to move so slowly and carefully. In this case, the fact the client was a nearly 200-year-old institution perhaps helped give the board a unique perspective on time and allowed them to see investing time would help ensure the fundraising efforts pay off—which it most certainly did.

Leveraging Money

Most PR and strategic communication practitioners can count on one hand the number of times in their careers they have enjoyed an abundance of money to work with on a campaign. Being given as much money as you think is required, or perhaps a little more, is a rare occurrence in the private sector and rarer still in the public and not-for-profit sectors. But it does happen and if it does, here are some of the ways you can leverage this most precious resource.

Buy Dominance

This first recommendation stems from the fact the competition for attention out there is fierce and getting fiercer. If you have money, leverage it by buying dominance. Use your financial strength to raise your voice above all others. Buy as much frequency as you can in as many different outlets as you can. Create an integrated plan and make it impossible for your audience *not* to come across your message a number of times each day for the duration of the campaign. Also, as mentioned above, use your budget to sustain your campaign longer than the competition. There is no substitute for the dominance money can buy in the form of frequent messages across multiple channels sustained for a longer period of time.

Buy Quality

A second strategic way to leverage a financial strength is to buy quality words and images for your campaign. Hire the best. Go for the highest level of quality you can afford. Make your messages the kind people will notice, remember, and talk about with others. Remember the TV commercial for Nespresso coffee makers starring George Clooney and Danny DeVito? It was a wonderful campaign featuring two of the highest-paid actors in Hollywood. Their performance created the kind of "buzz" that gets people talking and sharing.

Work that is emotional, dramatic, beautiful, and hilarious will always get attention and move audiences. Getting to this level of creativity will often cost more money. The best writers, photographers, video directors, and programmers command the highest fees. Celebrity endorsers rarely work for free. Printing on superb paper using four-colour process costs more than photocopying. Shooting in high-definition on location in Costa Rica costs more than industrial-grade video in a suburban studio. Investing in quality means your float in the speeding parade of the modern media landscape is one that will be remembered and will make a difference at the end of the day.

Buy Audience Insight
Finally, at the risk of repeating a point made in the section on time above, if money is a strength, consider investing your budget in audience testing and evaluation. Often, clients will have to forgo these expensive research methods for lack of budget. When you do have the budget, be sure to test your messages before the campaign and then evaluate the effectiveness of your efforts at regular intervals. You'll learn which of your messages are most effective, you'll be able to improve the messages that aren't, and you'll know which channels are actually performing to place your messages in front of the right audience at the right time. By investing in audience research, you'll reap big dividends in the form of messages that are continually improved and a media plan that continually generates more impact.

Every aspect of a modern communications campaign costs money, and you'll never have any trouble finding ways to spend those rare ample budgets. When you do have one, be strategic and focus some of your investment on a dominant campaign, high-impact messages, and ongoing research to monitor and improve your performance.

Leveraging People
Ours is truly a multidisciplinary field. The best marketing, fundraising, public affairs, communication, and public relations campaigns are the results of talented teams of people working together: from planners and creative types to people pitching reporters, CEOs to deliver great speeches at an employee meeting, and talented coders to build powerful online vehicles. Strength in people really does mean having an abundance of people to do the work and having high quality (e.g., skilled, motivated) people on your team. If your resource assessment points

to people as an area of strength, consider the following strategic directions to make the very most of this important resource.

Put Them to Work

Make sure you run the campaign in a way that lets the writers write, gets the spokespeople speaking, highlights the credible people who are the face of your campaign, and lets the people with access carry your message. The simplicity of this solution, of course, masks the complexity of the challenge. If the talented people are employees under your management, the task is relatively straightforward. Even so, you need to manage these people's workloads so they have quality time to devote to the task. You need to share your strategic intelligence with them so their work can be informed and strategic. You need to make the overall goals of the campaign clear to them so they are motivated to deliver their best work. Simply sending an email stating "write this for me by Friday" is not nearly enough to fully leverage strength in your employees.

If the quality people are employees of your organization but not under your management, the task becomes a little more complicated. Getting the skilled and trusted CEO to deliver that speech at the employee meeting is not a given. Getting the mailroom supervisor to agree to the extra work of inserting customized reminder cards in the fundraising letters won't necessarily be easy. The challenge here is to informally recruit these talented people to your team. You need to invite and motivate them to bring their strengths to your campaign. There are two essential steps to doing this. First, you must approach them as early as possible. Surprising your CEO by casually asking, "by the way, what are you doing this Friday at lunch?" is never a good idea. Second, you must tie your campaign and its outcomes to the overall mission and goals of the organization (remember that from the first part of this book?). You and the CEO and the mailroom supervisor all share some common goals, and your ability to convince them their participation in the campaign advances those common goals is the best way to motivate them.

Now if the people whose strengths you want to leverage are not formally part of the organization (e.g., they are volunteers or partners from other organizations), the challenge is even greater. Make sure you give yourself even more time to approach and motivate them. Notice again how strengths are interconnected and one strength (time) can be used to help leverage another strength (people). Much like employees not under your management, volunteers will need to be approached and motivated by presenting to them how the success of your campaign will advance goals and ideals you have in common. Volunteers will rarely donate their time and talent just because they are needed. Your victory has to be their victory. The goals and ideals will sometimes go beyond those of the organization you represent. They will often be broader, more universal goals like peace, freedom from hunger, justice, and compassion. You need to understand what motivates these potential team members and be prepared to demonstrate how your campaign can advance the causes they believe in.

Give Them Tools

More than just a timely approach and motivation, the people you want to leverage will need resources of their own. To go back to our gardening analogy, if these people are to help you with the harvest, they will need gloves, baskets, and clear instructions on what to pick and what to leave on the vines. If you want them to include an article in their newsletter, give them the article. If you want them to speak to their patients on your behalf, arm them with speaking points and a brochure or button to leave behind. If you want them to present, arm them with an amazing presentation, training, and logistical support. If you want them to share your messages via social media, you need to provide them with brilliant content to share. Once talented people say "yes," their contribution to the campaign will in large part be determined by your ability to provide them with the tools and support they need to shine.

THE WELL-ARMED MEMBER

A campaign my colleagues and I did on behalf of the Ontario Physiotherapy Association (OPA) is a good reminder of the importance of arming the people you want to leverage with the right tools. Our research revealed just what a tremendous resource the members of the OPA were; we learned how trusted they were by their patients and how much time they spent, on average, with each patient. To leverage these people, we developed a range of tools each member could use to join the campaign, including posters, flyers to hand out, and brief speaking points to foster a consistent message throughout the province. In a later edition of the campaign, we added messages members could share with patients online and via social media. We knew we had a strength in the people who were members of this association. With the right tools in place, we were able to "put them to work" and make the most of their numbers and the relationships they had forged with their patients.

You can find a more detailed case study of this campaign for the OPA in Appendix B at the end of the book.

Leveraging Vehicles

There's a reason why the root word for the verb "to seed" in Latin (*sema*) is also the root word for communication-related words like "disseminate" and "semaphore." A gardener without a means to get seeds into ground is as helpless as a communicator without the means to get messages out to an audience. Seeds that stay in their little paper envelope will have as much impact as words and sounds and images that stay locked in a communicator's mind. Seeds, like messages, need vehicles to carry them to where they can work their magic.

If your resource assessment pointed to existing communication vehicles as a real strength (e.g., they are well read or watched and their content is trusted and deemed relevant), you have a powerful resource on which to build your campaign. Here are some strategic directions to consider if you have strong vehicles to leverage.

Put Them to Work

Good vehicles are the result of careful planning and hard work. They are well known, trusted, and well read. They are also one of the most valuable resources to bring to a campaign since they can help to overcome weaknesses like lack of money, lack of time, or lack of people. A quality vehicle is a well-worn path to your audience you can use with confidence. The number-one way to leverage such a strength, of course, is to use it and put it to work.

Make quality vehicles the foundation of your campaign. If the quarterly employee meeting is a much-anticipated event by all, make sure you launch your campaign there and then. If the annual report is trusted and distributed to an influential list of people, be sure to add your campaign's messages to this year's edition. If your organization's Instagram account is creative and growing in traffic every year, make sure your messages are evident in that channel. Craft your messages so they will work effectively in your strongest vehicles. The key to this strategic direction, of course, is to know which of your vehicles are the strongest. Be sure to measure the success of each vehicle on a regular basis so you can spot your strengths and put them to work.

Extend and Expand

You can also go one step further to leverage the credibility and reach of strong vehicles by going beyond their original frequency and format to prepare special editions whose timing and content are more closely aligned to your specific campaign needs. Imagine, for example, a special quarterly meeting that comes between regularly scheduled meetings or a special semi-annual donors report.

Imagine a separate Facebook page or YouTube channel focused only on your campaign and its messages. These vehicles will borrow from the credibility and reach of the originals, all while creating some level of excitement and attention given their "special" nature. Make the most of what's working well.

Listen in

Strong vehicles can also be leveraged to gather strategic intelligence; that's another one of the many ways you can leverage one strength to help overcome a weakness. When the social media channels, publications, and activities you have developed earn the trust and engagement of the audience, you have an ideal strength you can use to dialogue with the audience. Go beyond mere readership surveys (which have their place, mind you). Leverage a strong vehicle by using it as a forum in which to find out where your audience stands on the critical issues facing your organization. Have the courage to ask provocative questions and listen carefully to the answers you get. You'll not only gather valuable strategic intelligence on biases, expectation, needs, codes, and habits, you'll also deepen your relationship with an important audience.

FROM MAGAZINE TO DIALOGUE

A great example of how to leverage a strong vehicle is the work my agency did for the Canadian Veterinary Medical Association and their monthly magazine for members. Survey after survey revealed it was well read and considered to be very credible. A strength indeed. The executive director, sensing the power of this magazine, introduced a new feature in which a fictitious case study was written to explore a critical ethical issue facing the members. Members could then write in and explain how they would handle the situation. The case studies were provocative, the members wrote in consistently, and the association was able to use the responses to spark important dialogue and to fine-tune its positions on these issues in a way that reflected members' opinions. There are many ways to have this kind of dialogue—and every organization should. The point here is that an existing vehicle was leveraged, allowing the association to move quickly, inexpensively, and effectively. They saw a key strength and they put it to work.

Leveraging Strategic Intelligence

Strategic intelligence—your organization's knowledge of the audiences you need to reach and the world in which they live and work—is also a resource, a strength that can be leveraged. That's why conducting a situation analysis is the essential first step of any strategy; without genuine strategic intelligence, you are merely counting on luck.

We've already covered ways to use your knowledge of the audience's biases, expectations, needs, codes, and habits. We've already talked about using knowledge of the external environment to anticipate change and get ahead of your competitors. Here is one more strategic direction to help ensure you really make the most of your strategic intelligence.

Follow Through

The key to fully leveraging strategic intelligence is to follow through. Make sure your action plan really does act on the strategic directions you worked so hard to set. If your strategic intelligence leads you in a direction that features a segmented campaign with messages tailor-made for each audience, don't give into the lure (simplicity, lower costs) of a one-size-fits-all campaign. If your intelligence points to an emerging threat posed by a new government and its priorities, don't wait until the new legislation is drafted and in-committee to start advocating. If your information tells you people will only pay attention to strong and provocative messages, don't settle for a dull campaign because the board is more likely to approve those messages.

Leveraging strategic intelligence means drawing fully from it as you create your directions and then respecting those directions as you plan and implement the actual campaign.

MESSAGES THAT ARE TRUE TO STRATEGY

A campaign my colleagues and I developed for a national professional association demonstrates the power of staying true to your situation analysis and the strategic direction it yields. Our audience research clearly showed grandiose messages about the members of this profession didn't ring true with the public (which helped explain why past campaigns for this association had not fully succeeded). Our research also revealed many people understood and valued all the many ways members of this profession contributed to the community—the work they often do for free that contributes to individuals and community-based organizations.

This strategic intelligence led us to a new creative strategy that celebrated the many ways members of the profession are making a difference to the community. We stayed true to this strategy and developed a three-year campaign that featured members of the profession and the community work they do. The messages were a hit both with the public audience and with members of the profession themselves, who fully supported the campaign.

Leveraging Goodwill

Goodwill is often one of the subtlest resources, and it's one that can change quickly from a strength to a weakness. As such, it's often less evident what to do with it when you have it in abundance. Remember goodwill is a resource that brings with it increased attention from your audience, a greater predisposition to perceive what you say as credible, and a greater predisposition to act. It is powerful, and your ability to leverage it fully will help empower your campaigns. Consider the following strategic directions to help you do this.

Focus on the Right Audiences

The first way to leverage goodwill is to make sure you focus your campaign on those audiences that know and like your organization. Start there and invest there. You'll generate greater return on your investment in the form of changed behaviour that benefits your organization. You'll also build momentum you can draw on as you move to reach other, more challenging audiences. After all, if you have a segment of the population that already knows your organization, supports your products and services, and has tattooed your logo on their arms, start with that segment; they are the ideal foundation on which to build the campaign. That's the reason, for example, Steve Jobs regularly announced the latest innovation from Apple at the annual Macworld conventions and, later, the annual Worldwide Developers Conference. The buzz started building from the core (pardon the pun) of Apple enthusiasts, whether consumers or developers, and would radiate out from there.

Tell Them about It

A second way to leverage goodwill is to build into your creative strategy the very information that earned the goodwill in the first place. Your organization has a long, proud history? Tell them about it one more time. You won some prestigious awards? Mention them in every ad and media release. You actively support charitable causes or sponsor an Olympic team? Don't hide it, flaunt it. By communicating to your audience the things they like best about your organization, your products, services, and mission, you'll strike a responsive chord,[1] win their continued attention, and make them feel good all over again.

As you prepare to use this strategic direction, be sure to remember the following characteristics of goodwill.

- Goodwill is earned slowly and carefully; this is not a "quick fix." Patience and persistence are required if you hope to build goodwill you can later leverage. Efforts to celebrate goodwill too quickly will often be met with skepticism.

- Any goodwill you generate will be based on the assessment of your organization and its activities that your audiences will carry out; they will determine whether or not they feel good as they emerge from that assessment. You can influence assessment through strong communication, but you cannot control the outcome.
- Goodwill also requires consistency. Audiences today are sophisticated and will quickly spot obvious attempts to curry favour on one front while concealing things on another. Trumpeting your "Top 100 Employers" ranking while closing down offices and laying off staff without proper warning and assistance won't work. Supporting a small environmental group while fighting in the courts to avoid fines over a toxic spill will have the same negative impact. Your audiences will spot the lack of consistency and will likely also post about it to their favourite social media channels.

In short, make sure the claims to goodwill that you present to the audience are consistent and genuine. Consumers, voters, donors, and citizens are increasingly sophisticated, skeptical, and vocal. Think twice, then, before stretching the bounds of credibility as you attempt to leverage goodwill. If you genuinely have goodwill with an audience, you can and should leverage it. If you don't, you'll need to build it first (but more on that later).

Find a Partner
Partnerships are a third strategic way to leverage goodwill. Those individuals and organizations that feel good about your organization are not only more likely to pay attention to your messages, they're more likely to agree to join you in your effort to spread those messages. A credible public health organization will find family doctors are willing to put up posters in their waiting rooms to help educate the public. Members who feel a deep attachment to an advocacy group will welcome the opportunity to wear t-shirts and affix bumper stickers to spread the messages. Other organizations that know and respect yours will be more open to the idea of sharing your social media messages or adding a banner on their website that directs visitors to yours.

The point here is that if goodwill is a strength for your organization, make sure you leverage it by making full use of partnerships in your campaign. Much as was the case with volunteers in the preceding section, potential partners must be approached early, they must be reminded of what you have in common, and they must be armed with the tools they will need (messages, vehicles, logistical information) to be a part of the campaign.

PARTNERSHIPS AND GOODWILL

The most impressive partnership I ever had a chance to be a part of was one forged by the Office of Consumer Affairs, an agency within Industry Canada that was mandated to educate consumers. In one year, this agency was able to secure the partnership of dozens of other federal departments and agencies who had information and tools that would be useful to consumers. All of this knowledge was brought together under a single web portal (the Canadian Consumer Information Gateway), and each partner was committed to maintaining their information and tools, and promoting the site. A year later, dozens more organizations—including NGOs, media outlets, and provincial governments—also joined the partnership, adding their content and resources to the partnership. The portal received awards, generated massive traffic, and helped hundreds of thousands of consumers. All this was possible because (a) the Office of Consumer Affairs had earned significant goodwill, and (b) they were able to find terrific partners and put them to work contributing valuable content and promoting the site.

Leveraging Internal Cohesion

Real internal cohesion happens when all the people needed for a communication campaign—staff, volunteers, decision-makers—agree on the direction of the campaign and agree to contribute fully to it. Cohesion typically (but not always) starts at the top of an organization and works its way down to the most junior staff. Leveraging this cohesion means leveraging the energy and commitment of all those people. Here are some strategic directions that can help you make the most of this resource.

Ask for More

One of the strongest ways to leverage the internal cohesion of your team is to engage them and ask for more. Whether in the mailroom, in the IT department, or at the front desk, people who know about and support a campaign will be willing to do those hundreds of little things that make a good campaign great. More importantly, they'll be more willing to work late, start early, and set other priorities aside to make sure the campaign succeeds. At the risk of sounding like a broken record, though, you can't take energy and commitment for granted, no matter how high levels of cohesion are. You must, as you do to recruit volunteers and partners, approach people early and clearly communicate the shared values that create the internal cohesion and how your campaign advances those values. Once that's done, ask. Let them know specifically how the work they do can make the campaign a success. Let them feel ownership in the success of the campaign.

To fully leverage the internal cohesion of senior managers and executives, you can also ask for more. In this case, ask for more of the hard resources you lack: time, money, people, and vehicles. Don't be satisfied with the budget you started the year with. Ask for the time to work in small steps or gather additional strategic intelligence if you need it. Put in a request for the added staff that will make all the difference. If you sense there is genuine support for the campaign at the highest levels of the organization, leverage it and get the resources you need to generate results.

This is not, however, an approach that should be taken on every campaign. You'll quickly erode any internal cohesion you had. Rather, wait until need is great and internal cohesion around the campaign is high. That's when it is most strategic to put a detailed argument together on how the additional resources will generate return on investment (in the form of moving the organization toward the achievement of its goals) and bring it forward.

Tell the Story

A subtler way to leverage internal cohesion around a campaign is to project that internal energy outward. The conviction and enthusiasm of internal staff and volunteers is contagious. A shared sense of mission and vision of the future can be harnessed to create compelling messages and dramatic spokespeople. If you sense internal cohesion is indeed one of the great strengths of the organization, look for ways to have the people within the organization deliver the message to those outside. Use their words and emotions in the messages you create for the campaign. The sincerity and passion will do wonders for motivating your external audiences.

COHESION AND LEARNING MORE

A great example of the power of internal cohesion came with my agency's work for the Academic Health Council, a regional, government-funded agency whose mandate was to foster inter-professional collaboration in healthcare. The organization retained our services to develop a strategic communication plan and campaign. There were two key findings from our situation analysis that came together quite nicely. First, we found the agency—being new—had very little reliable strategic intelligence on its audiences. Other than the insight of its leadership, all of whom had worked in healthcare for some time, the organization was lacking in terms of strategic intelligence on the very healthcare providers whose collaboration it was hoping to foster. We also found a high level of internal cohesion between

continued

the organization and the government agencies that funded it. The funders recognized the benefits of inter-professional collaboration to patient health, safety,
and the overall satisfaction of care providers; they wanted to see the organization
succeed and were prepared to help. The executive director of the new agency
was able to leverage this high level of internal cohesion by securing substantial
funding for a study of healthcare providers in the region. As the findings were
gathered, the agency was able to substantially sharpen its overall creative strategy and communication action plan—another elegant example of how leveraging
a strength (in this case, internal cohesion) can help an organization overcome a
weakness (in this case, strategic intelligence and stories to tell).

Leveraging Stories

The healthcare example leads us to the final resource area you need to consider as
you develop your strategy: stories to tell. In a way, stories are the easiest resource
to leverage; if you have stories to tell, tell them. It's a simple approach but remarkably few organizations do it well. Government departments are so busy listing
rules and regulations they often forget to talk about the people, the challenges,
and the opportunities behind those rules and regulations. Each one has a good
story that is never told. Not-for-profits often focus so intently on asking for money
and support that they never take the time to tell the often moving story of the
people who struggled to address a compelling issue and built the organization as
a result. Too few fundraising campaigns tell the real stories of how people's lives
have been changed by the organization. Even businesses that are too busy closing sales ("Hurry, buy today, act now, operators are waiting!") forget they have
many dramatic stories to tell—stories of innovation, guts, battles, and victories.

One of the principal reasons for the success of business leaders like Lee
Iacocca, Colonel Sanders, Richard Branson, and Steve Jobs is that they had great
stories to tell and they told them well. Audiences are drawn to good stories; great
stories helped to build Chrysler, KFC, Virgin, and Apple. Here's what you can
do to leverage this powerful resource.

Gather Great Stories

Great stories are relatively easy to find in any organization. A good story deserves
to be told, and the people within and outside your organization will naturally want
to tell it. The trick is to listen closely to what people are talking and writing about.

What do your employees, volunteers, and members discuss most often and
with the most energy and conviction? When asked, what stories do donors and

customers like to share? Increasingly, people turn to social media channels to tell their stories. Look for your organization's name in hashtags and the text. Pay attention to those stories and connect with the people telling them when you see an opportunity to share the story more widely. News reporters, of course, are highly skilled storytellers and most understand the qualities of a great story. That's just one reason why monitoring the news media is so important for organizations. If reporters find a great story within your organization, look for ways to share that story and build it beyond a two-minute news piece; what began as a news media story can quickly become a new page on your website or a series of tweets or posts. The key is to spot the great story early and to put it to work for the organization.

Tell Your Stories

A good story is a strength, and the #1 strategic direction to deploy when you have this strength is to leverage your stories at every opportunity. Strategic communicators will see every ad campaign, every speech, every post to a social media channel, every meeting with a reporter, every mailing, and every visit to the website as a chance to tell a story. Strategic communicators will dare to capitalize on these opportunities and to speak the language of storytelling. They will talk of victories and challenges instead of processes and outcomes. They will tell stories of how real people overcame challenges and achieved great results, rather than relying on tables of statistics without a face. They will look back decades or even centuries to tell stories of how the organization came about and set its course, rather than only looking back three months to report sales or contributions.

Great stories are personal, dramatic, and colourful. They can be told via every medium and every channel. Great stories are at times funny, romantic, heroic, or even tragic. They are never dull, and they always have an arc as people face challenges, find solutions, and triumph or start over. Most organizations have great stories. Only a few have the conviction and strategic know-how to put those stories to work for them.

Overcoming Weaknesses in Hard Resources

This section is not quite as pleasant to read as the preceding one, but it is likely you will turn to these strategic directions far more often in your career. An abundance of communication resources is a rare and wonderful occasion; modest resources are much more the norm. In particular, this section will focus on how to deal strategically with a lack of hard resources: time, money, people, and vehicles. The following section will explore how best to overcome weaknesses in soft resources.

Overcoming a Lack of Time

As mentioned above, working with an abundance of time is a rare privilege in public relations and strategic communication. More often than not, campaigns must be planned, created, and executed quickly to meet a particular deadline, capitalize on a great opportunity, or mitigate an emerging threat. There are, however, many approaches to overcoming a lack of time. Here are the most powerful strategic directions to consider as you develop your plan.

Grow Your Team

This is the most obvious solution and it works. If you're faced with tight deadlines and your in-house team is already pushed to the limit, you grow the team of people. If you need to undertake a communication tactic you have never attempted before, you grow your team to add people who specialize in this area. Most often, this will mean hiring a consultant or an entire agency so their people resources can be added to yours. Of course, finding and hiring a consultant or an agency can, in and of itself, take time. It's the reason many client organizations will regularly search a small and trusted list of agencies and contractors they can turn to quickly when they need to overcome a weakness in people. Your ability to respond quickly and jump into complex situations with confidence will make a big difference to the outcomes you generate.

Ask for More Time

If you enjoy a strength in internal cohesion and all the members of your cohesive team understand the project is important, you just might be able to ask those in charge for more time. In some instances, that won't be possible. The Olympic Games are scheduled years in advance and if your organization is going to be able to capitalize on the opportunity, you will have to be ready; asking in the International Olympic Committee for a few more weeks is not likely to generate much success! In many instances, though, deadlines are set by organizational leaders or committees. Those deadlines may well be flexible and putting together a strong case for why you and your team need more time may just be the most strategic approach to overcoming this weakness.

Enhance Your Tools

Tilling and planting a one-acre garden by hand takes an awfully long time. Doing the same thing with power tools, on the other hand, is much faster. In much the same way, new tools for your communication team may allow them to do more and do it more quickly. From digital video editing to online survey tools, social media channels, and colour laser printers, strategic communicators can increasingly do high-quality work more quickly and at comparable cost to older methods. The key is to rely on the members of your communication team. Your researchers, writers, designers, and event managers will likely know about the newest tools for their specialized work. Let them guide you in assessing and acquiring tools with the greatest potential for improving productivity and overcoming a lack of time.

Leveraging Existing Vehicles

Each new vehicle you develop will require time to conceive, design, test, approve, and deploy. On the other hand, those communication vehicles that are already part of your routine, proven, and funded can be deployed much more quickly. That's why most organizations have a small number of regularly published, broadcast, or updated vehicles they can use to communicate.

Being strategic means making the very most of your organization's existing vehicles, especially when time is limited. Those vehicles may not be as exciting as a brand-new vehicle, and they may not be ideal in terms of their overall positioning, their distribution schedules, and messaging, but they can help you get information out quickly and reliably when it matters most.

Overcoming a Lack of Money

Money is by far the most flexible resource a communication professional can deploy. You can often convert money into any of the other resources: time, people, vehicles, goodwill, and so on. What can you do when money is tight or entirely lacking? This is a near constant challenge for communicators, especially those working in the public and not-for-profit sectors. There are, however, very strategic approaches to overcoming this weakness. Here are the most promising directions to consider as you look for ways to overcome this weakness.

Slow Down

Money is especially important when deadlines are tight and results need to be generated quickly. That's when hiring an agency and paying to place an ad in tomorrow's daily newspaper makes the most sense. Moving quickly, however, costs more money. Quite often, timelines are not so tight, and an organization can afford to move a little more slowly and lower its costs substantially. These are the times when recruiting volunteers can be more strategic than hiring an agency. It's when building relationships with principal reporters can make more sense than buying advertising. It's when using social media and letting your messages spread slowly but surely can be a better approach than hosting a major event. If time is a strength and money is not, leverage the former to help you overcome the latter.

Be Choosy about Audiences

Each new audience you decide to reach out to and engage will necessarily grow your need for money. This is why having plenty of strategic intelligence can be so valuable. Leverage that intelligence and pick audiences that are truly important for your campaign: those that are predisposed to pay attention and close to taking action or establishing a strong relationship. Focus on those influencer audiences that can most dramatically reach and persuade your actor audiences. Select those enablers who matter most. Be certain, in other words, that every audience you reach out to is truly a "key" audience.

Look for Volunteers

This is one approach those in the not-for-profit sector know well. If you can't afford to pay people full wages to work on your campaign, look for those who are so committed to the cause and so drawn to the activity itself they will work for free or for a reduced amount. It's also an approach that organizations in the public and private sectors can consider. After all, people often dedicate time to activities that don't reward them financially. Instead, we undertake different tasks because we believe in the cause or purpose, we are looking to connect socially with others, or we like the activity and want to engage in it and have others appreciate our effort.

Whatever sector your organization is in, the key to success when looking for volunteers is to focus on finding people who like to do whatever it is you need done. Whether it's writing, photography, video production, or event management, find the people who love doing those things and who are looking for ways to do more of them. Often, those people will be students or recent graduates looking to enhance their portfolio and grow their network. They might belong to clubs or associations dedicated to the activity. Recognize what it is these people are most looking for (e.g., recognition, networking, social connections, pleasure), and find ways to build as much of these benefits as possible into the process.

Work as a Team

Most organizations have relatively small communication and PR teams. Often, a company with hundreds of employees will have four or five of those people focused on the task of creating messages, reaching out to audiences, and engaging in dialogue with them. If the campaign matters and the organization enjoys strong internal cohesion, consider growing the team by drawing from the pool of people within. Whether they're in IT, legal, engineering, sales, or HR, people have a wide range of skills and talents. Many can write well, build web pages, deliver powerful speeches, or help host a special event. Most importantly, they are all on payroll already so their contributions to your campaign will cost relatively little. All they need is an invitation to pitch in. Your work will be something fresh for them, a way to expand their skills and their network within the organization. Chances are, they'll see the opportunity to be creative and engage key audiences as something new, something fun, and something worth doing.

Overcoming a Lack of People

Communication is essentially impossible without people. You need people to create messages, distribute them, engage in dialogue, and evaluate the results. Not only do you need people to do these things, you need talented and creative people. Both quantity and quality matter a great deal for this resource. There are, fortunately, very effective and strategic ways to overcome a weakness in this resource area. Many of these were introduced in the preceding section but they bear repeating.

Grow Your Team

If you desperately need someone skilled in using the latest analytics tools to assess and improve your social media vehicles, you should consider adding that kind of person to your team. Yes, it takes money and enough internal cohesion to make it happen, but it's how organizations grow and adapt to changing conditions in their external environment. This strategy also requires the time to make the decision, recruit and hire the individual, and integrate them fully into your communication team. All of these investments will pay off once the new person or new people are on board.

Hire Talent

Hiring an agency or consultant to provide the services your own team can't is often a faster and less expensive way forward. Though it will have less lasting value than growing your team, individual consultants or agencies can deliver very specialized services, and they can do it quickly. That expertise comes at a price, however. If money is a strength and time is a weakness, this may be the more strategic way forward.

Slow Down

As was discussed earlier, working quickly is usually a more expensive way to get things done. It also often requires a bigger team. If time is a strength and people are a weakness, consider shifting gears so your campaign can be handled in house but in a matter of months rather than days or weeks.

Work as a Team

Here too, calling on colleagues from within the organization to participate in your campaign can be a solid way to overcome a lack of people on the communication team specifically. If internal cohesion is strong, many people in areas outside of communication may welcome the opportunity to be part of a campaign. You need only to invite them and make the tools they'll need available to them.

Find Volunteers

Finally, an organization with plenty of goodwill and a little more time can often have a considerable amount of work done by volunteers. Volunteers can include seasoned professionals and aspiring students. The work they can do is often inspired, creative, and cutting-edge. Generally speaking, though, it takes a little longer to recruit talented volunteers and to get work done through this resource; many of them will already have full schedules so dropping everything to pitch in is not an option. Be sure to plan accordingly and look for ways to speed up and simplify the work that needs to be done.

Overcoming a Lack of Quality Vehicles

A quality vehicle is one with the capacity to carry the messages you need to send, the readership you need to reach, and the credibility that allows your messages to be read, reflected upon, and acted upon. Not every organization enjoys such a vehicle. Certainly, any new organization will struggle for lack of effective vehicles but even some well-established organizations just have not invested the time and effort required to build vehicles with the capacity, readership, and trust they need. There are, however, effective and strategic directions to overcome this weakness.

Launch New Vehicles

This is a daunting strategic direction for any organization pressed for time and/ or money. It is a powerful strategic direction, though, because new vehicles often bring with them excitement and visibility. A brand-new website, a first Twitter account, or a first-of-its-kind special event will all generate buzz and likely enjoy greater attention simply because they are new and a "first." New vehicles won't have much in the way of positive expectations and trustworthiness (since these take time to establish), but they also won't be burdened by negative expectations or suspicion. You get to start with a fresh slate. People will pay attention for a short time and see the extent to which your new vehicle delivers useful, trustworthy, and engaging information. If you have the time, people, and money to develop a brand-new vehicle, this is a solid strategic direction.

Improve Your Vehicles

This solution can also take time and cost money. It also requires some strategic intelligence in the form of a good readership survey for the vehicle. Ask the intended audience why they do or do not read it. Get their sense of what is lacking and what is worth keeping. Then work to refresh, revise, and relaunch the vehicle. Again, if the organization has time as a strength, this approach can deliver solid results in the long run. The newly improved vehicle will attract attention much like a new vehicle would, and it'll deliver improved results for many months or years after.

Borrow Other Vehicles

This direction depends on having solid goodwill among other organizations that can also reach your core audiences. The solution is to leverage your goodwill and establish a partnership whereby your messages are communicated using the other organization's vehicles. In reality, this is the essence of media relations as a PR tactic. If you can establish goodwill with a CTV News reporter, you can leverage that goodwill and have them communicate your newsworthy messages to their audiences.

In much the same way, you may be able to use the newsletter of a schoolboard to get the message about your children's charity out to teachers and parents. You may be able to partner with the National Football League to have their players wear pink ribbons on their uniforms and raise the profile of breast cancer research. You may be able to get a local bank to help raise funds for your charity by placing small collection boxes on their counters. The list of potential partnerships goes on and is only really limited by the imagination of the communication team and the expectations of the audience. The key is to think broadly about what constitutes a communication vehicle: the jerseys of professional athletes and the countertops of a bank may not spring to mind as communication vehicles, but they both have tremendous reach.

Overcoming Weaknesses in Soft Resources

This section will deal with how best to overcome weaknesses in each of the soft resource areas: goodwill, strategic intelligence, internal cohesion, and stories. More often than not, solving weaknesses in soft resources will require an investment of hard resources.

- If you need to build your goodwill, you need to connect with audiences more, give back to the community, and communicate effectively about your efforts to do this. Doing so will require time, money, people, and vehicles.
- If you need more strategic intelligence, you need to conduct or purchase research. This requires time, money, and skilled people to find the data, analyze it, and make sense of it.
- If you need more internal cohesion, you will need to communicate more effectively so people inside the organization are more aware of, more supportive of, and more aligned with the organization's overall mission, goals, and objectives. You'll need time, money, people, and vehicles to make that happen.
- And if you lack stories to tell, you'll need to gather them and write them. You'll need time to do this, skilled people to do it, and quality vehicles to share the stories.

The surest way to overcome a weakness in soft resources, then, is to identify the weakness and then to build the store of hard resources so you can grow the quantity and enhance the quality of the soft resource. It may seem too simplistic an approach, but it works and works consistently. Of course, securing the hard resources you need depends on your ability to assess each of the soft resource areas and convince the leaders of the organization that the weakness in goodwill, strategic intelligence, internal cohesion, or stories to tell will have a significant and negative impact on the campaign.

OVERCOMING A LACK OF STRATEGIC INTELLIGENCE

I once conducted a campaign for the Canadian Dental Hygienists Association, a professional association with a very strategic executive director. Our work began with a thorough situation analysis and included the finding that the organization had a weakness in strategic intelligence. They didn't have recent and reliable research we could use to guide the development of our campaign messages or our media strategy. We needed to know more about their members.

What the organization did have, however, was a savvy executive director and terrific goodwill. The executive director agreed with our assessment, reached out to the organizations whose support she had gathered, and secured a sponsor to cover the costs of a member study. The story has a happy ending in that the organization was able to leverage its people resource and goodwill to strategically overcome a weakness in strategic intelligence. We, in turn, were able to leverage the results of the member survey to develop more powerful stories to tell. Good strategy is wonderfully integrated in this way.

KEY TERMS AND CONCEPTS

As you review this chapter for any tests or assignments, you will want to pay particular attention to the following terms and concepts introduced in the preceding pages:

- **leveraging time**
- **leveraging money**
- **leveraging people**
- **leveraging vehicles**
- **leveraging goodwill**
- **leveraging strategic intelligence**
- **leveraging internal cohesion**
- **leveraging stories**
- **overcoming a lack of time**
- **overcoming a lack of money**
- **overcoming a weakness in people**
- **overcoming weak vehicles**
- **overcoming weaknesses in soft resources**

QUESTIONS FOR CRITICAL REFLECTION

1. Of the hard resources considered in this chapter, which do you feel offers the most potential to bring a PR or communication campaign to a higher level? Why?
2. Of the soft resources considered in this chapter, which do you feel is the most powerful and valuable? Would you rather work with strong strategic intelligence, goodwill, internal cohesion, or stories? Why?
3. Assume your client has one key strength and one only: amazing, inspiring, and captivating stories to tell. They have little of any other key resource to work with. They ask for your advice on how to leverage this strength in the face of all their weaknesses. How would you approach this challenge?
4. If you could choose one weakness for your organization's hard resources, which would it be? What would be easier to overcome?
5. This chapter suggests the most practical way to overcome a weakness in soft resources is to invest in hard resources. Pick an example of a soft resource and describe how you would invest hard resources to enhance the quantity and quality of the soft resource in question.

NOTE

1. I borrow this wonderful expression from Tony Schwartz once again. Schwartz, T. (1973). *The responsive chord*. New York, NY: Doubleday.

CHAPTER SEVEN
Opportunities, Threats, and Strategy

You go out for your afternoon walk in the garden and notice a troubling trend affecting the plants and animals there. The milder winters and harsher summers have created ideal conditions for grubs. The pests burrow just under the grass and munch happily at the roots all spring, to be then dug up by the neighbourhood skunks and raccoons. Your carefully manicured lawn now looks like a battlefield. You have a threat (a competitor or adversary), and you need to either get out of its way or tackle it head on.

In terms of grubs, tackling them head on is a straightforward enough strategic direction that usually comes out the end of a lawn care company's hose. You spray the right insecticide at the right time of year, and your grass roots become poison for the little pests. It can work, but for many gardeners, the strategic direction comes with a price to the environment and makes this less in keeping with their long-term gardening goals. You might search for an organic option, but the outcome in terms of preserving an attractive yard is less certain.

You consider your neighbours and the alternative approach to mitigating a threat they have chosen—getting out of the way. In an approach worthy of a sage martial arts expert, they understand the grass is as much a part of the problem as the grubs. So they rip out the grass and plant clover and wild flowers, for example. Over time, they bring about an attractive green lawn cover grubs despise. The grubs don't eat, they die, end of problem.

These are two different strategic directions, but both are very effective in terms of yielding the desired outcome: an attractive lawn. The key is that both gardeners recognize, as with all threats, the status quo is not an option. The threat is real and imminent.

CHAPTER OVERVIEW

This chapter focuses on the trends and forces outside of an organization that can most affect the success of a communication or PR campaign. The discussion begins with a review of how some trends and forces (opportunities) can make it easier to succeed. Steps to capitalize on opportunities by aligning closely with the time, place, and idea at the heart of the change or trend are then discussed. Next, the chapter presents a similar discussion on trends and forces in the external environment that can make it more difficult for the campaign to succeed (threats). Strategic approaches to mitigating threats are presented, also linked to time, place, and ideas behind the force or trend. Examples of strategic responses to both opportunities and threats are presented.

LEARNING OBJECTIVES

1. Differentiate between trends and forces outside an organization that make it easier to succeed in communication and public relations (i.e., opportunities) and harder to succeed (i.e., threats).
2. Strategically align an organization's communication and public relations program with the place, time, and idea at the heart of an opportunity.
3. Strategically distance an organization's communication and public relations program from the place, time, and idea at the heart of a threat.
4. Manage the risk of overstating the extent of the alignment between an organization and an opportunity in its external environment.
5. Differentiate between different strategic approaches to mitigating threats in the communication and public relations environment. Select the optimal approach to mitigating specific threats.
6. Differentiate between opportunities and threats, and make strategic use of the ambiguity between the two concepts in your planning.

This chapter on opportunities and threats is quite different from the preceding chapter on strengths and weaknesses because, well, opportunities and threats are different. They spring from a different, exterior place; they affect organizations in a different way. Opportunities and threats compel organizations to respond differently than strengths and weaknesses.

STRATEGIC COMMUNICATION AND OPPORTUNITIES

Any change in the external environment that makes success more likely and easier for your organization is an opportunity. For communicators, opportunities generally do one of two things: (1) they grow the audience that can be reached and engaged, or (2) they make the audience more predisposed to pay attention or act in the way you've identified in your communication goals. Sometimes, a single opportunity can do both: grow the audience and make all of its members more predisposed.

Consider, for example, how the international success of a local tennis player would make residents of the home city more predisposed to pay attention to messages about tennis and more likely to visit a local club and perhaps join.

Opportunities can exist in all eight of the dimensions of the external environment you scanned in the first part of this book: political, economic, social/cultural, technological, demographic, competitive, news media, and natural.

- A political shift to the left might make elected officials more predisposed to pay attention to your message of social justice and to fund programs you support.
- A healthy economy makes people more predisposed to spend by supporting your charity. It might also grow the size of the market able to afford a trip to your resort.
- A change in the social values of your audience (e.g., an increase in environmental consciousness) could make them more predisposed to behave the way your organization needs them to behave (e.g., buying trucks with hybrid or electric engines).
- A radical new technology might predispose your audience to suddenly pay closer attention to the information you provide (e.g., abandoning the cassette tapes you used to send out in favour of a new, more inviting MP3 technology).
- A demographic shift can reshape your key audience and make the intended behaviour easier or harder to generate. Having more consumers than ever in the 75–90-year-old segment creates a growing audience of people to receive your messages about planned giving for your foundation.
- The decline of a strong competitor in the grocery business could significantly increase the amount of attention you can expect from your audience.
- The arrival of a new CEO with an illustrious past and impressive track record could make reporters more predisposed to pay attention to your messages and pass them along to the public.
- A hot, dry summer could raise the profile of the debate over global warming and increase media and public interest in the debate.

Now that you have a clearer sense of what an opportunity actually is, you need to find ways to capitalize on the trend or force as part of your strategic communication campaign.

Capitalizing on Opportunities

To capitalize on or make the most of an opportunity in the external environment, your organization needs to align with the trend or force creating the opportunity. You need to get as "close" to that trend or force as possible with the words, sounds, and images you create for your campaign. Generally speaking, an opportunity in strategic communication has three dimensions: a place, a time, and an idea. Once you've identified an opportunity (i.e., a trend or force in the external environment that will make your audience more predisposed to pay attention to your campaign and act on its messages), you capitalize on the opportunity by aligning your campaign with the place of the opportunity, the time of it, and/or the idea at the heart of the opportunity. The campaign, in other words, needs to be active and visible as close to the time and place of the opportunity as possible. The messages you communicate need to demonstrate how your organization's position and values are as close to the idea of the opportunity as possible.

Place

Capitalizing on an opportunity can mean getting close to that opportunity in a very physical, geographic sense. Getting messages to an audience—the business we are in—still often requires some physical presence for you or your message. If the members of a profession you want to reach are gathering for an annual conference in Montreal, go there. If young people are tuning out of television and spending time online, that's where your messages belong. In short, if the opportunity has a physical dimension, get as close to the physical manifestation as possible. Aligning with the place of an opportunity is why sponsors will pay millions of dollars to sponsor the Olympics; fans and television cameras will be in the stadium so it makes sense for the sponsors' logos to be there too. If a large, attentive, and favourably predisposed portion of your audience is scheduled to come together in a particular place, it makes strategic sense to align your campaign with that location.

Time

Aligning yourself chronologically with a trend or force is also an important part of capitalizing on an opportunity. Consider, for example, how potato chip companies are busy communicating in the weeks leading up to the Super Bowl. Aligning the timing of the campaign with a time of the year when millions are more likely to purchase potato chips is strategic. In the same way, communicating with an audience about investing to reduce taxes can be very effective in March and April, when those tax statements are causing much lost sleep. Campaigns to promote healthy eating for kids make sense in the fall when parents once again have to think about what to put in those lunch bags every day. So if the size, the attention, or the favourable predisposition of your audience is scheduled to peak at a particular time of year, it makes strategic sense to align your campaign with that time. That way, you can maximize the likelihood those people will pay attention and act on your messages.

Idea

Opportunities in the external environment often also include the widespread dissemination or adoption of a particular idea (e.g., a mood, idea, belief, value, or interest). Public opinion changes, people become more aware of something, public resistance to certain behaviour subsides, or public interest in an issue grows. Capitalizing on such opportunities comes with aligning your organization and your message with the *idea* emerging and spreading. Draw attention to how close, how alike, how in-tune your organization and the idea are. If gas prices are climbing and people are increasingly concerned about greenhouse gasses, focus your messages on how your new vehicle, your transit system, your fundraising campaign are in tune with that trend and able to save people money on gas while saving the environment (this assumes, of course, the marketing people did their homework and the engineering team has developed fuel efficient vehicles for you to promote).

A CASE IN POINT: CHILDHOOD OBESITY—HOW A HEALTH EPIDEMIC CREATES STRATEGIC OPPORTUNITIES

The **place** for this opportunity is in Canada and the U.S., where concern over childhood obesity is very high. Cities and neighbourhoods with a high percentage of lower-income families might be particularly affected, and so people in those places might be even more predisposed to pay attention.

There are many **times** when this issue gathers our attention; some of the key moments you might try to align your efforts with include the following: (1) when a new study documenting the depth of the childhood obesity problem is released; (2) when a news media outlet prepares to tackle the issue in a multipart series; (3) when new legislation or a new government program designed to address the issue is set to be debated or launched; (4) during the back-to-school season when parents are thinking about what their kids will eat for lunch; and (5) when a food company that targets kids (e.g., breakfast cereal, candy, fast food) launches a

continued

decadent new product or announces a healthier new policy on advertising. Each of these moments will feature a growth in the size of the audience you can reach and a greater likelihood the members of this growing audience will pay attention to your campaign and act on the information you share.

The **idea** behind this issue is narrowly defined as childhood obesity but can be quickly expanded to include obesity for people of all ages, diabetes, heart disease and other related conditions, education, child welfare, corporate responsibility, preventative health, and leisure activities. The key is that all of these secondary ideas are evidently connected to the core issue or idea. As such, the rise in interest around childhood obesity serves to expand the size and predisposition of the audience toward this central idea and those pertinent or related to it.

The **strategy** here, if you are attempting to promote a new product or service to help alleviate childhood obesity (perhaps a nutrition program for inner city schools), is to align your communications campaign with the place, time, and idea of childhood obesity. Launch the program in cities with a high proportion of obese preteens; announce the program in late August and early September, when parents' thoughts turn to their kids, or time the launch to coincide with a long-anticipated study on the incidence of childhood obesity; and focus your messages on the health risks of preteen obesity, perhaps securing the endorsement of physicians or advocacy groups representing people with heart disease and diabetes.

Effective strategic directions, then, begin with a thorough review of your situation analysis and the driving forces behind the opportunities you have identified. What is driving the growth in the size of the audience or its shift to paying more attention and being more predisposed to your messages? If what's driving the shift is happening at a particular place or time, capitalize by focusing your messages on that same place and time. If, on the other hand, what's driving the shift is the emergence of a particular idea, then you need to align yourself as closely as possible (and reasonable) to that idea.

A Word of Caution: "Tugging at the Leash"

Aligning with an idea can seem deceptively simple. "The audience cares about the environment? No problem: run some ads celebrating how much we care about the environment!" It sounds easy enough, but remember audiences are increasingly sophisticated and will know full well when your efforts to align with a popular idea are going too far and "tugging at their leash." The reaction when an audience knows it's being manipulated in this way—especially in this era of social media, in which everyone has a platform—can be swift and severe: ridicule, eroded trust, and perhaps even sanctions. The fines for false advertising will likely be miniscule compared to the lost goodwill from extensive media coverage and intense criticism from opposing groups.

To avoid these risks, be sure you remain objective as you consider which trends and forces in the external environment are most genuinely aligned with your organization. Maybe environmental protection is not a good fit for your steel mill but job creation is. That being said, organizations do change, of course, so a bold new strategic direction that aligns an organization with the shift to concern for protecting the environment might prove to be very effective. If that's the strategic direction, you need to ensure the entire organization is behind it so close scrutiny by consumers or the news media won't reveal any inconsistencies.

STRATEGIC COMMUNICATION AND THREATS

Now we come to the opposite of opportunities and, frankly, the reason most clients call PR agencies—threats in the external environment. Threats generally make the audience smaller (e.g., an aging population is a threat for manufacturers of baby cribs) or less predisposed to pay attention or take action (e.g., public and government concern over climate change may pose a threat if you manufacture two-stroke gasoline engines for lawnmowers, leaf blowers, and weed trimmers). The place, time, and idea of these threats will significantly add to the challenge of reaching and engaging these audiences.

Threats, like opportunities, can be found in any element of the environment.

What a Threat Looks Like

- Political: A new party in power is pro-business and sees your social program as merely an expense.
- Economic: The closing of a local factory means donors will have less money to spend and will have to choose between you and the others.
- Social/cultural: The public is increasingly skeptical of your profession's members and trusts its own abilities to find information and make decisions.
- Technological: A new online or mobile app offers the same benefits as your computer-based software but at a fraction of the cost.
- Demographic: The rapid aging of your membership base and the lack of interest among younger people means a demographic time bomb is tick-tick-ticking.

- News media: An angry radio show host seems intent on killing your project and dedicates the week's call-in-shows to what's wrong with the project and why municipal politicians should reject it.
- Competitive: A new charitable group begins canvasing from your traditional donor base. They're organized, effective, and their name is confusingly similar to yours.
- Natural: The increase in the number of cases of death and disease linked to a product you make or distribute is causing governments and public health advocacy groups to raise the level of critique and public scrutiny.

As was suggested by the lawn grubs analogy at the beginning of this chapter, there are essentially two ways to mitigate a threat: you can reduce the negative impact of a threat by tackling the threat head on (the fight response), or you can get out of the way of the trend or force (the flight response). Both the fight and flight responses have advantages and disadvantages; the choice should be strategic and not based on your level of anger or your need to prove just how tough you are. Pick the option that offers the greatest likelihood of success, the least risk of failure, and the lowest cost. The discussion of each approach in the section below should help you make the most strategic choice.

Flight: Getting Out of the Way of a Threat

The flight approach to mitigating a threat involves putting as much distance as possible between your communication campaign and the place, time, and idea at the heart of the threat. Your messages need to show how your organization is in no way aligned with the trend or force; often times, you will dispute or challenge the trend or force. The further away your organization is from the place, time, and ideas behind a threat, the better.

Place

Messages are very physical things—the stuff of sound, light, and touch. As such, crowded places are difficult spaces in which to communicate. Your message is less likely to be noticed, interpreted, remembered, or acted upon. The solution is often to move your messages to a less crowded place. Instead of setting up a booth at a large event, cluttered with competing voices and messages, design and manage your own event or purchase exclusive rights to sponsor an existing event. Both approaches will help gather a larger audience and keep it more focused on your campaign.

Likewise, certain physical environments are not conducive to gathering a predisposed audience: people in big cities are generally less predisposed to "right to bear arms" messages, whereas young people at a concert are less likely customers for the bathtub you can walk into securely. A conference on youth obesity is no place to announce your new triple-bacon burger (as compared to, say, the pork producers' conference). Strategically, you want to steer clear of places filled with audiences that are, at best, disinterested in what you have to say and, at worst, downright hostile to it. The secret, of course, is to discover where exactly that is for your audiences and finding effective ways to get your messages to the right audiences in a different place.

Time

Of course, not all places are crowded with competing messages or resistant audiences all the time. That's why the strategic thing to do in many cases is to put some time between your campaign and the threats. Wait until a few weeks after Earth Day to announce the expansion of the municipal dump. Give donors time to pay off their Christmas credit card bills before sending your fundraising appeal. Try to get your message out about your product *after* the blockbuster movie that features your organization as the villain is safely out of the theatres.

Idea

Finally, and most importantly, if a threat in the external environment is built around a particular idea, you may find the most strategic approach is to distance your organization from the idea. You need to create and communicate messages that clearly demonstrate how your organization is *not* a proponent of the idea and how your actions do *not* contribute to the idea. Indeed, you may want to demonstrate how the beliefs and actions of your organization contribute to the very *opposite* of the idea—maximizing the distance between your organization and the idea behind the threat. This is often the strategic direction that gets labelled as "spin." Remember there are limits to how far you can go with this approach before you begin "tugging at the leash" and potentially eroding the public's confidence and trust (i.e., goodwill).

To illustrate this, consider the threats involved in announcing the expansion of a municipal dump. If your strategic intelligence tells you there is public concern over municipal dumps, you can only go so far in distancing your proposal from the idea. Suddenly announcing you're shrinking the dump would be untrue; announcing you are actually increasing the size of a nature preserve would also be a stretch (though the expanded nature preserve may be a part of measures taken to compensate for the expanded dump). In either case, a PR campaign founded on a lie or a tug at the leash will likely only serve to draw fire in the long run. The better strategy here is to gather more strategic intelligence and learn more about the aspects of a municipal dump to which the public objects most (e.g., the odour, the loose litter surrounding the site, impact on ground water) and to focus your messages on specific steps being taken to address those specific concerns. In this way, you are indeed distancing your organization from specific ideas (e.g., that dumps are smelly) and pointing to specific measures (e.g., burning the methane off) to maintain your goodwill. If that methane gas can be used to generate electricity, then your story just got even better, as it helps you align the municipal dump with an opportunity at the same time as you distance it from a threat. Strategy can sometimes be so elegant.

Note here how resources and environment can interact in many complex ways. Having resources like strategic intelligence and a great story to tell allows you to mitigate a threat. This, in turn, helps build goodwill—another important resource.

Fight: Challenging a Threat Head-on

Now we come to that aspect of strategic communication (and notably public relations) that fits more neatly with the military or sport analogy referred to at the very start of this book—the pitch battle between two organizations for the hearts, minds, and wallets of the same public. It's rarely the most common strategic approach to mitigating a threat, but the decision to fight head-on can be the most strategic approach in certain cases, so it's always important for an organization to be ready. From a strategic communication perspective, tackling a threat head-on generally involves one of three approaches:

1. challenging the competitor's story with a better story of your own;
2. eroding the competitor's goodwill so its attention and influence are diminished; or
3. finding a way to remove your opponent's voice from the public sphere altogether.

Each approach has advantages and disadvantages so choosing strategically between them should be based on a careful review of all three options; don't settle for imitation, luck, or habit with this key decision.

Challenging the Competitor's Story

This strategic direction requires your organization to undertake a considerable amount of communication as you counter the claims of your opponent or competition, set the record straight, and get your argument or perspective out into the open. The approach is essentially one of public debate—of showing the audience how your story, your campaign is more closely aligned with *their* way of thinking, their values, and their priorities than the competitor's. At the same time, you articulate how the competitor's particular position or call to action runs *counter* to the audience's ways of thinking, values, and priorities. In this way, your campaign is mitigating a threat (the competitor's messages) by capitalizing on an opportunity. Notice how valuable a situation analysis becomes when you can make use of both a threat and an opportunity you spotted with your research.

Generally speaking, this strategic direction works best when you have the resources to speak more loudly and more often to more people than the competition; it's rarely a good strategy when you are David and they are Goliath. For communicators who love to communicate, this strategy is often the most fun. You get to sharpen your pencil and create all kinds of powerful messages and the opportunities to send them out.

Of course, this strategy also works best when you *genuinely* have a better story to tell than the competition. The public will ultimately decide who wins the debate. Losing the debate is both counterproductive and expensive in the long run.

Eroding the Competitor's Goodwill

Goodwill predisposes an audience to pay attention and to change their behaviour in a way that will make your organization successful. In short, an organization with strong goodwill is more influential than others. The audience is listening, and they are more likely to agree with what they hear because of how they already feel about the organization sending the messages. A strategic direction to consider, then, and one political parties excel at, is to erode the goodwill your competitor has earned. The fight is not so much with the messages of your competitors as with the messenger.

Eroding the goodwill a competitor enjoys essentially involves communicating in a way that challenges the credibility of the organization and the values it claims to hold. A science-based organization might challenge the scientific credentials of a critic. A political party may take aim at the wrongdoings of a rival party's leader. A corporation might like to remind customers of the environmental laws broken by a competitor and wonder what it says about the competitor's commitment to the environment. The list goes on.

You'll notice even from those brief examples this strategy is risky. To challenge another organization's or individual's credibility and values brings with it two important risks: (1) your competitor might fire back with similarly harsh attacks on your own credibility and values, and (2) the audience might judge your attack to be "below the belt" and question your values and credibility in launching this kind of campaign. In either case, your own goodwill could suffer significant damage. In other words, this second approach to fighting a competitive threat should be approached with great caution. These kinds of attacks can act much like a powerful pesticide: it gets rid of the weeds while taking down every flower and vegetable in the garden as well.

Diminishing the Competitor's Voice

The third possible approach to fighting a competitive threat is to diminish or even eliminate the competition's voice—its ability to fight with messages. Often, an appropriate way to diminish the voice of an opponent is to look for legal means to get it done. If the opponent is committing a hate crime or slandering your organization, you just might have a case worth pursuing. Sometimes money is a resource that can be leveraged to silence an opponent. That's why sponsors or major sporting events will pay a premium price for category exclusivity, ensuring competitors are not visible and not heard at all during the event or accompanying television broadcast.

As you consider this third approach, be sure to bear in mind most people who live and work in this country favour an approach to strategic communication that takes on competitors in an open forum, rather than a behind-closed-doors attempt to silence an opponent. Canadians generally prefer organizations that are willing and able to fight arguments with counterarguments; to win debates with smart, high-profile messages; and to trust the audience to see how their client's proposals ultimately make more sense for them. This kind of free exchange of ideas is, after all, the very foundation of modern democracy. Though a legal solution can make sense for cases of slander, defamation, and hate crimes, Canadians will generally respond more positively to organizations that can out-think and out-communicate their competitors. The goal of the campaign, after all, is to ensure long-term success, and the high road is always the best path to that destination.

OPPORTUNITIES AND THREATS: A QUESTION OF PERSPECTIVE

Imagine your morning walk in the garden reveals your neighbour, who recently inherited a small fortune, has decided to spend her new money by building an addition onto her modest bungalow. The plans call for a monster house that will tower above your garden. You're concerned because the same garden now bathed in sunlight much of the day will sit in the shadows of the addition; the environment in which your garden now grows will suddenly change quite dramatically. You are now faced with one of two options.

The first and most common option is to see this sudden change in the environment as a threat—a change that will make it harder for you to succeed. You can get out of the way of this threat by moving the garden to a different, sunnier part of the yard or a new, sunnier neighbourhood. You could also tackle the threat head-on by taking your neighbour to court if the house design doesn't meet municipal guidelines.

The other option, of course, is to see the change in environment as an opportunity. How might this change in the environment make it easier to achieve your original goal (a colourful, fragrant retreat)? Could there be a variety of shade-loving flowers that will thrive in this new environment and bring you even more colour? In other words, how can you *align* your gardening plans with the trend in the environment? How can you go in the same direction, and choose the place and time that are most conducive to success?

As this example illustrates, most trends or forces in the environment can represent both an opportunity and a threat. The difference lies in your perspective: how you see it and what you decide to do about it. In this way, opportunities and threats are fundamentally different from strengths and weaknesses. A strength is a strength; a weakness is a weakness. You measure, you assess, and you determine whether the quantity or quality of the resource is high enough. With opportunities and threats, however, your judgement and experience will influence what you find and how you choose to cope with it. If what you perceive is an opportunity, your strategic direction is clear: align yourself with the opportunity you see in the environment. If you perceive a threat, prepare to fight or take flight. Just be sure to question your first response and see if a change in perspective might not yield an even better solution.

The example of staging an event the same weekend as the opening of a new IKEA outlet mentioned earlier in the book is worth remembering here: the store opening was certain to draw attention from consumers and the media; it was a threat that would compete with our event and limit the exposure we could create for our client. We rethought our initial approach and recognized the IKEA store opening could also be an opportunity for us to draw benefit from all the attention the new store would generate. We aligned our event with the time and place of the IKEA store opening and generated strong results for our client.

KEY TERMS AND CONCEPTS

As you review this chapter for any tests or assignments, you will want to pay particular attention to the following terms and concepts introduced in the preceding pages:

- time
- place
- idea
- alignment
- distance
- challenging a competitor's story
- eroding a competitor's goodwill
- removing a competitor's voice
- changes in the environment that are at once a threat and an opportunity

QUESTIONS FOR CRITICAL REFLECTION

1. Based on your current knowledge of the political, economic, social/cultural, and technological fields in your city, what do you feel could be the most important opportunities and threats for a campaign to boost use of rapid transit in that city? What will make it easier for you to succeed? Harder for you to succeed?

2. Imagine a local business group launches a campaign to promote the establishment of medical marijuana dispensaries in your neighbourhood. You have been asked to develop a strategy to counter this campaign and keep the dispensaries out of the neighbourhood. You decide to tackle the threat of marijuana dispensaries in your neighbourhood head-on and now must prepare to compete for the public's support with the local business group. Reflect on the three strategies presented and choose between (1) challenging the opponent's story, (2) eroding the competitor's goodwill, and (3) removing the competitor's voice. Which approach or blend of approaches would you take and why?

CHAPTER EIGHT
Presenting the Strategy

The hard choices are all made. You are informed and confident you are heading in the right direction, setting a new standard for garden beauty by making the most of your resources, fixing and adding the resources you need. You've scanned the environment exhaustively and are prepared to align yourself with opportunities in the environment while mitigating the threats out there.

The challenge now is to convince the whole family your strategic gardening plan is sound. You need their support and their effort to bring it all to life. You call a family meeting and prepare for the presentation that will make or break this year's garden. You know successfully presenting the strategy is the first step in ensuring its successful implementation.

CHAPTER OVERVIEW

No matter how brilliant, creative, and well-informed your strategy is, you can never expect the document and the thinking behind it will "sell itself." Strategies need to be sold. They need to be carefully presented, and those who will decide whether or not to implement a strategy must be convinced of the soundness and the necessity of the approach you put before them.

This chapter walks you through the steps of presenting the most effective strategic communication plan possible, to make it as easy and quick as possible for you to secure approval to proceed. We begin by presenting the ideal structure for a strategic communication or public relations plan: the main ingredients and the optimal order for those ingredients. Next, we consider the role of principal messages in a plan, and we discuss ways to "find" those messages for the campaign in the research you did to identify strengths and weaknesses, opportunities and threats. Finally, we end the chapter by considering how best to present a creative strategy, which is a vital portion of your strategic communication plan. This is where the creative ideas everyone is looking for will live, so presenting them effectively is an important step in securing the approval of that plan.

LEARNING OBJECTIVES

1. Structure and write your plan in a way people will want to read and will understand.
2. Ensure all of the ingredients of a complete communication or PR strategy are included in the document or presentation you write.
3. Complement the strategy you create with a series of effective key messages. Present those messages in the most effective ways.
4. Locate the central ideas for your campaign's central messages within the research findings you gathered to identify your strengths, weaknesses, opportunities, and threats.
5. Present your creative strategy in an effective manner to ensure it is understood and valued.

WHAT DOES A STRATEGIC COMMUNICATION PLAN LOOK LIKE?

As mentioned earlier in the book, a strategic communication plan is more than a strategy. Ideally, the strategic communication plan will follow the same CARE model that has given structure to this book. Your plan should identify the specific changes in awareness, motivation, action, and relationship you hope to bring about. It should also provide a detailed list of the audiences you intend to reach and engage. You'll recall, of course, these two topics were covered in detail in the first half of the book; strategic thinking is not possible without them. Your plan should also carefully assess the resources the organization can deploy as it communicates, noting the particular strengths and weaknesses among those resources. A strategic communication plan should also carefully describe the external environment in which the plan will be implemented, noting the opportunities and threats present in that environment.

This summary of intended changes, description of principal audiences, assessment of resources, and description of the external environment are best placed early in the plan (i.e., immediately after the introduction) as the decisions that follow should all be based on what your exploration of the four elements revealed. You can combine the four subsections into a single section (i.e., situation analysis), or you can keep them as separate sections (i.e., change, audiences, resources, and environment).

The next major section of the strategic communication plan should be the strategy itself. This is where you can sum up the findings of your situation analysis and answer the pressing question: what should we do about this? Describe the strengths and propose strategic directions to leverage those resources. Describe the weaknesses and propose how you will overcome them. Describe the opportunities in the external environment and propose ways to capitalize on them. Finally, describe any threats in the external environment and propose strategic directions to mitigate those threats.

Once the strategic directions are presented, you can then move to the action plan. This is where you will present the actual communication and PR tactics you propose to undertake. As will be covered in Chapter Nine, tables are a proven way to present each tactic in detail without overwhelming the reader with page after page of text. In addition to the individual tactic tables, however, it is important to provide an overall look at the proposed budget for the campaign, as well as timelines for the implementation.

After all this, a conclusion and some appendices are usually required to close off the document.

WHAT DOES A STRATEGY LOOK LIKE?

Though the entire strategic communication plan can be quite long for larger campaigns, the specific section on strategy is often quite short and to the point. It is the distillation of a lot of work into a concise statement of strategic thinking. There is no need here to restate what's in your situation analysis. You merely need to build upon it.

An effective way to present a communication strategy to clients is in the form of a series of brief statements of: (a) the key findings from the SWOT analysis and (b) what you propose they do about those findings. Typically, these are organized into four familiar categories.

- Begin by listing the **strengths** you found and how you propose to leverage them. This is where you present the strategic directions that outline how you intend to put resources to work and build the campaign or program around your principal strengths.
- Next, present the central **weaknesses** you found and how you propose to overcome them. These strategic directions indicate how you intend to supplement or improve the quality of the resources your client needs but does not currently have at their disposal.
- Third, list the primary **opportunities** you found in your situation analysis and present strategic directions that show how you propose to

capitalize on them. State how your client can best align their campaign to the time, place, and ideas behind the opportunities.

- Finally, list the main **threats** you found and how you propose to mitigate them. These strategic directions indicate how your client can distance their organization from a threat (its time, place, or idea) or tackle the threat head-on by challenging or silencing it.

Assuming you have identified perhaps one or two principal findings under each of the four categories, you will have a list of perhaps eight to ten strategic directions to present to your client. There is no magic number to aim for here, however. Nor will there necessarily be a finding for each of the four categories. Maybe you're fortunate enough to have strong opportunities on which to capitalize and no real threats to mitigate. A client may have plenty of strengths to leverage and no real weaknesses to overcome; it happens.

If you find yourself, however, with 10 or 20 strategic directions to realize, chances are you aren't being discriminating enough in your selection of just the *key* strengths, weaknesses, opportunities, and threats. You'll want to make sure the findings you choose to build your strategic directions upon all have the following features.

Clear Direction

There should be no question that a strength is strong (in terms of quality and abundance) or a weakness is weak. Likewise, make sure the opportunities you select will really make it easier for your campaign to succeed and the threats will so impede your efforts they can't be overlooked. Avoid findings that are borderline.

Reliable Sources

Your assessment of strengths, weaknesses, opportunities, and threats must be based on recent and trusted information, not hearsay or assumption. If you're not quite certain the key audience is getting older faster than the general population, you would do well to double-check your facts or turn to more reliable findings to build your strategic directions. If you are not entirely certain there is sound and recent evidence to support your claim, it may be best to do more research before you propose a strategic direction based on that finding.

Strong Potential

The findings you choose to build your strategy around need to be resources or trends and forces in the external environment you can truly work with. Avoid, in other words, strategic directions that attempt to capitalize on opportunities or mitigate threats you really can't do anything about; they're rare but they exist. If, after reflection and some brainstorming you really can't figure out what to do with the opportunity or threat, it's perhaps best to move on. Likewise, beware strategic directions built on leveraging or overcoming resources over which you really have no control. If the strong resource is not for you to leverage or the weak resources are not something you can improve or add to, shift your focus elsewhere.

Sustainable Directions

More often than not, your strategic communication plan will be designed to achieve some long-term goals. The change you will want to bring about will be needed many months or years after the campaign has ended. That's why it's important to ensure the condition you describe and on which you want to build a strategic direction is one that will endure for some time. After all, deciding to switch your garden to growing flowers that require lots of water after a single afternoon of rain is not necessarily a wise thing to do in the desert. Focus on resources and environmental conditions you can count on for at least the duration of the campaign.

Even so, you may be left with a list of strategic directions too long to implement all at once. You'll need to use your judgement here to focus on a smaller number so as not to spread yourself too thin. As much as possible, go for the findings that give you the clearest direction, greatest reliability, most potential, and longest-lasting sustainability.

Once you have distilled your findings to a tight list of strengths, weaknesses, opportunities, and threats, consider presenting them by placing them in a table with two columns. The left-hand column lists the key findings, while the right-hand column shows what you intend to do with these. Table 8.1 shows some examples of findings and strategic directions you can use to work with.

Notice how many of these strategic directions are very close to actual tactics—specific recommendations for communications vehicles or activities. That is one of the real beauties of a strategic approach to planning—good work in one phase very much guides you to the next stage. A good situation analysis guides you to a strategic direction which, in turn, leads you to your action plan. Often, if you have difficulty with the second or third stage of your work, the answer lies in the previous stage.

TABLE 8.1: STRATEGIC DIRECTIONS TO WORK WITH KEY STRENGTHS, WEAKNESSES, OPPORTUNITIES, AND THREATS

KEY STRENGTHS	HOW TO LEVERAGE THEM
People: Skilled and trusted CEO	We will plan and implement regular meetings between the CEO and staff, select investors, and retail partners
Stories: A rags-to-riches story of a small-town farmer who invents an ecologically friendly way to protect gardens from pests	Place the founder and his story at the centre of all key messages through media relations and advertising
KEY WEAKNESSES	**HOW TO OVERCOME THEM**
Goodwill: A new organization that few potential customers have heard of	We will plan a national media tour and concurrent advertising campaign to introduce the company brand and its founder
KEY OPPORTUNITIES	**HOW TO CAPITALIZE ON THEM**
Social: Consumers are increasingly concerned about environmental sustainability and the safety of the food they eat	The single key message of this campaign will be that this is a non-toxic and biodegradable way to protect plants from pests
Competitive: Earth Day is a period of intense communications on the need to protect the environment	The launch campaign will begin with sponsorship of local Earth Day events in ten key markets and roll out in the weeks after Earth Day to capitalize on the afterglow
KEY THREATS	**HOW TO MITIGATE THEM**
Technological: Gardeners are increasingly turning to online communities to ask questions, share advice, and assess new products	Our online channels will feature advice and an opportunity for visitors to pose questions; we will also monitor other sites to challenge and correct misconceptions about the product on the web
Economic: The product is roughly twice as expensive as regular pesticides, and a projected economic downturn could shrink the segment of the market that can easily afford the incremental costs	The product will be positioned as a high-end solution and advertising messages will be targeted to homeowners with combined annual income in the top third of household incomes

CREATIVE STRATEGY: CORE MESSAGES TO COMPLEMENT THE OVERALL STRATEGY

You have reviewed your situation analysis and developed innovative ways to leverage your strengths, overcome your weaknesses, capitalize on opportunities, and mitigate any threats in the external environment. In short, you now have a tight and realistic list of strategic directions that will guide the development and execution of the communication campaign or program. Since this is a strategic communication plan, you will want to complement these broad strategic directions with a creative strategy: a list of the core messages at the heart of your campaign. The creative strategy is your chance to craft powerful messages that will bring your strategic directions to life. This is often where clients get most excited about a plan; they can begin to imagine what it will all look and sound like.

One of the best ways to present your creative strategy is to return to the stations along the continuum from awareness to habit and relationship that were discussed earlier.

Awareness → Motivation → Instruction → Action → Habit/Relationship

Basically, you can use these categories to organize and present your core messages. What will you say to create a base level of awareness? How will you motivate the audience? How will you present the steps they need to take? By going through your messages and noting the section each message is in, you will help the reader of the plan understand how one message can build on the previous and what the intended effect of a particular message is. Remember as you prepare this section of your plan the first word in "core messages" is "core." Don't try to include absolutely every point your campaign or program has to get across. Rather, focus on those messages that matter most—the messages at the very heart of the campaign. Fewer messages will help focus the reader, your communication team, and, in the end, the audience as well.

As you write the core messages for your campaign, be sure to make full use of everything you have learned from your situation analysis. The messages you choose, like the vehicles and activities you create, should be geared to leveraging strengths, overcoming weaknesses, capitalizing on opportunities, and mitigating threats. The creativity comes when you choose just the right words and images to express those very strategic messages.

Consider, for example, a legendary campaign by the Wendy's chain of fast-food restaurants to differentiate themselves from intense competition in the take-out restaurant market. The strength they decided to leverage was the story behind their burgers: the larger and fresher beef patty Wendy's used. The opportunity they identified was in the competitive environment: none of their competitors were talking much about the beef patty that is, after all, the heart of any hamburger. The creative strategy centred on leveraging that strength and capitalizing on the opportunity by focusing the public's attention on the competitive advantage of a larger, fresher beef patty. The ad agency was then charged with finding a creative and memorable way to communicate this core message, and the successful "Where's the beef?" campaign was born. A brilliant creative strategy resulted from a careful situation analysis.

The good news here is that if the strategic directions you have developed are sound and based on a quality situation analysis, they contain the seeds of the optimal creative strategy. Go back over your situation analysis and strategic directions, and you should find hints for all the messages you need to succeed. Here are some tips on how to approach this.

Finding Core Messages in Strengths and Weaknesses

To start with, review the strengths you have identified and the ways you intend to leverage them. As was suggested earlier, the most successful campaigns are usually built on these strengths.

- If you have, for example, strong communications vehicles you intend to leverage, be sure to tell people these trusted and familiar vehicles will be home to a new campaign.
- If you have great people on your team, remind your audiences these people are well known, trusted, and worth paying attention to.
- If goodwill is the strength you intend to leverage, remind your audiences of how it is your organization earned that goodwill in the first place. Tell them of the products they love, the service they value, and the contributions you make to the community. Use testimonials from members of the community to drive home the goodwill you have earned.
- If internal cohesion is the strength, show it off. Tell all your audiences the organization is solidly behind this. Let your employees and volunteers tell the outside world why they are so proud to be a part of the organization and the campaign.
- If you are blessed with ample and high-quality strategic intelligence, use it to accurately reflect the audience and their priorities in your messages. Hold a mirror up to the audience and watch how they are drawn to it.

Demonstrate to the audience you understand what they are thinking, what they value, and what keeps them up at night. These kinds of messages resonate with an audience; they attract and hold attention.

- Finally, and most evidently, if you have a great story, tell it. Make the heroic, comic, romantic, and dramatic aspects of your organization the very core of the campaign.

As compared to strengths, weaknesses may not appear to be a particularly good place to look for key messages. After all, telling your audiences your vehicles are not particularly good or your goodwill in the community is lacking is not likely to endear them to you. Consider that many of these weaknesses may be the result of ineffective communications in the past. The community may not know or like the organization because you *haven't* effectively told them about the good things you do. Make sure your core messages overcome this past omission. Help the audience see what they've been missing.

The other way weaknesses can yield messages is by focusing your messages not on the weakness but on how you plan to overcome it. Your audiences will likely be happy to hear you acknowledge your weaknesses and then learn about the new and improved website coming this spring, the new fundraising program you have started to benefit the local veteran's hospital, or the new measures you are taking to listen more carefully to customers and get a better sense of what they want to see in future products and services. Look through your list of strategic directions designed to overcome weaknesses and you are likely to find several positive messages to include.

Strengths and weaknesses, then, can be the source of important messages. Telling audiences about the resources you have and about your efforts to improve and augment the resources you lack is a sound way to engage them and to advance your efforts to leverage strengths and overcome weaknesses.

Finding Core Messages in Opportunities and Threats

You may also find that the most important messages to communicate are those that emerge from the strategic directions designed to capitalize on opportunities and mitigate threats. Your efforts to align your organization with the *idea* behind an opportunity you have identified will likely be the most effective way to position the organization and motivate the audience. Likewise, your efforts to distance your organization from a threat or to challenge that threat head-on will also be the raw materials of many core messages.

Consider how oil companies have responded to growing consumer concern over greenhouse gas emissions and their impact on climate change. The trend is a significant threat to companies that drill for and distribute fuels that emit tons of carbon and greenhouse gases each day. It's a trend that could fundamentally change North Americans' relationship with oil and gas, and companies can't afford to stand still. And they haven't. For a few decades, they challenged the threat head-on and called into question the link between greenhouse gas emissions and climate change. They challenged the other side's story and called into question the competition's credibility. They have largely lost that battle and suffered some loss of goodwill in the process. More recently, they've been crafting messages designed to get out of the way of the threat, promoting "cleaner burning" gasoline, for example, to distance themselves. Oil companies also participate in a variety of programs to protect the environment, trying to put some much-needed distance between themselves and the threat of public concern over climate change. Shell tells us about its efforts to drill wells with less impact on the environment. British Petroleum (BP) tells us its famous brand now stands for "Beyond Petroleum" and uses a flower as its logo. As was cautioned earlier in the book, there is a risk in going too far with efforts to align with an opportunity and distance an organization from a threat. In the wake of the oil spill in the Gulf of Mexico, BP's efforts to distance itself from the threat posed by growing concern for the environment could have been interpreted as insincere.

One of the secrets to successfully communicating messages that align your organization with some ideas and distance the organization from others is credibility. Organizations that have secured credibility can do great things through communication. Those that lack credibility will have a major barrier to overcome. To secure credibility, you must first convince the audience the organization is knowledgeable and shares their values. If the organization indeed satisfies both criteria, you have a strength to leverage, so tell the world about it. If, however, the organization isn't yet perceived as credible and sharing in the audience's values, you have a weakness to overcome. In this case, be sure to tell the audience how you intend to overcome that weakness. Ensure you do this by presenting the audience with credible and appropriate messages. It's not enough to *claim* your organization cares about the environment or is dramatically different from the competition. You must *prove* it. And you must do so in a credible way. The take-away here is to include evidence in your core messages. The actions of your organization, the raw statistics you can gather, the decisions made by organizations—all speak volumes about the organization whether you like it or not. In aligning with opportunities or distancing from threats, be sure to turn to this evidence to construct a compelling and credible argument.

For the most part, then, the core messages that emerge from your strategic directions geared to capitalizing on opportunities and mitigating threats will be messages that motivate the audience. These are the messages that will prove to the audience they can benefit from doing business with your organization—they can get more of what they want and less of what they fear. These motivational messages are, of course, the crux of any creative strategy. Remember as you write them that they must be focused on how the audience benefits, not how your organization or your client will benefit.

The final component of a creative strategy is the call to action. More good news—the raw materials you will need to craft your call to action are also contained in your situation analysis. You'll find it under the section titled "Outcomes." To the extent your outcomes are expressed as audiences changing their behaviour in some way (e.g., getting airline passengers to stop bringing liquids in their carry-on luggage), you now have a precise call to action to communicate. When crafting your call to action, be sure you are clear as to when, how often, and for how long you need the audience to adopt the desired behaviour. After all, getting airline passengers to not bring liquids on board only once is hardly an accomplishment. The next time they fly, you're back at square one.

As you prepare a list of your core messages, remember to organize your thinking and your messages along the action continuum: (1) awareness, (2) motivation, (3) instruction, (4) call to action, and (5) habit and relationship. Most campaigns will include some messages in all five groups, but chances are many of your messages will be focused on getting the audience over one particular hurdle—the hurdle that confronts them most at this time. If the audience is aware but not yet motivated, motivational messages should command most of your resources. If members of your audience have taken action once but haven't yet formed a strong habit or relationship, you'll want to focus on messages that thank them, offer incentives, and foster dialogue. Remember also that if your organization has time as a strength, you may choose to move the audience across the continuum slowly, in distinct phases. Be sure to reflect which messages will be communicated in which phase of the campaign if this will be your approach.

A Theme to Unify and Summarize the Campaign

The final stage of developing a creative strategy is to find a theme for the campaign. Much like in music, literature, or theatre, a theme is a unifying factor woven into every stage of the work. A theme makes the work of art unified and more powerful. A theme is repeated and becomes one of the most memorable parts of the audience's experience.

In much the same way, a theme in a communication campaign ties the various messages and vehicles of the campaign together. It is woven into every vehicle and repeated often enough that it becomes one of the most memorable parts of the campaign. When advertisers develop a theme for an ad campaign, they often use that theme as the slogan or tagline at the end of each ad. The famous M&M slogan, "Melts in your mouth, not in your hands," comes to mind.

In PR and strategic communication, our communication vehicles are often quite different from advertisements, so catchy slogans are not always called for. That's why you may prefer to subtly weave the theme of the campaign into each vehicle you create. The closing lines of the president's speech will echo the theme, so will the opening paragraph in the media release, the home page of the website, and a whole series of tweets you have planned.

The theme is an idea, in many ways, the "big idea" at the heart of the entire campaign or program. It is not a specific group of words like a slogan is, however. That being said, you may find yourself repeating certain words from the theme over and over. In the hospital example mentioned earlier in the book, the campaign theme was all about caring. That word and derivatives of it (notably "care," "delivering care," and "healthcare") were featured prominently in every vehicle we developed for that client. We chose the theme because it was a powerful idea and one that fit perfectly with the internal cohesion of the organization. Every ad, every speech, every media document, and every brochure became unified by constantly iterating the campaign's theme. And, yes, when the campaign called for advertisements, we included a tagline ("the future of caring") with the idea.

Final Thoughts on Presenting a Creative Strategy

There is a tendency when developing creative strategy to spend more time looking for just the right pun, the niftiest alliteration, or the catchiest rhyme and rhythm, rather than building the most strategic key messages. Remember powerful creative writing is essential to getting and holding attention but, in the end, moving your audiences across the action continuum requires *both* style and strategy. Audiences pay attention because your messages are clever, funny, sad, interesting, or surprising. Audiences change their behaviour, however, because your messages convince them your organization is credible and aligned with their values. They change because your messages demonstrate, in a logical and compelling way, the change in behaviour you are suggesting will bring them more of what they want in life and less of what they don't want. And, in the end, audiences will keep behaving in a way that allows your organization to be successful because they are certain your organization values them and listens to what they have to say.

So start by making sure the core messages you develop in your creative strategy are truly the ones that will make the most of the resources you have, help you overcome weaknesses, and align your organization with opportunities, while distancing it from the threats out there. Later, when it comes time to implement the campaign, turn to the most talented and creative writers and designers to make sure those strategic messages truly dazzle the audience and earn their valuable attention.

KEY TERMS AND CONCEPTS

As you review this chapter for any tests or assignments, you will want to pay particular attention to the following terms and concepts introduced in the preceding pages:

- direction
- reliability
- potential
- sustainability
- key messages
- theme

QUESTIONS FOR CRITICAL REFLECTION

1. In this chapter, we discussed the importance of narrowing the list of strategic directions in a strategy by considering the direction, reliability, potential, and sustainability of the trend or force at the heart of a strategic direction. Of the four factors listed, which do you feel is the most important to consider and why? Which quality do you feel is most essential when determining if a trend or force is appropriate to link to a strategic direction?

2. Imagine your client is a new, technology-based company designing small, electric cars that are remarkably affordable and that perform in ways that meet or exceed consumer expectations. Think of the strengths, weaknesses, opportunities, and threats confronting such a company. Now, find the key messages within those four categories of information. What must this new company communicate in order to succeed?

3. Given what you know about the current external environment into which small, electric cars would be marketed, what might be an effective theme for a strategic communication campaign to promote these cars? What might be a clever way to express this theme in an advertising slogan?

CHAPTER NINE
From Strategy to Action Plan

The sketch of the new garden is done. You have a clear picture in your mind of the kinds of plants and animals you want to have as your companions this summer. You can almost taste the cucumber and dill salad that will emerge from the ground at the back of the house. You've even figured an automatic sprinkler system will help you overcome the lack of time and mitigate the effects of the harsh sun. How strategic. Of course, the sketch and your imagination are just the beginning. Now comes the detail that will ensure this strategic plan comes to life. How much will the sprinkler system cost? Who will install it? When will you start the cucumber seeds? When will you bring them outside? Will you buy a small dill plant or grow it from seed too? And when will be the best weekend to plant each? As a seasoned gardener, you know full well detailed and optimal answers to these questions are absolutely essential. You get out your almanac, seed catalogue, and calculator and get busy developing your gardening action plan.

CHAPTER OVERVIEW

We now arrive at the stage in the strategic communication planning process where many people want to start: listing the communication tactics that will bring the campaign to life. Rather than providing a list of the very best tactics, however, this chapter will guide you in the process of *selecting* the very best tactics for the campaign you are planning, for the audiences you need to engage, and for the environment in which your campaign will run. You will also learn a three-stage approach to action planning to ensure you and your colleagues make optimal choices that build off of all the planning work you have done up to this point. Finally, you will be introduced to a simple way to format action plans that has served my colleagues and me very well as we developed complex strategic campaigns for a wide range of clients. It's a proven template, and one flexible enough to fit any PR tactic you can imagine.

LEARNING OBJECTIVES

1. Thoroughly review the situation analysis you have conducted and the strategy you have developed to set the stage for developing a strategic communication action plan.

2. Apply strategic principles as you work to select the optimal tactics to bring your strategy to life.
3. Organize and run an effective brainstorming session to generate possible communication tactics for your strategic communication plan.
4. Carefully review your list of possible tactics and distill it to the most optimal ones given the resources you can deploy, the audiences you seek to engage, and the environment in which the campaign will run.
5. Present your strategic communication action plan in a manner that is clear, concise, and persuasive to managers and clients.

THE END OF THE STRATEGY DEVELOPMENT PROCESS

And so we come to the end of the strategy development process—the process on which this book is focused. The information has been gathered. The findings have been analyzed. The thinking is complete. Your strategic directions are down on paper and ready to share. You're confident the recommendations rest on a sound analysis of the organization's resources and a thorough scan of the external environment. You are also confident the intended changes and the audiences driving all of this are anchored in the mission and vision of the organization. All that remains is to build upon this solid and strategic foundation with an action plan of optimal tactics.

If you've followed the steps proposed in this little book, you should now know the following about your strategic communication plan:

- the reasons you're communicating;
- the audiences you need to reach and why;
- the very strongest resources you have to deploy and how you can best do that;
- the gaps in your resources and what you will do to overcome those;
- the opportunities in the external environment on which you want to capitalize and how you can do that;
- the threats in the environment you need to pay attention to and what you will do to mitigate them; and
- the key messages you need to deliver in order to bring your strategy to life.

What a powerful place from which to start your action planning! All that gathering of information and thinking has made it relatively easy for you to now propose the actual tactics around which to build your campaign or program.

THINKING ABOUT THE ACTION PLAN

As mentioned at the very start of this book, the purpose here is not to tell you how to run PR campaigns; there are many books that discuss the merits of different tactics available to you and many others that walk you through the steps of how best to get the work done. This chapter will share with you, however, some overarching strategic principles that are the mark of the best and most effective strategic communication campaigns. Consider these as a starting point as you move from solid strategic directions to your selection of optimal tactics to bring your communications strategy to life.

1. Direct Your Messages Strategically

You put a great deal of thought into each audience you would include in your campaign. Make the most of that effort by carefully directing your messages to just the right audience. Never, in other words, have an audience wondering, "Why did they send this to me?" Find the most reliable, cost-effective, and potent vehicles to reach each audience specifically, rather than relying on a shotgun approach that throws every message at every audience.

2. Diversify Your Vehicles

Never assume the members of a particular audience will all turn to a single medium in the same way. Rather than a single superhighway, build a network of small roads that reach out to individual homes and business, making it easy for people to access your messages at the time and place that suits them best. Look for the two or three ways to reach a particular audience and, if you can afford it, use them all. An old saying sums it up neatly: "Don't place all your eggs in one basket."

3. Run Programs, Not Campaigns

Moving an audience from awareness to habit or relationship takes time. Think of your strategic communication plan as a long-term effort to communicate and build relationships, rather than short-term campaigns to yield one-time successes. The most profitable relationships are those that last for years, not weeks. The most successful "campaigns" are those with time to make an impact and that can be evaluated and adjusted on an ongoing basis. By thinking in terms of sustained programs instead of monthly or quarterly campaigns, you give yourself the best chances of success.

As you continue your efforts over months or even years, never assume the audience is as sick of your messages as you are. Stay on track and give those messages time to get out, sink in, and have their effect. Ideally, try to plan around three-year cycles: time to launch a campaign, monitor its performance over the first year, adjust, and carry on for another 18 months. Messages that change too frequently are often more expensive and confusing to a busy audience; they can add to the sense of being overwhelmed and surrounded by clutter. The A&W chain of restaurants, for example, ran a very consistent series of ads and special events featuring their friendly "root bear" character for more than 40 years.[1] Each ad was distinctive, but the themes and the personality established for the brand were consistent throughout. That consistency in messaging over many years is a hallmark of a strategic communication program.

4. Listen in Order to Understand Deeply

In formal and informal ways, be sure to listen deeply to your audiences. Give your audiences easy ways to talk back to you and feed into your communication planning process. Make listening an ongoing process rather than a once-each-year process. With so many organizations now communicating daily on social media, the bar is set high and audiences that feel their voice doesn't matter to you will simply tune out and turn elsewhere. What's more, by listening closely, you can understand your audiences more deeply and fine tune your messages and action plan, generating more action and less frustration on both ends.

Listening deeply takes time and money but it is an important way to build valuable resources you can use. It's how genuine strategic intelligence is gathered. It's how goodwill is nurtured. Listening deeply to employees and volunteers is how internal cohesion grows. What's more, listening deeply often allows organizations to discover the very best stories they have to tell. Any activity that can grow your stores of strategic intelligence, goodwill, internal cohesion, and stories to tell is an activity worth doing and worth doing well. Make sure you create opportunities and channels to allow your audience to reach in at least as often as you reach out to them.

5. Build Quality into Every Vehicle

All communicators must take the time to build genuine quality into everything they do. Our world is increasingly cluttered with ineffective messages: messages that aren't original or attractive, messages that aren't effectively directed to the right audiences, messages riddled with errors, omissions, and evasions. This sense of clutter is driving many of your audiences to tune out completely—a lose-lose proposition. Make sure you take the time and invest the resources to make the words and images attractive, delightful, dramatic, and memorable. Be inspired by the early advertising pioneers who quickly learned the power of dramatic messages that crisply and memorably communicate a powerful and resonant message. Insist on quality vehicles that can attract audiences (not repel them), encourage people to talk about the vehicles, and continue to work long after they've been heard or seen. Simply put, after all the time and energy you spend analyzing the situation and building a powerful creative strategy, do justice to that strategy by making sure it is brought to life using the best possible words, images, sounds, and experiences you can afford. The best way to attract and keep butterflies in your garden is to build a beautiful, welcoming butterfly garden, filled with food and shelter.

6. Time Your Campaign Strategically

Notwithstanding the earlier advice to plan programs rather than campaigns, the reality of budgets and business cycles is such that most programs include cycles of high activity followed by more quiet periods—campaigns within a program. Given this reality, be sure to go back to your assessment of the environment and remember strategic timing will allow you to move closer to the time of your opportunities and further away from the time of your threats. Be mindful also of when your audience will be most predisposed to pay attention and to act. In such a cluttered and fast-paced environment, sensitivity to the audience's rhythm and the activities of those competing for attention can make all the difference. If you don't know your audience's rhythms—those moments when they are most likely to pay attention—you have a weakness that requires research to overcome.

ACTION PLANNING IN THREE EASY STEPS

As you prepare to move from your strategy to a detailed action plan, consider the following stages for your work.

Stage 1: Brainstorming Potential Tactics

To begin the action planning process, organize a brainstorming[2] session. Bring together the principal members of your team and review all the strategic directions and any strategic intelligence related to your audiences. Use the brainstorming session to arrive at a preliminary list of tactics, ensuring these have the potential to bring to life the strategic directions you developed and, of course, also have the potential to reach your key audiences (that's what the strategic intelligence will tell you). Remember tactics are more specific than strategic directions. A tactic is a communication vehicle or activity you will deploy to get core messages out to the audiences that matter.

Remember also to have fun with the brainstorming process. Do it as a group, keep the atmosphere lively, and ensure everyone has plenty of snacks to fuel their brainstorming. Keep an open mind and don't shy away from jokes and silly comments—they often have a kernel of wisdom that you can mine. Don't criticize your own ideas before you share them, and don't criticize the ideas of others after they put them on the table. What you want at this first stage is a long, creative, and surprising list.

THE JOKE THAT SET THE STAGE FOR A GREAT CAMPAIGN ...

I once led a brainstorming session to develop a strategic communication plan for the Canadian Veterinary Medical Association (CVMA). We gathered a group of creative people, ate plenty of snacks, and answered a series of provocative questions designed to generate ideas. One of those questions was simply this: "If the CVMA were to develop a television series, what would it be?" This was when one of the leading series on television was *ER*, which featured a cast of characters who worked in a Chicago hospital's emergency room. One of the first answers to the question I asked was "*ER* for vets!" We all had a good chuckle and began describing some of the scenes that might appear in the series. Later, as I reviewed the detailed notes from the brainstorming session, I was struck by the idea of a series like *ER* featuring veterinarians. I loved the way the show portrayed physicians and nurses. It was gritty, realistic, and noble. These were real people doing demanding and important work. That idea—portraying veterinarians as gritty, realistic, and noble, as real people doing demanding and important work—became the foundation of our creative strategy. We later hired one of Canada's leading photographers, Ted Grant, whose work had included incredible books of photographs of doctors working in Canada and around the world.[3] Because I had worked with Ted's daughter in an earlier job (and met him at the time) and because he had a pet that was cared for by a veterinarian whose work he appreciated and valued, Ted agreed to do the photoshoots for us. It was a real privilege as this would be the only time in his career Ted did any commercial photography. The resulting ads were remarkable. We eventually chose three outstanding black and white photographs of actual veterinarians with their patients and their patients' owners. All three perfectly captured the mood and the essence of the campaign.

Stage 2: Distilling the Preliminary Lists

The second stage of the action planning process is to carefully review your possible tactics and distill the preliminary list to those that are reasonable given the resources you have and those you lack. There's no sense planning a massive event that would take a staff of 50 to carry out when the communication team consists of you and 2 volunteers. This distillation can be done by the same team of people you gathered for brainstorming or by a smaller team of more senior people. If you opt for gathering the same group of people who brainstormed the list, be sure to give them some time to take a break and reflect; at least a few days should be inserted between Stage One and Stage Two.

When you do gather to distill your preliminary lists of possible tactics, be sure to look carefully at each possible tactic and ask yourself if you have the resources (e.g., time, people, money, vehicles, strategic intelligence, goodwill, internal cohesion, and stories) to implement the tactic well. Be sure to have budgets, calendars, organizational charts, and research reports on hand to help with this assessment. Needless to say, this second step is not quite as much fun as the first, but it can help you avoid great pain later on.

Stage 3: Refine the Short List

The third stage of the action planning process involves going through your shortened list of tactics and refining it to ensure the tactics within meet the criteria mentioned above. As you decide whether or not to include a tactic in your action plan, ensure that tactic meets the following criteria:

1. The tactic is truly directed to specific and appropriate audiences.
2. The list of tactics includes a diversity of ways to reach each audience.
3. The blend of tactics will ensure an effort to communicate that will continue for an appropriate length of time—a sustained program rather than a short-term campaign.
4. The action plan will include sufficient interactive tactics to allow you to listen deeply to the audiences, learn from them, and deepen your relationship.
5. The final list of tactics in your action plan will be short enough to allow you to invest the time and money to ensure quality messages and quality vehicles.
6. The timing of each tactic is built strategically around the timing of your competitors' efforts and the rhythms of your audiences.

It seems like a tall order, and it is. Strategy demands you be selective. Your resources are limited, so you need to ensure you invest those resources in the optimal way. The good news is the process you have undertaken to develop your strategic communication plan is designed to lead you to this short list of optimal tactics. You have a solid situation analysis as the foundation, a smart strategy, and a detailed action plan with the very best tactics on it.

WHAT DOES AN ACTION PLAN LOOK LIKE?

Tactics are the stuff of action plans. They are specific communication vehicles and activities distributed or presented to specific audiences in an effort to leverage strengths, overcome weaknesses, capitalize on opportunities, and mitigate threats. So, to return to an earlier example, the regular meetings between our dynamic and trusted CEO and employees represent an important and very strategic tactic. That much we know. What we don't yet know is how many meetings will we schedule? When? Where? Lasting how long? Requiring how much budget to implement? The answers to these questions are to be found in your action plan. This part of your document is where the details live.

Similarly, planning a website that includes a forum for visitors to pose questions is a strategic idea. Now you need to map out exactly how much money such a site will require, who will develop it, and when the work needs to be done. Details, details, details.

This book is not intended to guide you on deciding how much money you should spend on a website or how often meetings between employees and CEOs should be scheduled. Frankly, each case is unique, and many other books have much to say on these precise tactical topics. Nonetheless, an action plan must include enough detailed information to win the support of decision-makers in the organizations (i.e., the enablers who approve budgets, staffing requests, and high-profile campaigns). The action plan must also have enough detail to truly guide the work of your communication team in the weeks and months ahead. At a minimum, your action plan should include the following information for each tactic you recommend:

- Start by simply **listing** the tactic you recommend, and identifying the **audience** the tactic will reach (e.g., quarterly CEO presentations designed to reach employees).
- Include a brief summary of the **strategic rationale** for the tactic. Explain to the reader why the tactic is strategic at all (e.g., a way to build more internal cohesion, boost employee retention in a competitive

labour market, and leverage the speaking skills and trustworthiness of the CEO).

- Add in a more **detailed description** of the tactic in terms of **who, what, where, and when** (e.g., meetings to be held in the movie theatre in the building adjacent to ours; meetings will be held on the last Friday of each quarter from 9:30 until 10:30 a.m., to be followed by an informal coffee break; CEO to lead the meeting though other senior managers will be invited to present, as required; two-way webcasting to be provided for employees in our field offices across Canada; assistance with the agenda, speaking notes, and presentations to be developed by communication services staff).

- And, of course, the description of the tactic must include a **proposed budget** for the tactic (usually for a one-year period, since budgeting is most often done on an annual basis). The budget section should include a basic breakdown of costs to help readers understand and, hopefully, approve the budget. For example, explain the theatre rental will cost $4,000; A/V equipment rental $8,000; refreshments $2,000; and webcasting will cost $4,000. The total budget for the year will be $18,000.

In short, your strategy tells you and your readers where you need to go for the organization to succeed. The action plan tells them precisely how and when you intend to get there.

Formatting the Action Plan

No matter how much time and effort you put into developing your action plan, you will find this amount of information written out in complete sentences and paragraphs makes for a very long and not very readable document. In fact, plans written out this way will likely be so long clients won't read them thoroughly or carefully.

The solution is to condense and compress this information. Bulleted lists replace full sentences and paragraphs. Compact tactic tables summarize all of the information in a concise, readable format. A sample tactic table is presented in Table 9.1, and a blank version is included in Appendix C. It's simple to create in a word processor, makes your action plans look much cleaner and more organized, and saves considerable time for both the writer and the reader.

TABLE 9.1: SAMPLE TACTIC TABLE

TACTIC: MEDIA CONFERENCE	AUDIENCE: REPORTERS, READERS, LISTENERS, AND VIEWERS

Details:
- We will gather key reporters who have interest in this topic and ensure they are aware of the new developments and motivated to report on it. This will help us leverage the reach and influence of these reporters.
- The event will be held at the National Press Theatre, from 9:30 to 11:00 a.m. on Friday, November 4.
- The Minister and Deputy Minister will both be speaking, as will the CEO of the Consumer Association.
- We will prepare a list of anticipated questions from reporters and provide key points for effective answers to those questions. We will also brief all speakers on these questions and proposed answers.
- The speeches will focus on the positive impact of the new investment regulations for both consumers and financial institutions.
- The backdrop will feature the cover of the final report and name/logo of each participating organization.

Budget:	Timing:
Venue Rental, Food, and AV: $1,500	Book Facility and AV: October 7
Writing and Translating Media Documents: $5,000	First Draft of Media Documents: October 14
Pitching the Media: $3,500	First Draft Media List: October 21
Managing On-site: $2,000	Briefing All Speakers: October 28
Media Monitoring and Reporting: $4,500	Final Media Documents: October 30
TOTAL: $16,500	Distribute Advisory and Pitch: October 30

CONCLUSION

Communicators often spend much of their planning time on action planning. Much of that action planning is not nearly as strategic as it could be. Indeed, the emphasis on action planning and the lack of emphasis on strategic thinking is precisely why this book was written. Action planning without a strategy is essentially drawing up a list of tactics you feel you can do. As was explained at the very start of this book, the tactics you include in your plan will often be the same tactics you have used in the past. Sometimes, they will be the tactics you have seen another organization use with good results. And, yes, at other times you will need to implement a tactic that was little more than an idea someone in the organization had on their way to work. What they are far less likely to be, however, are the optimal tactics the organization should be implementing.

The approach presented in this book sees action planning as a final stage in a comprehensive and strategic planning process. When action planning is built on a thorough situation analysis and a series of powerful strategic directions, the lure of relying on habit, emulation, or luck is greatly reduced. Starting with a situation analysis and building off an effective strategy make action planning much simpler and quicker to complete. You know what you want to do and you know precisely why. The optimal tactics seem to flow out of your strategy, which flows out of your situation analysis.

There is no question, though, that detailed, thoughtful action planning is a key step in the process. Details matter. Knowing exactly who will do what, where, when, and at what cost is essential to running PR campaigns that deliver. The more questions you can answer with precision during the planning stage, the smoother implementation will be.

KEY TERMS AND CONCEPTS

As you review this chapter for any tests or assignments, you will want to pay particular attention to the following terms and concepts introduced in the preceding pages:

- **strategic communication program**
- **strategic communication campaign**
- **listening deeply**
- **strategic timing**
- **brainstorming**
- **distilling long lists**
- **refining short lists**
- **tactic table**

QUESTIONS FOR CRITICAL REFLECTION

1. The start of this chapter listed all of the information gathered by a strategic communication planner: the reasons you're communicating at all; the audiences you need to reach and why; the very strongest resources you have to deploy and how you can best do that; the gaps in your resources and what you will do to overcome those; the opportunities in the external environment on which you

want to capitalize and how you can do that; the threats in the environment you need to pay attention to and what you will do to mitigate them; as well as the key messages you need to deliver in order to bring your strategy to life. Choose what you feel are the three most valuable or important of these assets and describe how they can be put to work in the development of a detailed action plan.

2. Do you agree diversifying the vehicles you use to reach a particular audience is a worthy strategic approach? If you can use a single vehicle to reach an audience, why also use different vehicles to reach the same group? Discuss the advantages or disadvantages of diversifying communication vehicles and point to a recent and successful strategic communication campaign to support your argument.

3. List what you feel are the three or four most effective ways an organization can listen deeply to its audience to better understand that audience. Which vehicles and activities would you recommend and why?

4. Your preliminary list of potential tactics to reach an audience of senior citizens across the country includes (a) social media posts, (b) a website, (c) direct mail cards mailed to their households, (d) media relations, (e) a speech by your CEO at a local seniors' residence, (f) a hot air balloon that will visit local hot air ballooning festivals with the name and logo of your program on the side, (g) a series of posters to be installed in local shopping malls across the country, and (h) a newspaper advertising campaign that will include daily and weekly papers across the country.

   Use the evaluation framework presented in this chapter to rank order these tactics from the least strategic to the most strategic. Be sure to consider all of the criteria in the evaluation framework.

   - Is the tactic truly directed to specific and appropriate audiences?
   - Does the tactic offer diversity in the ways you will reach the audience?
   - Will the tactic contribute to a blend that can ensure an effort to communicate will continue for an appropriate length of time?
   - Is the tactic interactive enough to allow you to listen deeply to the audiences, learn from them, and deepen your relationship?
   - Is the tactic simple enough to implement to allow you to invest the time and money to ensure quality messages and quality vehicles?
   - Is there a way to ensure the timing of the tactic so you can work around the timing of your competitors' efforts and the rhythms of your audiences?

NOTES

1.   Retrieved July 30, 2017, from http://www.awrootbeer.com/aw_history.php.

2.   Lehrer, J. (2012, January 30). Groupthink: The brainstorming myth. *The New Yorker*. Retrieved July 30, 2017, from http://www.newyorker.com/magazine/2012/01/30/groupthink.

3.   Retrieved July 30, 2017, from http://tedgrantphoto.com/books%20and%20DVD.htm.

CHAPTER TEN
Evaluating Strategic Communication Campaigns

It's late fall. The garden is now empty of plants. You walk around your garden slowly, reflecting on the busy spring and summer you had. You're eager to start planning next year's garden but know evaluating this year's effort is the first step to an effective plan for next year.

You start by reflecting on the goals you set out with and the extent to which you brought about the changes you hoped to bring.

- *If you set out to create fresh food, how much fresh food did you create? How delicious was that food? How special were the meals built on produce from the garden?*
- *If you set out to create medicinal plants, how much medicine did you create? How effective was the medicine? How did your family members' health fare as a result?*
- *Maybe you set out to grow colourful flowers for hats and home decorating. In that case, you think back on just how many flowers you were able to cultivate and how colourful they were. How did the hats look this year? How did the house look and smell? Did friends and family notice them, appreciate them, and comment on them?*

As you continue to evaluate the year's gardening effort, you reflect on the many species of plants and animals you hoped to bring to your garden this year, as well as on those you were determined to keep out. What plants and animals did you see? Were they the right ones? What strategies for attracting some plants and animals worked? What strategies for deterring others also worked? And, of course, what strategies did not work?

You think back on the resources you deployed to prepare, plant, tend to, and cultivate your garden this year. How well were you able to use your time, your friends and family members, the tools you gathered, and the land you set aside? What got in the way of effective use of these resources? What resources disappointed you and should be replaced or refurbished next year?

Finally, you think about the environment in which you gardened this past year. You think about the weather, the sun, the rain, and the wind. How did these conditions compare to what you expected? How well did your efforts to capitalize on the opportunities and mitigate the threats really work?

It's late in the day, and it's getting a little darker and a lot cooler outside. You leave the garden and step inside. You grab your workbook and pen and get to work evaluating the gardening season that has just ended. You realize this is not only the end of one gardening season; it is the start of the new gardening season.

CHAPTER OVERVIEW

This chapter focuses on the critical process of evaluating a strategic communication campaign and the important links between evaluating a past campaign and program and planning for the future. The chapter uses the same framework for evaluation as the earlier chapters used for strategic planning. The questions you must answer as you evaluate are all focused on the intended changes, the key audiences, the resources, and the external environment. In this way, the work you put into your evaluation becomes the foundation for the strategic plan of the next wave of your communication campaign or program.

This is not, however, intended to be a chapter about research methodology. Many fine books have been written on how best to plan, implement, and analyze the findings from quantitative methods like surveys and qualitative methods like in-depth interviews and focus groups. Be sure to also make full use of these more focused resources as you plan to evaluate your strategic communication campaign.

LEARNING OBJECTIVES

1. Determine effective ways to assess the extent to which the intended changes identified for a strategic communication campaign have been realized.
2. Explore ways to conduct research with the key audiences of a strategic communication program or campaign as a means to assess the initial plan and prepare for the evolution of the campaign or program.
3. Evaluate the extent to which the original assessment of resources was correct and the strategic efforts to leverage strengths and overcome weaknesses were effective.
4. Evaluate the extent to which the original scan of the external environment was correct and the strategic efforts to capitalize on opportunities and mitigate threats were effective.

5. Identify effective ways to evaluate the extent to which strategic directions were implemented and the effectiveness of each strategic direction in terms of reaching the key audiences and bringing about the intended changes.

THE CARE MODEL AS A FRAMEWORK FOR EVALUATION

The CARE model used as the foundation for this book was originally developed as a way to structure strategic communication planning efforts. By focusing attention on the changes a campaign is intended to bring about, on the audiences that need to be reached and engaged, on the resources the communicators can deploy, and on the external environment in which the campaign will unfold, the model helps communicators gather the information they need most and use it to craft effective strategic directions.

Those same four categories—the elements of strategic communication—also serve as a very effective structure for efforts to evaluate those same communication and PR campaigns. In essence, the model proposes four sets of essential questions for any evaluation of a PR or strategic communication campaign:

- Did the campaign bring about the **changes** you intended it to bring about?
- Did the campaign actually reach and engage the **audiences** identified in the plan and were those, in fact, the most important audiences to reach with this campaign? Was the information you gathered on each audience correct? Was the role you accorded to each audience the correct role (i.e., actor, influencer, or enabler)?
- Were the **resources** deployed for this campaign as strong or as weak as you anticipated? Were there other strengths you could have leveraged or weaknesses you should have overcome? Were your efforts to leverage the strengths and overcome weaknesses effective?
- Did the fields in the external **environment** serve as opportunities and as threats in the manner you anticipated? Were there other opportunities out there you could have capitalized on or threats you should have mitigated? Were your efforts to capitalize on opportunities and mitigate threats effective?

There are two significant advantages to using the CARE model to frame both your strategic planning and your evaluation. First, the evaluation uses concepts and categories you are already familiar with, and second, the evaluation yields a report of findings that will serve as the foundation for the next strategic communication plan you develop for this program.

A FIVE-STAGE FRAMEWORK FOR EVALUATION

Stage 1: Evaluating the Intended Changes

As suggested above, the first stage in evaluating a strategic communication campaign developed using the CARE model is to review the extent to which the intended changes you set out to bring about with the campaign were, in fact, brought about. Each intended change is an objective you can now measure against. Has the change happened? Has it happened completely or partially? Has it happened once or does a new pattern appear to have been established? If a numerical target was set, has that target been achieved? This is one of the most significant advantages of using the CARE model as the framework for strategic communication planning: You already know what to measure and why. You began planning by determining if a particular change in awareness, motivation, action, or relationship was needed for the organization to succeed. Now you can evaluate the extent to which that change was brought about.

For example, if the intended change of your campaign was to increase the number of young engineers who join their provincial professional association, then the first step in evaluating the campaign is clear: Count the number of young engineers who joined and compare it to the numbers from previous years. The behaviour either changed or it didn't. The relationship between the provincial association and the engineer either exists or it doesn't. The thinking you did as you set out to develop your strategic plan now serves you as you evaluate the campaign.

The beauty of behaviour is it usually leaves a trace. It is often fairly straightforward and objective to evaluate the extent to which a particular behaviour occurred or didn't. When members join, they leave a trace (e.g., an account is set up with their name, money changes hands, a membership card is issued). When young people pick a college or university for their studies, they leave a trace (e.g., an application and cheque are received, a file is opened with that student's name, a letter of acceptance is sent). When voters choose to support a particular candidate for mayor, they leave a trace (e.g., a completed ballot placed in a ballot box). When the ultimate measure of a strategic communication campaign is a particular behaviour or a particular relationship, there is very often a simple yet precise way to measure the success of that campaign. Action leaves a trace.

The first stage of your campaign evaluation, then, will be to review the intended changes you set out to realize, identify what traces those changes would have left, and find the trace.

Having said this, if the intended changes you set out to bring were not rooted in behaviour or relationship, but rather in awareness or motivation, then you will have to work harder to gather the data you need to prove your success or failure. You will likely have to undertake primary research with the core audiences from the campaign. A survey of members, public opinion polling, or qualitative research will allow you to assess whether the campaign has indeed increased people's levels of awareness and enhanced their motivation to change in the ways your campaign is trying to bring about. Ideally, your budget and people resources will allow you to run a survey or focus groups before and after the campaign; pre- and post-studies are often the surest way to measure change in the attitudes and awareness of audiences.

Stage 2: Connecting with Key Audiences

Your strategic communication plan will not only allow you to clearly identify the changes you intended to bring about. It will also allow you to identify the precise audiences you needed to reach and engage and to know what specific changes to look for as indicators your campaign was successful (e.g., take action, influence others, enable the campaign). A solid approach to evaluating your campaign is to connect with a sample of each audience's members and determine the extent to which your campaign did indeed reach them and encouraged them to take action, influence others, or enable the campaign.

The main questions you need to answer include the following:

- Did they receive and notice the information you sent?
- Did they read it, watch it, or listen to it? Did they click on the links?
- Was their level of awareness and motivation affected in a positive way?
- Were the instructions presented clear and complete to the audience?
- If they were categorized as an actor audience, did they act at all on the information you sent?
- If they were categorized as an influencer audience, did they indeed communicate with others about your organization, your products and services, or your cause? Do they feel they were influential as they spoke to others?

- If they were categorized as an enabler audience, did they actually play the role of enabler for your organization and for this campaign? Did they approve what you hoped would be approved? Did they feel well informed and engaged as they did this?

This kind of audience-centered evaluation will also allow you to validate a number of assumptions at the heart of your strategic communication plan.

- Are these indeed the principal audiences? Can they play the roles you imagine them playing?
- Are your vehicles able to actually reach these audiences?
- Is the writing, design, and coding in your vehicles able to deliver the kind of experience these audiences find irresistible and will actually read or watch?
- Are your messages clear, compelling, and persuasive?
- Are your assumptions about the audience's biases, expectations, needs, codes, and habits correct?

In terms of research methods, both surveys and focus groups can be an effective way to ask these kinds of questions from most audiences. Surveys bring the advantage of a larger sample of respondents and greater precision in terms of results. Qualitative research brings the advantage of depth of understanding, revealing not so much what percentage of people read the web page thoroughly but why they did and why others didn't. If time and budget allows, you should consider running both types of studies and then bring the data from both methods together for analysis.

Audiences, like modern society as a whole, are continually changing, especially as concerns communication. That's why it's important to undertake this kind of research every two to three years if possible. Data about core audiences that is more than three years old may well prove to be so outdated it is more of a nuisance than a resource.

Stage 3: Focus on Resources

A major part of any strategic plan is to carefully assess the resources deployed by communicators, identifying strengths and weaknesses, and then finding ways to leverage the strengths and overcome weaknesses. Given the centrality of these processes in strategic planning, it should come as no surprise that evaluating the effectiveness of each resource is an important part of a strategic evaluation process.

When evaluating resources, it's best to rely on the insight and experiences of both a sample of your key audience members and of the members of your communication or PR team. Ideally, the members of your core audiences will participate in a focus group or survey process separately from the members of your team; that way, the discussion stays focused and participants feel free to share their sentiments about the campaign without the fear of upsetting those who worked on the campaign. As Table 10.1 points out, each of these two groups should focus on assessing different resources and answering different sets of questions. Combined in this way, the collective insight of those who created the campaign and those who received and engaged with its messages will be a powerful force in continually improving the results of the campaign.

TABLE 10.1: ASSESSING RESOURCES

HARD RESOURCE	WHO SHOULD ASSESS?	QUESTIONS TO ANSWER
Time	Team members	• Do you feel you and your colleagues had adequate time to plan, create, produce, and distribute the message and vehicles used for this campaign? • In what stage of your work do you feel you needed more time? • How do you feel the final products and the outcomes of the campaign would have been different had you had more time?
Money	Team members	• Do you feel you and your colleagues had adequate financial resources to plan, create, produce, and distribute the message and vehicles used for this campaign? • In what stage of your work do you feel you needed more money? • How do you feel the final products and the outcomes of the campaign would have been different had you had more money to spend on this campaign?

continued

People	Team members	• Do you feel you and your colleagues had enough talented people to plan, create, produce, and distribute the message and vehicles used for this campaign?
		• In what stage of your work do you feel you needed more team members or team members with different skill sets? Was the gap more in the number of people working or the skill sets of those people?
		• How do you feel the final products and the outcomes of the campaign would have been different had you had more talented people?
Vehicles	Key audiences	• Did the principal vehicles we used for this campaign actually reach you?
		• Did you notice these vehicles? Did you read them or watch them?
		• How inviting and how effective did you feel these vehicles were?

SOFT RESOURCE	WHO SHOULD ASSESS?	QUESTIONS TO ANSWER
Goodwill	Key audiences	• How well do you feel you know this organization, its work, its people, and the impact of its work?
		• Do you feel knowing more about the organization might have made you more likely to read or watch its messages? Why or why not?
		• Overall, how would you assess the values of this organization and its performance in terms of living up to those values?
		• Is this an organization you would be proud to be associated with? Why or why not?
		• What is one aspect of this organization you feel everyone should know about? Why is that?
Strategic Intelligence	Team members	• How well do you feel you and your colleagues understood the key audiences you were addressing with this campaign?
		• Are there aspects about this audience (e.g., their biases, expectations, needs, codes, and habits) you wish you had known more about as you were developing the campaign?
		• How well do you feel you and your colleagues understood the principal trends and forces unfolding in the external environment for this campaign?
		• Are there fields within the external environment (i.e., political, economic, social/cultural, technological, demographic, competitive, news media, and natural fields) you wish you had known more about as you were developing the campaign?

Internal Cohesion	Team members	• How effectively do you feel the various members of our team worked together on this campaign? • Do you feel all members of the team agreed on the general direction and intended changes of the campaign? Why or why not? • Do you feel all members of the team agreed on the need for all of us to work together to bring about the intended changes? Why or why not?
Stories	Key audiences	• Thinking back to the messages that were sent to you as part of this campaign, how clear did you find these messages? • How compelling were the messages? Did you want to read them? Did you read them? Why or why not? • How much of an impact did the campaign's messages have on your attitudes and your behaviour? Were they effective in motivating you to change? Why or why not?
Strategy	Team members	• In our original strategic plan, we determined the following resources were strengths (list them here) and the following resources were weaknesses (list them here). One year later, do you feel this assessment was correct? If not, what type of resource do you feel is worthy of being reassessed and why? • Our original strategic plan called for the following strategic directions (list strategic directions related to the resources here). At this stage of the campaign, which of these strategic directions do you feel have been fully implemented? Have the resulting changes met, exceeded, or failed to meet our expectations? • At this stage of the campaign, which of these strategic directions do you feel have not been fully implemented? Why do you think that is? What is preventing the team from fully implementing this strategic direction?

There are many questions to answer here and a great deal to be learned by answering them. This third stage of the evaluation process is often the most daunting and the most valuable.

Stage 4: Focus on the Environmental Scan

Much as it is important to evaluate the original assessment of resources and the team's ability to effectively leverage and overcome those resources, it is equally important to evaluate the original environmental scan (e.g., was it complete, was it accurate?) as well as to evaluate the extent to which the campaign was able to capitalize on the opportunities and mitigate the threats originally identified. This fourth stage of the evaluation process is best done by the members of the PR and communication team and by members of the leadership team at the client organization. Given how complex and diversified the external environment tends to be for most campaigns, having a larger group at the evaluation table helps to bring more knowledge and insight to the process. Table 10.2 summarizes who should be involved and what questions need to be answered.

TABLE 10.2: THE ENVIRONMENTAL SCAN

ENVIRONMENTAL FIELD	WHO SHOULD ASSESS?	QUESTIONS TO ANSWER
Political	Team members Executives	• Do you feel you have a good grasp of the key political trends and forces operating on this organization today? • If yes, what do you feel are the most influential trends and forces we need to consider (prompt for municipal, provincial, and federal governments)? • If not, what are some of the key aspects of the political environment you feel we should know more about (prompt for municipal, provincial, and federal governments)?
Economic	Team members Executives	• Do you feel you have a good grasp of the economic trends and forces affecting this organization today? • If yes, what do you feel are the most influential economic trends and forces we need to consider (prompt for the economy as a whole and the sector in which the organization operates)? • If not, what are some of the key aspects of the economic environment you feel we should know more about (prompt for the economy as a whole and the sector in which the organization operates)?

Social/Cultural	Team members Executives	• Do you feel you have a good grasp of the social and cultural trends and forces affecting this organization today? • If yes, what do you feel are the most influential social and cultural trends and forces we need to consider (prompt for broad social/cultural trends and those affecting the organization's key audiences specifically)? • If not, what are some of the key aspects of the social/cultural environment you feel we should know more about (prompt for broad social/cultural trends and those affecting the organization's core audiences specifically)?
Technological	Team members Executives	• Do you feel you have a good grasp of the technological trends and forces affecting this organization today? • If yes, what do you feel are the most influential technological trends and forces we need to consider (prompt for broad technological trends and those affecting the organization's operations, products, and services specifically)? • If not, what are some of the key aspects of the technological environment you feel we should know more about (prompt for broad technological trends and those affecting the organization's operations, products, and services specifically)?
Demographic	Team members Executives	• Do you feel you have a good grasp of the demographic trends and forces affecting this organization today? • If yes, what do you feel are the most influential demographic trends and forces we need to consider (prompt for broad demographic trends and those affecting the organization's core audiences specifically)? • If not, what are some of the key aspects of the demographic environment you feel we should know more about (prompt for broad demographic trends and those affecting the organization's core audiences specifically)?

continued

Competitive	Team members Executives	• Do you feel you have a good grasp of the competitive trends and forces affecting this organization today? • If yes, what do you feel are the most influential competitive trends and forces we need to consider (prompt for broad competitive trends and those affecting the organization's key products and services specifically)? • If not, what are some of the key aspects of the competitive environment you feel we should know more about (prompt for broad competitive trends and those affecting the organization's products and services specifically)?
News Media	Team members Executives	• Do you feel you have a good grasp of the news media trends and forces affecting this organization today? • If yes, what do you feel are the most influential news media trends and forces we need to consider (prompt for broad news media trends and those reaching the organization's key audiences specifically)? • If not, what are some of the key aspects of the news media environment you feel we should know more about (prompt for broad news media trends and those reaching the organization's main audiences specifically)?
Natural	Team members Executives	• Do you feel you have a good grasp of the natural trends and forces affecting this organization today? • If yes, what do you feel are the most influential natural trends and forces we need to consider (prompt for broad natural trends and those affecting the organization's key operations and key audiences specifically)? • If not, what are some of the key aspects of the natural environment you feel we should know more about (prompt for broad natural trends and those affecting the organization's principal operations and core audiences specifically)?

Strategy	Team members Executives	• In our original strategic plan, we determined that the following fields in the external environment were opportunities (list them here) and the following fields were threats (list them here). One year later, do you feel this assessment was correct? If not, what field in the external environment do you feel is worthy of being reassessed and why? • Our original strategic plan called for the following strategic directions (list strategic directions related to the external environment here). At this stage of the campaign, which of these strategic directions do you feel have been fully implemented? Have the resulting changes met, exceeded, or failed to meet our expectations? • At this stage of the campaign, which of these strategic directions do you feel have not been fully implemented? Why do you think that is? What is preventing the team from fully implementing this strategic direction?

This discussion will likely take three to four hours to complete, and maybe longer, depending on the number of participants. It's exhausting, but a thorough review of the external environment is essential for effective strategy. As an added bonus, this kind of frank discussion among colleagues from the PR or communication team as well as executives from elsewhere in the organization has a wonderful way of boosting the sense of connection and teamwork among participants; the return on investment is both enhanced strategic intelligence and enhanced internal cohesion. It is, in short, time well spent.

Stage 5: Content Analysis of the Campaign Vehicles

Clearly, in-depth discussions with colleagues, audience members, and executives play a vital role in effectively evaluating a strategic communication plan. There is, however, another way to evaluate aspects of a strategic communication campaign that is equally rewarding and that doesn't require quite as much time and involvement from very busy people.

Content analysis is a well-established research technique dating back at least to 1952 and the publication of Bernard Berelson's *Content Analysis in Communication Research*.[1] Unlike surveys and focus groups, which draw data from participants, content analysis is a method that draws data from actual communication vehicles. It is a way to study, to sum up, and to find patterns in what an organization actually communicates via the various vehicles and activities that together make up a communication campaign or program.

Content analysis is a proven way to assess an organization's PR or strategic communication campaign. The questions content analysis will allow you to answer are fundamentally important to communication and focused on the following four aspects of the campaign:

1. What were the **key messages** communicated by the campaign and how do these compare to the stated messages in the campaign's strategic plan?

2. What were the **key communication vehicles** used to reach and engage each of the audiences identified for the campaign? How do these compare to the original strategic plan for the campaign?

3. **How often were the key messages communicated** by the campaign and what was the schedule of this communication? How did that compare to the action plan?

4. **How was the total budget for the campaign allocated** in terms of the share accorded to each audience and to each communication vehicle or activity?

Essentially, the content analysis is a way to assess the extent to which the actual campaign was consistent with the strategic plan developed for that campaign. This may seem like an irrelevant assessment; after all, the plan is there, it's official, and the communication team must follow the plan. That's true in principle, but in the real world of PR and strategic communication, life gets in the way. Deadlines are missed. Messages change as they are approved. Plans change as feedback from early vehicles and activities is received. It's always a good idea to go back and assess the extent to which the actual campaign compared to the plan that was developed. This can be especially valuable if the plan fails to meet its goals and generate its intended changes. With this kind of assessment completed, you will know what elements of the *actual* plan were implemented, what worked, and what didn't work; you won't make the mistake of assessing the hoped-for plan and looking there for what might have gone wrong.

OBJECTIVITY AND EVALUATING STRATEGIC COMMUNICATION CAMPAIGNS

The CARE model is a very helpful framework for evaluating strategic communication campaigns. The blend of a rigorous content analysis and in-depth discussion with members of the communication team, executives within the client organization, and members of the key audiences will yield real insight into what worked, what didn't, and what can be improved as the campaign moves forward. Be prepared for surprises, however. Communication is a very difficult process to predict; keep an open mind and you'll learn much more from the process.

One of the best ways to ensure you keep an open mind when evaluating is to back away from evaluating any projects you are too close to. Strategic communicators should be prepared to step away from the evaluation if they played a key role in developing the strategic plan and implementing it. When you are too close to a campaign, interview participants (whether organization executives or members of the audience) will find it difficult to be completely open about what they feel worked and didn't work. You will likely also be too close to the process to effectively run a content analysis of the vehicles you helped to create. If you have a large enough team, have someone else lead the evaluation process—someone who perhaps was only lightly involved in the campaign or not at all involved. If your team is small, consider hiring an outside agency or consultant to lead the charge. Make sure they have had no role to play in the planning and implementation of the campaign so they can be completely objective as they assess the campaign and the strategy behind it.

KEY TERMS AND CONCEPTS

As you review this chapter for any tests or assignments, you will want to pay particular attention to the following terms and concepts introduced in the preceding pages:

- intended change and campaign evaluation
- key audiences and campaign evaluation
- resource assessment and campaign evaluation
- environmental scan and campaign evaluation
- advantages of using the CARE model to frame both your strategic planning *and* your evaluation
- surveys

- **focus groups**
- **research interviews**
- **content analysis**

QUESTIONS FOR CRITICAL REFLECTION

1. The elements of strategic communication (change, audiences, resources, and environment) can also serve as a framework for evaluating a communication campaign. In your opinion, which of the four elements is most likely to lead to recommendations to improve future campaigns? Why do you think that is?

2. What is the main advantage of using the same four-part framework to both plan your strategic campaign and to evaluate it? Can you think of any disadvantages of using the same framework for two very different processes?

3. Given the kind of information you hope to receive from an evaluation of a strategic communication campaign, which research method do you feel would make the most sense in terms of consulting with members of your key audience? Would you prefer using individual interviews or focus groups with multiple members of your audiences? Why is that and how do you feel the result would differ based on the method used?

4. Of the five stages proposed for the evaluation framework (evaluating the intended changes; connecting with key audiences; focusing on resources; focusing on the environmental scan; and content analysis of the campaign vehicles), which do you feel is most likely to yield real insight and point the way to improving the campaign? Why is that? What is it about the stage you feel gives it the added potential?

NOTE

1.   Berelson, B. (1952). *Content analysis in communication research*. Glencoe, IL: Free Press.

CONCLUSION TO PART II

To borrow from the gardening analogy that has shaped much of this book, we now come to the end of the year. It is early winter, the garden has been harvested, the preserves set aside, the lessons learned, and the foundation already put in place for a plan to guide next year's effort.

We have covered a good deal of ground over these many pages. Although this book is divided into two parts and ten chapters, there is only one process: strategic communication planning. Each type of information you learned to gather in Part I contributes to a single strategy. Each of the steps you followed in Part II of the book similarly contributes to a single strategic communication plan.

If I can offer a final piece of advice to help you become a more effective strategic communication planner, it would be this: Pay attention to the sudden ideas that emerge when you least expect them. Note the "a-ha moments" you will no doubt experience as you gather, analyze, and fashion the information you gather into a coherent series of strategic directions. Though there is a precise order to the chapters and the steps presented in this book, there is simply no telling when the moments of true inspiration will come. As you embark on a strategic communication planning process, it's important to expect the unexpected. Have your cellphone, laptop, or a small pad of paper beside you at all times. At any moment, your mind will reflect on how to leverage a strength in a brand new way. You will suddenly know how to overcome a weakness through a creative and ground-breaking approach. When you least expect it, the single best way to capitalize on an opportunity will become clear to you, or the most creative way to mitigate a threat will pop into your mind. Pay attention to those moments, make a few notes, and know your efforts at gathering, analyzing, solving, and organizing are paying off. Enjoy these moments, and be grateful so many people chose to share their thoughts and information with you at the very start of the planning process.

EPILOGUE
Reflecting on Ethics and Strategic Communication

It's the middle of winter. Your garden lies sleeping under several feet of snow. Your tools are in the shed, maintained and ready to go for another season in a few short months.

You've just used a jar of tomatoes that came from your garden to make a wonderful spaghetti sauce you'll enjoy later in the day. The colour and the smell are rich and promising.

As you stir the sauce and enjoy the aroma, you reflect on gardening once again. This time, you reflect on the ethics of gardening. On what makes a garden "right" and how those same qualities have a way of yielding the best fruits and vegetables, the brightest flowers, and the healthiest butterflies and birds.

You reflect on the importance of respecting nature, the plants and the animals you hope to attract and nurture each year. You understand these species do you a favour by growing, living, and thriving in a small lot of land you have set aside for them.

You reflect on the importance of always thinking in the longer term. Gardening needs to be sustainable. Success is measured over decades or even centuries, not one season at a time. The choices you make now may well affect the soil, the plants, and the animals you want to nurture for years to come. The quick fix shot of fertilizer or weed killer may, in the long run, do more harm than good.

You breathe in the aroma and start to think about getting the pasta ready to eat.

ON GARDENS, ETHICS, AND STRATEGIC COMMUNICATION

This book is many thousands of words long and contains the information you will need to think strategically about communication and public relations. There are information and tools here to help you plan a truly strategic campaign, to help you evaluate that campaign, and to allow you to use that evaluation to fuel the next edition of the plan.

There is only one, brief section in this book on the ethics of strategic communication. The topic is important, rich, and worthy of an entire book. There is, however, an idea in this book which connects very well to the question of ethics. That idea is the very analogy that started this work and lent it the small blocks of text on every new chapter's first page: gardening. That idea is an appropriate way to end this book.

The ethics of communication at the heart of this book calls for a focus on nurturing audiences rather than merely targeting them. It is an ethics that understands audiences have a choice and will inevitably go where the conditions are most respectful, profitable, and enjoyable; and they do. As any former executive from a bankrupt corporation, former leader of a disbanded charity, or former official from a government voters sent packing will tell you, efforts to conquer an audience are more often than not ineffective in the long run.

When we think of communication as a gardener thinks of a garden, truth becomes essential and automatic. Lying to an audience is like using too much fertilizer (there's a pun in there somewhere, perhaps) and burning the very plants you're trying to nurture. When we think of an audience the way a gardener thinks of a plant or animal they are trying to nurture, creative messages that sow fear or merely titillate quickly lose their appeal. The short-term gains of these approaches are quickly surpassed by the long-term pain that follows when an audience turns its back on your organizations and all of its messages.

In the end, the gardener understands success depends on the health, vitality, and success of the plants and animals they want in their garden. Communicators need to come to the same conclusion: Their success inevitably depends on the health, vitality, and success of their audiences. Their concern for and respect for the audience must be sincere and reflected in every strategic decision they make. Suddenly the urge to target, manipulate, and overwhelm the audience is replaced by a determination to share clear information, present logical arguments, listen continuously, and understand deeply. Short-term campaigns become long-term programs with rhythms and cycles throughout. When communicators approach their work like gardeners, success is measured not in weekly sales figures or monthly donation charts. Success, instead, is measured in lasting relationships between an organization and its audiences—relationships forged out of two-way communication and built on trust and mutual benefit.

Respecting the audiences is not only the right thing to do as communicators; it is by far the most strategic and effective approach to take.

APPENDIX A
Glossary

Action: Action is a step on the continuum that begins with awareness and ends with habit or relationship. When a member of a key audience takes action, he or she changes behaviour in the way intended by the strategic communication campaign. Though it is not yet a habit (see below), adopting the desired behaviour once as a result of the campaign is a critical first step in creating a habit and repeated behaviour over time.

Audiences: In the context of strategic communication planning, audiences represent one of the four elements of any plan (along with intended changes, resources, and environment). Audiences are the individuals and groups to whom the messages of a campaign or program must be directed in order to ensure the success of the effort. Audiences include those whose behaviour and relationship with the organization you hope to affect (referred to as the "actors"). Audiences also include those individuals and organizations that can reliably influence your actor audiences (referred to as "influencers"), as well as individuals in positions of leadership and authority who can fundamentally allow the campaign to proceed or block it entirely (referred to as "enablers").

Audiences are also closely tied to the external environment; opportunities are most often changes that will increase the number of members of a particular audience and/or increase the extent to which those members are predisposed to pay attention to the campaign and act on its messages. Threats, on the other hand, are often forces and trends that reduce the size and predisposition of an audience.

Awareness: Awareness is one of the foundations for success in any strategic communication or public relations campaign or program. An audience most often first needs to be aware of an organization before that organization can persuasively call for a proposed change in behaviour or relationship with the organization. Generally speaking, we pay more attention to and are more persuaded by messages from an individual or organization with whom we are familiar. We are also more likely to change our behaviour or relationship if we are aware of the option to make the change and the benefits this change might bring about. Lack of awareness, on the other hand, makes success in strategic communication and public relations nearly impossible.

BENCH analysis: BENCH analysis is a particular approach to researching the members of a key audience to better understand how they will respond to messages sent as part of a strategic communication or public relations campaign. BENCH is an acronym and stands for "biases, expectations, needs, codes, and habits." Each of these five aspects of an audience will play a part in determining whether or not a campaign's messages reach them, how they interpret that message, and whether they choose to act on the message in any way. Research designed to identify and deepen the communicator's understanding of an audience along these five dimensions is highly effective in enhancing the effectiveness of a given message or campaign.

Capitalize: To capitalize on an opportunity is to maximize the positive impact a trend or force outside the organization will have on the organization. Opportunities are those trends and forces that will grow the size of a key audience and render those people more likely to pay attention to the campaign and to act on the messages of the campaign.

Capitalizing on an opportunity most often involves aligning the strategic communication campaign—its messages, timing, vehicles, and activities—with the time, the place, and the idea at the heart of the opportunity. When successful, capitalizing on an opportunity will increase the likelihood an opportunity will actually occur (e.g., becoming a sponsor of an event to ensure the event does go ahead) and will increase the impact when it does occur (e.g., running an advertising campaign to ensure the audience knows about your sponsorship).

Change: The change or changes to be brought about by a strategic communication campaign or program represent the first and most fundamental choice for any strategic planner. Strategic thinking demands a clear sense of the goals and objectives against which the effort will be assessed. A strategic communication planner will want to focus intended changes on raising levels of awareness and building strong motivation among audience members, and providing clear instruction of what changes are required, as well as when and how those instructions are to be implemented.

Competitive: The competitive field of the external environment refers to those organizations that compete for the attention and the engagement of the audiences your organization hopes to reach and engage. Often, these are business competitors after the same market as your organization, but competition goes beyond this to include any organization actively seeking to communicate on similar topics to those covered in your campaign and hold the attention of one of your audiences. If your client is a large chain of bookstores, for example, you need to compete with other bookstores, book publishers, libraries, and online bookstores as you set out to reach and engage an audience of active readers. You will also have to consider magazines, social media fields, and websites that also reach active book readers. The competitive field is extremely important to consider when developing a strategic communication plan for the simple reason most individuals with whom you will want to communicate will be continually overloaded with far too many messages sent to them by far too many organizations and individuals.

Content analysis: Content analysis is a powerful methodology for studying any large group of texts (e.g., works of art, news media articles, social media posts, etc.). It is primarily a quantitative research methodology that relies on counting the number of times a particular term, phrase, pattern, or idea was expressed in the texts being analyzed. For strategic communicators, content analysis is an important part of a thorough evaluation process. The various texts created for a particular communication campaign or program can be assessed to determine the extent to which the ideas expressed in those vehicles actually correspond to the core messages intended for the campaign.

Demographic: The demographic profile of a group of people looks at the most fundamental aspects of that population: the number of people; birth rates and mortality rates; the distribution of those people around the city, province, or country; the age distribution and gender distribution of the population; and the martial status of the population. Some definitions of the term "demographic profile" will go beyond these fundamental measures to consider the racial profile of the population, as well as levels of education, employment, and income. The demographic field is one of the areas of the external environment strategic communication planners will want to study carefully, noting important changes to the profile of the audiences they hope to reach and engage.

Economic: The economic field of the external environment considers all of the trends and forces that affect the amount of money members of your key audiences will have and, hence, the likelihood they will agree to spend that money. Most public, private, and not-for-profit organizations will, at some point, run a campaign whose intended change will be to affect the manner in which members of the key audience spend their money; soliciting donations, sales, and taxes or fees for service are all quite common outcomes of strategic communication campaign.

External environment: The external environment represents one of the four elements of strategic communication. The environment refers to the conditions outside of the organization behind the campaign or program. Communicators will want to pay particular attention to conditions in certain fields of the external environment that can have a significant impact on the attitudes, behaviour, and relationships of core audiences. These fields include the political, economic, social/cultural, and technological fields. Also of importance to communicators are conditions in the demographic, competitive, news media, and natural fields of the external environment. Those conditions will lay the foundations for the opportunities and threats that will then guide the development of strategic directions for the campaign.

Focus group: A focus group is an important method used by researchers to gather qualitative data. Focus groups typically bring participants together around a table to discuss points raised by a moderator. Increasingly, teleconferences and web-based conferences are being used to virtually gather participants from a wider geographic area and to make their participation easier. The power of focus groups stems from the careful transcription of every word spoken by the participants. The analysis of those transcripts focuses less on the precise number of people who answered one way or another and focuses more on the meaning of the answers delivered by participants and patterns in those different answers.

Goodwill: Goodwill is not only a crucial resource for strategic communicators, it is often one of the desired outcomes of a successful PR or strategic communication campaign; building goodwill is often why an organization chooses to run such a campaign or program in the first place. Goodwill is the measure of the extent to which members of a particular external audience know about a particular organization, cause, or movement and the extent to which they like or positively assess that organization, cause, or movement. In this respect, building goodwill is often the foundation for changing the behaviour of a core audience or changing the nature of the relationship those audiences have with the organization, the cause, or the movement. If I know about a local group trying to create jobs for unemployed youth in my community and I like the people running the group and the purpose of the group, I am much more predisposed to help fund the group or perhaps participate in their program.

Habit: In the context of strategic communication, "habit" refers to specific behaviours members of a key audience undertake on a regular basis. Quite often, when an intended change in behaviour (e.g., purchasing a particular brand, taking specific measures to protect the environment, or promoting health) becomes a habit, the campaign that brought it about truly becomes successful.

Instruction: In the context of strategic communication, "instruction" refers to the complete list of steps a member of a core audience must complete in order to bring about the change in behaviour or change in relationship intended by a PR or strategic communication campaign. Instruction is also a critical point along the action continuum, and effective strategic communication plans are careful to develop a complete list of instructions and express them in clear and engaging ways.

Intended change: The intended change of a strategic communication or public relations plan is best understood as the "reason(s) why" an organization is choosing to invest its time and money in a campaign to communicate certain messages to certain audiences. In many ways, the intended change of a campaign can be referred to as the goals and objectives of the campaign, the mission of the campaign, or the desired outcome of a campaign. Both words in this expression are important. The word "change" suggests campaign success will be measured by the extent to which the level of awareness, the attitude, the behaviour, or the relationship of a particular audience has changed as a result of the communication; the word "intended" suggests this change has been carefully selected and lies at the heart of the strategic choices made in writing, designing, and distributing the messages of the campaign.

Internal cohesion: Internal cohesion is a subtle resource strategic communicators can deploy. It can best be described as the condition within an organization where most people agree on a destination and agree to pick up a paddle and contribute to getting the organization there quickly. Internal cohesion is expressed both by how people within an organization feel and what it is they do with that sentiment. When an organization is able to deploy internal cohesion, more people are able to contribute to a communication campaign or program. The people within that organization are also more likely to pay attention to the messages they receive from the organization and more likely to act on those messages.

Key messages: The key messages for a communication campaign or program are one of the most important parts of a creative strategy. These messages are essential to the communication campaign or program succeeding and bringing about its intended changes. Key messages should be written to move the audience along the action continuum, ensuring members are aware, motivated, properly instructed, and effectively called to action. These principle messages can be inspired by the strengths an organization can leverage, by its efforts to overcome weaknesses, and by how the organization will capitalize on opportunities and mitigate strengths. Key messages emerge, then, from the communication strategy for a campaign or program.

Leverage: To leverage a resource is to put that resource to work. In the context of strategic communication, the challenge for communicators is to identify the strongest resources they can deploy and then find effective ways to make the very most of those resources; it means focusing the action plan on those tactics that draw most fully from the identified strengths.

Mitigate: Mitigating is a strategic process of reducing the negative impact an external threat can have on your organization and your campaign. In the context of strategic communication, threats are most often forces and trends that will reduce the size of a particular audience and/or render those people less likely to pay attention to the messages of a campaign and less likely to act on those messages in the manner intended by the planners.

Mitigation can come in many forms, including distancing the time and location of a campaign from that of the threat. It can also come in the form of distancing the messages of a campaign from the idea at the core of the threats. When successful, mitigating a threat will reduce the likelihood a threat will occur (e.g., putting a fence around the swimming pool) and will reduce the impact when it does strike (e.g., teaching everyone in the home how to swim).

Money: For the strategic communicator, money is one of the simplest and most valuable resources. Budgets are often set far in advance of a campaign and are most often fixed for the year in which the investment will take place. This makes knowing how much money can be deployed a relatively simple assessment. Some organizations budget more flexibly than others, though, so budgets can sometimes change as the fiscal year unfolds, which can add an element of uncertainty to assessing this resource.

Motivation: Motivation is the willing recognition by an individual that a particular change in their behaviour or relationship will likely bring about direct benefits for them. When motivated, individuals will change their behaviour or change the nature of their relationship of their own accord; no threats or manipulation are required to bring about the change. Motivation is the second point along the action continuum.

Multiplier effect: The term multiplier effect refers to the potential for some audiences to take a message sent to them and redirect it to a larger audience, hence multiplying the impact of the campaign. Some editors and reporters, for example, have a significant multiplier effect when they take your press release and decide to develop and run a news story based on the idea. Bloggers and opinion leaders of all types can also have a multiplier effect, as they share what they have found in your messages with the audience they have gathered. Assessing the potential for multiplier effect is one of the strategic ways to determine if a particular key audience should indeed be part of a campaign or perhaps left off the list to preserve resources for more effective audiences.

Natural: The natural field of the external environment includes all those aspects of life on the planet that fundamentally affect our ability to live here. These include safe water, stable climate, healthy soil, animal life and plant life on the planet, as well as small organisms like viruses and bacteria that can dramatically affect human health. These very basic elements of the natural field can dramatically affect the success of many campaigns since they will dramatically affect the life, work, health, and death of members of your core audiences.

News media: The news media is the field of the external environment most often associated with the practice of public relations. The field comprises all the people who work for the public and private news media outlets in Canada, including in newspapers, magazines, radio, television, and online news sources. Whether the campaign you are planning will include a media relations component or not, it makes sense to carefully scan this field and understand what messages are currently circulating about the topic or issue your campaign intends to address. The biases your audience members bring to the communication process will often be shaped in part by what they read, hear, and see in the news media. Depending on the topic and on the relations your organization currently has with the news media, this field may also be home to a powerful resource you can use to spread your messages or a powerful competitor you will have to contend with as you seek to mobilize your key audiences. Developing a clear sense of the news media's priorities, principal players, practices, and potential reach will be an important part of any strategic communication planning process.

Opinion leaders: Opinion leader is a term used to denote individuals who are widely regarded by their peers as being well informed and, therefore, having credible opinions on issues that matter. The issue can be any issue that interests an individual, although the term is typically used in the context of politics and marketing. Opinion leaders are often identified by the way they consume a good deal more media than most people, most often media focused on their particular topic of interest and expertise. Opinion leaders are also more active than most in sharing their opinions. They are more likely to post comments, write letters to the editor, and speak about the topic to friends, family, colleagues, and others who share their interest. The term and the concept of a two-step flow of communication (from mass media to opinion leaders and then to opinion followers) is largely credited to sociologist Paul Lazarsfeld. Lazarsfeld explored and developed the concept in 1944's *The People's Choice*, which he co-wrote with Bernard Berelson and Hazel Gaudet, and then expanded in 1955's *Personal Influence*, which he co-wrote with Elihu Katz.

Overcome: To "overcome" a weak resource is to find strategic ways to enhance the quality and or quantity of that resource before deploying it. Overcoming a weakness makes strategic sense because it recognizes the negative impact that can follow from trying to deploy a resource that is not up to the challenge; it seeks to avoid the negative impact by proactively enhancing the quantity and quality of that resource in order to ensure it is up to the challenge at hand.

People: In the context of strategic communication management, "people" refers to the individuals an organization can deploy as it seeks to plan, prepare, and implement a public relations or strategic communication program or campaign. Most often, the people are employed by the organization and have a clearly defined role in the communication process. Planners should also consider, though, the role volunteers and partners can play in greatly expanding the total number of people who can be deployed. The planner will want to assess the number of people available, as well as their actual availability for the assignment and their skills and expertise in the activity planned for them.

Political: The political field of the external environment is comprised of all the people who work in the public sector in Canada, be they in the federal, provincial, or municipal system. These people include elected officials but also include members of the public service who work to interpret and enact the many decisions made by those elected officials. Whether your campaign includes elected officials and public servants as key audiences or not, a scan of the political field may well be in order. The members of your key audiences will very likely be influenced by the laws, policies, and procedures of the three levels of government. Many of our behaviours are limited by laws (e.g., driving a car without a seatbelt on) and other behaviours are directly brought about by policies and legislation in support of those behaviours (e.g., sending kids to school, paying taxes, trying to quit smoking). Understanding what the current laws, policies, and procedures are doing to the likelihood of people responding to your messages in the way you intend is critical to effective strategic planning.

Publics: Publics are groups of people who are of particular, strategic importance to an organization. They are often, but not always, the same groups of people who constitute core audiences for that organization. In some cases, an important public is not a core audience; their sentiment and behaviour needs to be monitored carefully but the organization decides its resources can be better spent reaching out to and engaging different groups. Essentially, if a group of people can be affected by the organization or if that group could affect the organization, then they should be considered an important public. If a group of people needs to change its awareness, its attitudes, or its behaviour in order for the organization to succeed, then the organization will want to communicate effectively with the group. It is this strategic desire or need to communicate with one or more publics that defines the group of people as a core audience.

Relationship: Relationship, in the context of strategic communication, refers to the nature of the link between an organization and members of its audiences. Relationships vary in strength and duration but stand apart from a one-time transaction or interaction. Generally speaking, where a relationship exists, the audience members with whom an organization has formed a relationship are more likely to pay attention to messages from the organization, more likely to assess the messages as credible, more likely to respond to the messages, and more likely to change their behaviour or the nature of their relationship along the lines of what the messages intended.

Research interview: Research interviews are a proven qualitative research method with several advantages over focus groups. Because they are individual conversations between a moderator and a participant, there is no chance the

answers of one participant will be influenced by the answers of another participant. What's more, the introverted members of the group you want to study will
likely be more comfortable in a one-on-one interview setting than in a focus
group and so will be more likely to accept your invitation. This advantage is particularly important when the subject of discussion is personal and private (e.g.,
sexual behaviour, drugs, alcohol, abuse, etc.). The disadvantage of one-on-one
research interviews, of course, is the time required to use this method. Whereas
a 90-minute focus group can gather data from 8 to 10 participants, 8 to 10
one-on-one interviews will take much longer to conduct (e.g., 20 to 30 minutes
multiplied by the number of interviews you conduct). Much like focus groups,
there is a growing tendency to conduct one-on-one research interviews over the
phone or using a web-based channel such as Skype.

Research panel: A research panel is a powerful method of quantitative and/
or qualitative research. The members of a research panel are selected from a
given group (e.g., members, donors, employees) who have an important quality in common. Rather than sending these people a single survey questionnaire
or inviting them to participate in a single focus group, the panel—much like a
committee—can be called upon multiple times to provide feedback and answers
on questions and challenges that matter to them. Given the total commitment
of time asked of panel members, some form of incentive is usually offered (e.g.,
money, discounts, special privileges, recognition, etc.). Panels have the advantage of allowing participants to learn about the organization or issue much more
deeply than one-time research participants. Unlike a committee, a research panel
should be randomly selected, and its members should reflect the demographic
profile of the group they are drawn from.

Resources: In the context of strategic communication, the resources an organization has to deploy in a public relations effort are one of the four elements that must
be considered carefully. In particular, communicators need to have adequate hard
resources they can deploy, including time, money, people, and communication vehicles. Communicators also benefit when they can deploy a number of soft resources,
such as goodwill, internal cohesion, strategic intelligence, and stories to tell. Hard
resources can be measured with confidence and rely less on subjective evaluation.
Soft resources, on the other hand, are more difficult to measure accurately and
are more tied to subjective assessment. The thorough and objective assessment of
resources is a critical stage in the strategic communication planning process as only
resources correctly assessed as strengths can then be leveraged effectively and only
those correctly assessed as weaknesses can then be overcome successfully.

Sample: Sample is a research term that means the specific individuals from a particular group who will be studied as part of a research project. If your goal is to learn about the media habits of baby boomer women in Ontario, for example, you will likely not choose to speak to every woman in the province born between 1945 and 1965; that would be too many participants, demanding too much expense and requiring too much time. Most researchers opt for a random selection of participants who fit the profile required by the study (e.g., demographic profile or behavioural profile). If the selection of the sample is truly random and every person who fits the profile has an equal chance of being invited to participate in the study, the results you generate from your study should be very similar to the results you would have generated had every individual who fits the profile participated (what is referred to as a census approach to sampling). Sampling, then, is a proven way to overcome weaknesses in money and in time when conducting research.

Social/cultural: As the name implies, the social/cultural field is effectively the intersection between two distinct fields. The social field refers to those norms, tendencies, tastes, and expectations widely shared among the members of a social group (e.g., a generation, a nation, a linguistic group, a gender, etc.). Many of our individual actions and choices are greatly influenced by the social trends and forces where we live; that's why understanding the current social trends and forces is such an important step in strategic communication planning. The cultural field, on the other hand, refers to the panoply of clothing, meals, gathering places, books, movies, songs, web pages, and social media channels with which we surround ourselves. We study this field to get a sense of what is happening in the social field. Our cultural activities tend to reflect and deepen social trends and forces. Studying these two fields together will sharpen your understanding of key trends and forces influencing your core audiences.

Stories: Good stories to tell are perhaps the single most valuable resource a strategic communicator can deploy. Having all the best vehicles, plenty of money to buy advertising, and a skilled team of PR professionals ready to mount a national series of press events is of little consequence if you have nothing to say. Stories make or break modern communication campaigns and programs. These can include stories related to the product or service being developed by the organization, the people who work there, and the people who have been helped by what the organization does. Often referred to as "content," the term "stories" is favoured here because it builds in the recognition that stories are one of the most ancient and effective ways to present content. Stories have memorable characters, rising tension, and emotional climaxes. All of these qualities can and should be built into any strategic communication campaign.

Strategic intelligence: In the context of strategic communication planning, the term strategic intelligence refers to the knowledge an organization has about the current conditions both inside and outside the organization. Assessing strategic intelligence involves evaluating how well the people in the organization understand the current state of the resources they can deploy and how well they understand the current conditions in the external environment. Building strategic intelligence involves an ongoing program of research and monitoring. This is a critical resource to build since knowing about strengths and weaknesses, opportunities and threats is the first step in developing strategic directions that will allow an organization to leverage, overcome, capitalize, and mitigate. Strategy depends on solid strategic intelligence.

Survey: A survey is one of the principal methods used by researchers to gather quantitative data. Survey questionnaires are presented on paper, using electronic channels (e.g., email, web pages, social media posts), via telephone, or face-to-face. Surveys typically contain straightforward questions that can be answered quickly using brief answers, selecting from multiple choice or assigning numerical scores (i.e., on a scale of 1 to 10 …).

SWOT analysis: SWOT analysis is a common method used to assess the resources an organization can deploy and the environment in which it operates as a first step in setting strategic directions. The range of items considered as resources is very wide, which is why this book focuses on the resources of greatest use to communicators. Similarly, the external environment of any organization is vast, complex, and ever-changing. Strategic planners do well to focus on those fields of the external environment most likely to contain opportunities and threats that will affect the organization. The SWOT analysis, then, is the summary of the findings from the process: the key strengths and weaknesses with which an organization must work, as well as the key opportunities and threats to be considered. Note a SWOT analysis is a vital step in developing strategy, but it is not a strategy in and of itself.

Technological: The technological field is just as vast as the others and easily the field that transforms at the most rapid pace. The impact of science and technology on modern life is clear. Technology is constantly changing the ways we play and work, the ways we learn and connect with others, the ways we move ourselves, and the food and materials we need. Not all of this activity, of course, will directly affect any one strategic communication campaign. But nearly every strategic communication campaign will be profoundly influenced by changes to the technological field. The secret, as with all fields in the external environment, is to quickly single out those changes that matter to you and to your client or employer. If developments in technology affect the way you can reach and engage your key audiences, if they affect the way the organization works or the lives of the audiences, then that aspect of the field should be studied closely.

Theme: A theme is a unifying factor woven into every aspect of a strategic communication plan. A consistent theme makes a campaign or program more unified and more powerful. Ideally, the theme is a powerful idea that ties the various messages and vehicles of the campaign together. It is woven into every vehicle, repeated often enough it becomes one of the most memorable parts of the campaign. A theme is not a slogan; however, the idea at the heart of a campaign theme can be used to inspire the slogan used for the campaign.

Time: In the context of strategic resources for communicators, time refers to the amount of time an organization can dedicate to a particular campaign or effort. Assessing the time available should include consideration of the time required to plan a campaign or effort, to develop and approve all the campaign materials, to deliver those materials, and to allow audiences to engage and respond to the materials. This process extends for the life of the campaign, which will vary widely by the type of campaign and the organization.

Vehicles: In the context of strategic communication planning, vehicles refer to the list of dedicated communication vehicles and activities an organization can deploy to communicate the messages of its campaign or program. For a vehicle to be considered a resource, it should be a vehicle entirely owned or at least shared by that organization so it can reliably control the content audiences will see and experience. The *Toronto Star* may be a strong vehicle to reach homeowners in the GTA, but it is not a resource that an organization (other than Torstar Corporation) can reliably control. Accessing the *Toronto Star* will require other resources, such as money, a great story, and people to tell it. A business's own website or a magazine published by a not-for-profit are both examples of vehicles that could be considered resources and assessed.

APPENDIX B
Case Study

A STRATEGIC COMMUNICATION CAMPAIGN FOR THE ONTARIO PHYSIOTHERAPY ASSOCIATION

Canada, like many modernized nations, is home to a number of different health-care professions, each offering a particular range of services and treatments to their patients. In the province of Ontario alone, 26 different professions are recognized and regulated under the *Regulated Health Professions Act* (RHPA) and other health profession Acts (e.g., *Medicine Act, 1991*).[1] The associations who represent these professions often engage in promotional campaigns to demonstrate the value of and differentiate their profession's services in a crowded market while educating the public who make healthcare choices. In 2009, the Ontario Physiotherapy Association (OPA) approached Delta Media, Inc.—an Ottawa-based strategic communication firm—to develop a campaign that would specifically address the challenge of ensuring strong demand for the services offered by their members. The OPA board had identified promoting the value of physiotherapy services as a top priority and had authorized a substantial investment of 15 percent of their total budget in an annual campaign to make it happen.

Delta Media's work on the campaign began with a thorough situation analysis of the current challenge faced by the OPA. The process included an extensive literature review (including internal OPA documents and external documents from the Government of Ontario and the news media), as well as in-depth interviews with a number of key staff and members of the OPA board.

Intended Changes

The intended changes of the campaign were clarified and included changes to the awareness, attitudes, and behaviour of the key audiences. The campaign was intended to:

- increase the extent to which residents of the province were aware of the health benefits of physiotherapy;
- increase the extent to which Ontarians valued those services; and
- increase the number of Ontarians choosing a physiotherapist and increase the number who value physiotherapy so much they would advocate for more access to those services through public funding (government) and private insurers.

Core Audiences

After a review of demographic data and discussions with the leaders of the OPA about the profile of physiotherapy patients in the province, the core audience for the campaign was identified as women who were part of the baby boomer generation. These women (born between 1945 and 1965) were selected for their potential to significantly increase demand for physiotherapy services in two separate ways:

1. as active women in their 40s, 50s, and 60s, they themselves were at an age where their demand for services that improve mobility and reduce pain would be increasing; and
2. as women often make or influence the healthcare choices of their families, they could also influence their children, spouses, and parents to choose the services of a registered physiotherapist.

A secondary audience was also identified for the campaign: physiotherapists in Ontario. Membership in the OPA is not mandatory, so the audience included both OPA members and practising physiotherapists who were not members. The intended changes for OPA members included that these people:

- become aware of and support the campaign;
- learn how to participate and play an active role in the campaign; and
- recognize and value their association is communicating on their behalf.

Similarly, the intended changes for non-OPA members in this audience was that they too become aware of and support the campaign, play an active role in the campaign, and recognize the OPA is communicating on their behalf. In addition, it was intended non-members would also recognize the value being offered by the OPA and consider joining the association.

Resource Assessment

The strategic communication planning process also included a thorough assessment of the resources at the disposal of the OPA and its agency. That assessment identified a number of strengths the organization could leverage, along with an area of "potential strength" that would require effort before it could be leveraged.

Time was seen as a strength for two reasons: the agency was given a full year to plan, develop, implement, and evaluate the campaign; and the OPA was committed to a multi-year effort to raise demand for physiotherapy in Ontario.

Money was assessed as a moderate strength; the annual budget was assessed as adequate and the fact the association was prepared to invest similar amounts each year of a multi-year campaign added an important measure of stability to the funding.

The **people** involved in the campaign were also assessed as a strength. These included knowledgeable and experienced staff at the OPA office, as well as an experienced agency team. Most importantly, the assessment captured the fact that the 5,000 members of the OPA were also a tremendous asset. Physiotherapists are opinion leaders on matters related to health, mobility, and recovery. Their education and professional experience both work to make them highly credible and informed.

The **vehicles** at the disposal of the OPA to reach and engage the two key audiences were also assessed as strengths. Membership surveys conducted by the OPA had shown high levels of readership and trust for the association's internal vehicles, including electronic and print vehicles. Given the budget set for the campaign, radio was identified as an ideal vehicle with which to reach the baby boomer women identified as the core external audience. Listenership of radio was strong among women of this age group, particularly among those stations focused on attracting this audience. It was also important to note that most radio stations in Ontario had a strong listenership within Ontario (with the possible exception of some stations in Eastern Ontario, which borders Western Quebec); most listeners, then, would be residents of Ontario. The cost of radio advertising was also quite competitive, and the agency recognized a province-wide campaign was possible within the budget.

Goodwill for the physiotherapist profession was assessed as a mix of strengths and challenges. In terms of recognition and trust, physiotherapists were ranked fourth by Ontario residents who were polled by the OPA; only physicians, nurses, and dentists were ranked higher. Nonetheless, the same survey did show some challenges, including misperceptions about access (with more than three-quarters of respondents mistakenly believing they require a referral from a doctor to be treated) and underestimation of the education required to become a physiotherapist (with more than one-third of respondents failing to understand that a Master's-level university degree is now required to practise in Ontario). These challenges helped set the stage for the creative strategy developed for the campaign.

Strategic intelligence was assessed as a clear strength for the OPA. The association was armed with recent, high-quality data on the attitudes and the actions of both key audiences. The data was used in many aspects of planning and creating the campaign.

Internal cohesion was also found to be a clear strength for the OPA. The commitment to the campaign among management and the board was very strong. In addition, support for the campaign among OPA members was also very high. There was a clear consensus within the profession that greater awareness, visibility, and differentiation were required. Given the strength of the members as a communication vehicle, the internal cohesion was vital to the success of the campaign.

Stories to tell, however, were assessed as a "potential strength." There was a clear sense among OPA staff and board members that each member of the profession had powerful stories to share about patients who regained strength, mobility, health, and confidence thanks to the care they received from their physiotherapist. Beyond this anecdotal evidence, stories had not been previously gathered in a coordinated way that could be shared. Stories would be needed to bring the scientific evidence of effectiveness and value to life.

Environmental Scan

The agency also conducted an extensive scan of the external environment into which the campaign would be running. The intent was to identify the opportunities that could be leveraged and the challenges or threats to be mitigated. The chief findings of the environmental scan are summarized below.

The **political** environment was assessed to be quite problematic in Ontario in 2009. The government of the day was running historic budget deficits and was clinging only to a minority position in the Legislative Assembly, making the future of the government uncertain. Adding to the political uncertainty at the time was the fact the government had partially delisted physiotherapy for some segments of the population in 2004 so patients now had more limited access to physiotherapy using the province's health insurance plan (OHIP); patients needed to rely more on their own funds or their employer's health insurance program. Adding to the political threat was the increasing pressure on hospitals to balance their budgets and the reduction of ambulatory services offered in this sector including out-patient physiotherapy clinics. Finally, the system of Community Care Access Centres that coordinated home care in the province lacked the funding required to allow for full access to physiotherapy for these patients, further reducing demand for services. There was, however, one significant opportunity in the political environment at the time. The provincial government had recently passed legislation expanding the scope of practice of the physiotherapy profession, demonstrating the government valued those services as part of the health system in Ontario.

The **economic** field of the external environment in Ontario at the time of the campaign was much more positive, with a drop in the unemployment rate and, hence, an increase in the percentage of residents who potentially would be covered by employer healthcare plans. At the same time, though, disposable income was declining and debt levels for individuals were climbing. The economic situation was volatile.

The **social/cultural** field of the economic environment was assessed as a moderate threat, owing to the growing use of alternative medicines by Canadians at the time. A poll by Ipsos-Reid found Ontarians who were more affluent were also more likely to seek healthcare advice from less traditional sources. In 2006, the Fraser Institute found more than half of all participants in their study had reported using at least one alternative therapy in the year prior to the survey—an increase of 4 percent from 1997. The most used alternative forms of therapy reported included massage therapy and chiropractic care—two therapies that were felt to compete with physiotherapy in certain respects. The same Fraser Institute survey found, however, that confidence in physicians remained strong in Canada, with 73 percent of respondents indicating they had "total" or "a lot" of confidence their doctor could help them manage their overall health. Since physiotherapy is also part of the more traditional healthcare system and since many referrals to physiotherapists are provided by physicians, this finding was assessed as a moderate opportunity.

The **technological** field of the external environment was assessed as a moderate opportunity. The growth in online channels to reach both the public at large and members of the OPA were seen as a solid opportunity to increase reach while maintaining or even lowering the costs of communication. Online media were becoming more popular with the public at large but research suggested the baby boomer women selected as a key audience for the campaign were less likely to be early adopters of web-based and social media channels; those would come later.

The **demographic** field of the external environment was the site of a major opportunity; aging baby boomers were beginning to create a growing pool of

Ontario residents aged 65 and older and those in that growing pool did have access to provincial health insurance (OHIP) to cover some of costs of physiotherapy. There was also recognition, however, that the demand for the services offered by physiotherapists would grow quickly, and the profession needed to be ready, especially as older members of the profession would start to retire at the same time as demand increased. The active lifestyle of the baby boomer generation meant strong demand for physiotherapists, related to sports injuries and mobility issues.

A media analysis by Delta Media showed the **news media** field of the external environment was the site of a steady level of coverage of physiotherapists and their work, much of it positive in tone. A good portion of the coverage focused on success stories, as athletes, celebrities, and politicians were reported to be returning to health thanks to the care they received from a physiotherapist. Much of this coverage, however, was described as "tangential," with stories centred on the recovering person and not specifically about physiotherapy. Nonetheless, the steady level of media interest and coverage was assessed as a moderate opportunity.

The **competitive** field within the external environment featured competing voices both inside and outside the physiotherapy family. Within the family, there were campaigns being planned by the College of Physiotherapists of Ontario— the regulatory body for physiotherapists in the province, which protects the "patients' rights to safe, competent and ethical care by supporting physiotherapists to maintain the standards of practice of the profession and by holding them accountable for their conduct and practice."[2] The College of Physiotherapists of Ontario (CPO) had planned a province-wide awareness campaign, featuring posters and brochures in physiotherapy clinics across the province, designed to raise the profile of the profession and of the role the CPO plays in ensuring accountability, quality, and safety. Though the intended changes and creative strategy were clearly in keeping with the planned OPA campaign, the agency hired by the OPA wanted to ensure the media and timing of the campaigns were planned to complement one another rather than compete for attention. Another competing voice within the physiotherapy family at that time was the Canadian Physiotherapy Association (CPA). The CPA represents physiotherapists in all Canadian provinces and territories and also engages in strategic communication campaigns to raise the profile of and public trust in the profession. Here too, the need was for careful integration and coordination to reduce the risk of confusion and to allow each campaign to reach its full effect. Both these competing voices were ready to cooperate with the OPA and so were assessed as moderate opportunities to coordinate and build cumulative impact.

There were other healthcare professions that were seen as important competitors to the physiotherapy profession in Ontario; many of the provincial and national associations representing these professionals were involved in campaigns similar to what the OPA and its agency were planning. The environmental scan noted all of the competing campaigns used similar clinical terminology and images. The OPA would need to take a different approach to ensure the campaign stood out.

Our scan of the **natural** environment revealed no trends or forces that would have significant impact on the campaign.

In short, the environmental scan revealed an external environment with many important opportunities for the OPA to capitalize upon, along with a small number of challenges or threats that would need to be overcome.

Strategy

A total of six strategic directions were proposed for the campaign, each responding to one or more of the findings from the situation analysis. The six strategic directions were:

1. Engage
2. Differentiate
3. Build value and demand
4. Focus
5. Coordinate
6. Integrate

Together, the six strategic directions would form the basis of a powerful and very strategic campaign. Each direction will be discussed briefly to explain the links to the situation analysis and expand on the ideas for each.

Engage

The strategy developed recognized the 4,500 educated and skilled members of the OPA were an important resource that needed to be fully leveraged for this campaign. The first step in engaging OPA members to become part of the campaign, however, was to ensure they were aware of the campaign, excited and motivated to play a part, and armed with communication tools they could use. The specific intended change of this strategic direction was to "turn OPA members into passionate advocates" for the profession and the healthcare it can offer. Engagement was not only the first strategic direction on the list prepared by the agency; it needed to be the first strategic direction implemented.

Differentiate

This strategic direction made clear the intention of the campaign to promote the value of physiotherapists without in any way demeaning the other health professionals listed as competing voices. The emphasis would be on stressing the post-graduate, university-educated status of physiotherapists and the trust and collaboration they have earned from the country's medical doctors. Differentiating physiotherapists from the many competing professionals also meant making clear the wide range of ailments and conditions they can treat and the wide range of services they can offer. A theme for the campaign emerged early in the planning process: "Discover all the ways a physiotherapist can help." The campaign would surprise the audience by introducing a range of ailments and conditions not typically associated with physiotherapy that physiotherapists can and do treat. A list of derived benefits of physiotherapy was also developed early and became a vital part of the creative strategy: "Strength, freedom, confidence, movement, and health" would be the benefits promoted in the campaign. Finally, a Unique Service Proposition (USP) was developed to sum up one of the core messages of the campaign: "Only a registered physiotherapist offers the benefits of a specialized university degree in physiotherapy and clinical experience."

Build Value and Demand

This strategic direction also guided much in the creative development for the campaign. The campaign would use a three-step approach to first build awareness of the unique qualifications of Ontario's registered physiotherapists (i.e., how they are trusted, highly-educated, and able to offer a full range of services). Next, the campaign would build the perceived value of physiotherapy treatment for patients (i.e., promoting the derived benefits). Finally, the campaign would call on the audience to increase their demand for physiotherapy services. This would come in the form of turning more often to a physiotherapist, paying for those services with their own money if need be. Increased demand would also come in the form of advocating for greater government funding of physiotherapy services and greater access to physiotherapy through employer health insurance plans.

Focus

As mentioned earlier, the core audience for the campaign was clearly identified as baby boomer women in Ontario. This large demographic segment not only was approaching an age when their demand for physiotherapy services would increase, but they could influence the healthcare choices of their children, their spouses, and their aging parents. The combined potential impact of this effort would be significant. That's why a strategic direction to carefully focus the campaign on this core audience was ideal as a way to overcome a limited budget for the campaign. A modest budget invested in only a few, carefully selected vehicles will yield a larger impact.

Coordinate

The fifth strategic direction called for the OPA and its agency to carefully coordinate the campaign with those planned by the Canadian Physiotherapists Association (CPA) and the College of Physiotherapists of Ontario (CPO). The coordination would help ensure these two other campaigns could fully function as opportunities rather than threats. In particular, the strategic direction called for close work with the CPA and CPO to ensure the messages of all three campaigns were complementary, that the timing was coordinated to reduce competition for attention, and that opportunities to share resources could be fully explored.

Integrate

Finally, the sixth strategic direction called for the OPA to carefully integrate its many outreach activities to build the cumulative impact of them all and ensure messages worked well together. In particular, it was noted that the OPA's efforts in media relations, government relations, web development, student engagement, and member recruitment could and should all be integrated with the campaign to ensure creative strategies and timing were optimized.

Action Plan: The First Three Years

The campaign for the OPA unfolded over three years and included a wide range of tactics intended to reach and engage both the internal and external individuals and organizations identified as core audiences. The blend of communication vehicles and activities evolved somewhat as the campaign unfolded, reflecting changing budgets and evaluation of each year of the campaign.

Internal Campaign

Dedicated iBlasts and Issue of Physiotherapy Today

Articles announcing the campaign were written and sent to all members of the OPA via the *Physiotherapy Today* newsletter. In addition, shorter announcements were made and distributed through regular iBlast emails to members. These channels were also used extensively throughout the first three years of the campaign.

PowerPoint Slides for Incorporation into Upcoming Events and Presentations
For both the annual provincial conference of the OPA and smaller meetings of local and regional chapters, PowerPoint slides were developed to announce the campaign and share campaign messages with members as part of these events. This tactic was used for the first year of the campaign only.

Contest to Gather Success Stories for Use in Future Campaigns (2009 and 2010)
The OPA and its agency recognized the need to gather actual success stories for use as the campaign unfolded. A special contest was developed to gather these stories and to further engage members. The contest ran in the first two years of the campaign, inviting members to submit their stories and secure the agreement of their patients to have the stories shared. Entries were all published to the campaign website and a prize was awarded to the stories deemed to be the best of the entries for the year, as voted by members. All those who submitted an entry were rewarded with a campaign water bottle bearing the campaign slogan ("Physiotherapy: Stronger in so many ways").

External Campaign

Dedicated Website (www.discoverphysiotherapy.ca)
A dedicated campaign website was developed by the agency and became a central hub for the campaign. All other internal and external vehicles for the campaign included mention of the URL to build maximum traffic and engagement. The site was designed and redesigned annually to reflect the creative strategy for that particular year, in terms of colours, images, and text.

Online Tools for OPA Members (2009, 2010, and 2011)
The dedicated members' section of website included links to tools members could use to build the visibility of the campaign among their patients, family members, and friends. The tools allowed members to share links to online versions of the campaign's advertisements, as well as content for short posts that included key messages and images from the campaign. These changed each year of the campaign to keep up with the evolving creative strategy and the growing potential the new online and social media channels offered.

Posters for Clinics (2009, 2010, and 2011)
The campaign also included a poster each year, depicting one of the principal

messages of the campaign for that year. In Year One of the campaign, the posters were mailed to each clinic in the province and were very well received and used by members, as will be discussed in the evaluation section below. The cost of mailing was substantial, though, so in subsequent years, members were invited to order their posters from the OPA office; in this way, only those committed to displaying the posters would then be sent one. This approach was also well received.

Brochures for Clinics (2009)

In the first year of the campaign, a small brochure was printed and shipped to each clinic in the province. The brochure reiterated the key messages of the campaign and featured many of the same photos and graphic elements as the poster.

Multi-market Radio Campaign on Stations that Attract Women Baby Boomers (2009 and 2010)

For the first two years of the campaign, radio advertising was deemed to be the most cost-effective way to reach a high number of baby boomer women in Ontario. The low cost of producing radio advertising (especially as compared to television) was also a reason for this decision. Radio stations in markets across the province we carefully selected to ensure a strong presence of the key audience among the station's listenership. The agency reviewed the listener profiles of a large number of stations and presented a recommended list of stations to the client. A series of ads were produced to reflect the diversity of ways that women in the baby boomer demographic segment can benefit from physiotherapy.

Ad in Canadian Living Magazine Ontario Edition (2010)

In the second year of the campaign, a modest increase in the campaign budget allowed for a new channel to be added to the campaign; specifically, a print ad in the Ontario edition of Canadian Living magazine was purchased and run during the same period of time as the radio campaign. The ad featured a similar message as the radio spots and allowed all members across Ontario to get a sense of the campaign's creative strategy regardless of what radio stations they listened to. The print ad was ideally directed to baby boomer women, who make up the majority of the magazine's readership.

Multi-market Television Campaign on Shows that Attract Women Baby Boomers (2011)

In the third year of the campaign, the decision was made to switch to television as the principal channel for the campaign. The decision was based on a number of factors, including an increase in the budget available for the media buy and the need to keep members of the OPA engaged in the campaign and wanting to participate in it. The OPA and its agency sought out proposals from the major television networks in the province, compared the reach of each proposal in terms of the baby boomer women audience, and determined which proposal offered the best return on investment for the campaign. In the end, a blended media buy involving stations from two of the networks was selected for maximum impact. Given higher production costs, a single television commercial[3] was written and produced, as compared to the three radio spots produced for each of the first two years. The creative strategy for the commercial allowed a single message to communicate the benefits of physiotherapy to baby boomer women, their parents, their spouses, and their children.

Internal Results of the Campaign

The OPA and its agency conducted a rigorous evaluation of each year of the campaign. The evaluation focused on understanding what aspects of the strategy were effective at reaching and engaging members of the OPA and what needed to be improved. The annual evaluation helped to ensure each year of the campaign was more effective than the previous year in terms of reach and of the impact of the campaign on OPA members.

Highlights of the findings from the first four evaluations conducted include the following:

- A survey of OPA members in 2012 showed only 4.9 percent were not at all aware of the campaign; in contrast, three-quarters of survey respondents reported being aware or very aware of the campaign. Clearly, the internal campaign was effective in reaching members.
- The radio spots created for the first three years of the campaign were well received by the internal audience, with more than 90 percent of OPA members rating them as "entirely appropriate" or "appropriate" for the profession. A similar percentage of respondents felt the radio spots reflected very well or well on the profession.

- The campaign poster was also well received by OPA members, with 87 percent of survey respondents indicating the poster and its messages was "entirely appropriate" or "appropriate."
- In terms of OPA members participating in the campaign, the results after two years were quite mixed; on the one hand, more than 70 percent of members reported putting up the campaign poster in their clinic and nearly 36 percent reported they had visited the campaign website. On the other hand, fewer than 4 percent had downloaded any of the electronic campaign materials from the OPA member website (e.g., campaign banners and buttons) and posted them to their clinic website or Facebook page.
- In 2012, when the campaign moved to television from radio, the results in terms of member awareness of the campaign remained strong, with 76 percent of respondents indicating they were aware or very aware of the campaign.
- The number of respondents who reported learning about the campaign from social media activity grew substantially in 2012, with close to 13 percent of respondents suggesting the OPA's Facebook page, Twitter feed, and LinkedIn profile were the source of their information. In later years, the reported reach and influence of social media channels would continue to grow and prompt other changes to the media strategy.
- The move to television generated renewed excitement among OPA members, with a sharp increase in respondents who reported learning about the campaign through word of mouth and with a significant increase in visits to the campaign site, where nearly 25 percent of respondents suggesting they had gone to view the TV commercial.
- OPA members strongly endorsed the creative strategy used in 2012 for the TV commercial. Fully 95.9 percent of respondents rated the ad's message as appropriate or entirely appropriate for the profession. Similarly, 94 percent of respondents agreed the quality of the messages in the commercial were good or very good. In addition, more than 97 percent of respondents felt the production quality of the spot reflected well on the profession. Given the positive reviews and the high costs of production, the same TV commercial was aired in the 2013 campaign.
- Member participation in the campaign remained a challenge, with a promising improvement between 2012 and 2013. In the first year after the move to television (2012), nearly 60 percent of members indicated they did not directly participate in the campaign in any way. The 40 percent of members who did participate were most likely to share a link

to the television commercial on Facebook or email a link to a friend, colleague, or family member. By 2013, the percentage of members who reported they did not participate in the campaign had dropped to 52 percent, thanks to an increase in the number of respondents who reported sharing the ad via Facebook.

- The biggest challenge with the move to television from radio was the more geographically focused media buy that was required, given television advertising is generally more expensive than radio. The media buy was focused on larger urban centres in the province (i.e., Toronto and Ottawa), which meant members in smaller communities were less likely to see the ad. To compensate for this, a print ad was also purchased in a widely available magazine reaching baby boomers (*Zoomer* magazine), and a daily newspaper in the Windsor market, where the large presence of American TV networks erodes the audience for Canadian channels.

External Reach of the Campaign

- The campaign generated significant and focused reach in the years it was run primarily on radio. The final year of the campaign on radio (2011) saw the ad run on 12 radio stations in key cities across the province, as well as 1 magazine and 1 newspaper. The combined focused reach of these outlets was 435,000 women baby boomers. With the number of times the ad was aired on each station, the total impressions generated by the campaign that year reached 2,568,728 women baby boomers.
- The first year of the campaign running on television saw the campaign achieve a total Gross Ratings Points (GRPs) of 1,220, meaning, the average woman aged between 50 and 70 in Ontario (the key audience for the campaign that in 2012 numbered 2.3 million people[4]) had more than 12 opportunities to see the ad.
- The number of unique visitors to the campaign site did increase substantially when the campaign was moved to television. In the month of October, traffic to the site increased by nearly 70 percent in 2012, as compared to 2011.

NOTES

1. Ministry of Health & Long-term Care. (2017). *Health workforce planning and regulatory affairs division: Regulated health professions*. Retrieved July 19, 2017, from http://www.health.gov.on.ca/en/pro/programs/hhrsd/about/regulated_professions.aspx.

2. College of Physiotherapists of Ontario. (2017) *About the College*. Retrieved July 20, 2017, from http://www.collegept.org/aboutus/AbouttheCollege.

3. To view the OPA TV commercial from the campaign, visit: https://www.youtube.com/watch?v=t_8Mty2q-LI.

4. Statistics Canada. (n.d.). Table 051-0001: Estimates of population, by age group and sex for July 1, Canada, provinces and territories, annual (persons unless otherwise noted). Retrieved July 30, 2012, from: http://www5.statcan.gc.ca/access_acces/alternative_alternatif?l=eng&keng=1.8&kfra=1.8&teng=Download%20file%20from%20CANSIM&tfra=Fichier%20extrait%20de%20CANSIM&loc=http://www5.statcan.gc.ca/cansim/results/cansim-0510001-eng-4799617959870078780.csv.

APPENDIX C

Tactic Table Template

Tactic:	Audience:
Details: • • • 	
Timing:	Budget:

INDEX